COLERIDGE: CRITIC OF SHAKESPEARE

Coleridge: critic of Shakespeare

M.M.BADAWI

FELLOW OF ST ANTONY'S COLLEGE, OXFORD

CAMBRIDGE
AT THE UNIVERSITY PRESS
1973

Published by the Syndics of the Cambridge University Press
Bentley House, 200 Euston Road, London NW1 2DB
American Branch: 32 East 57th Street, New York, N.Y. 10022

Library of Congress Catalogue Card Number: 72 86417

ISBN: 0 521 20040 7

Printed in Great Britain
by W & J Mackay Limited, Chatham

Contents

FOR MIEKE

Acknowledgements

This book is based on a thesis which earned the degree of Ph.D. from the University of London. It was made possible through a most generous scholarship from the University of Alexandria to whom I wish to record here my very warm gratitude. I also wish to express my thanks to the University of Oxford and St Antony's College for granting me leave of absence for the academic year 1970/1, thus enabling me, among other things, to get this work ready for publication. To the governing body of St Antony's College I owe the further debt of a grant to help cover the typing expenses.

M.M.B.

St Antony's College
Oxford
November 1972

Abbreviations

The following abbreviations of some of Coleridge's works are used in references:

AP: *Anima Poetae*, ed. E. H. Coleridge (London, 1895).
AR: *Aids to Reflection and Confessions of an Inquiring Spirit* (London, 1904).
BL: *Biographia Literaria*, ed. J. Shawcross, 2 vols. (Oxford, 1907).
CL: *Collected Letters of Samuel Taylor Coleridge*, ed. E. L. Griggs (Oxford, 1956–71).
CN: *The Notebooks of Samuel Taylor Coleridge*, ed. Kathleen Coburn (vol. I, 1957; vol. II, 1962).
MC: *Coleridge's Miscellaneous Criticism*, ed. T. M. Raysor (London, 1936).
Method: *S. T. Coleridge's Treatise on Method as published in the Encyclopaedia Metropolitana*, ed. A. D. Snyder (London, 1934).
Omniana: *Omniana or Horae Otiosiores*, ed. Robert Southey, 2 vols. (London, 1812).
Ph L: *The Philosophical Lectures of Samuel Taylor Coleridge*, ed. Kathleen Coburn (London, 1949).
SC: *Coleridge's Shakespearean Criticism*, ed. T. M. Raysor, 2 vols. (London, 1930).
TT: *Specimens of the Table Talk of Samuel Taylor Coleridge*, ed. H. N. Coleridge, 4th edn. (London, 1851).

Other abbreviations:

Hazlitt: William Hazlitt, *The Complete Works*, ed. P. P. Howe (London, 1930–4).
Hooker: *The Critical Works of John Dennis*, ed. E. N. Hooker, 2 vols. (Baltimore, 1939–43).
Ker: *Essays of John Dryden*, ed. W. P. Ker, 2 vols. (Oxford, 1900).
MLN: *Modern Language Notes* (Baltimore, 1886–).
OED: *Oxford English Dictionary*.
PMLA: *Publications of the Modern Language Association* (Baltimore, 1886–).
Raleigh: *Johnson on Shakespeare*, ed. Sir Walter Raleigh (Oxford, 1946).
Richardson: William Richardson, *Essays on Shakespeare's Dramatic Characters with an Illustration of Shakespeare's Representation of National Characters in that of Fluellen*, 6th edn. (London, 1812).
Smith: *Eighteenth Century Essays on Shakespeare*, ed. D. Nichol Smith (Glasgow, 1903).

The references to Shakespeare's text are all to the Globe edition.

Introduction

At the beginning of this century David Nichol Smith claimed that the publication of Dr Johnson's *Preface to Shakespeare* in 1765 marked the end of a stage in the history of Shakespearean criticism, and that after that date there was a new mode of approach to Shakespeare. This new mode, he alleged, was similar to that of Coleridge. But in 1931, armed with an impressive amount of scholarship, R. W. Babcock stepped forth with his study of the Shakespearean critics of the last third of the eighteenth century. In it he put forward the theory that when we have studied the works of these minor critics we find nothing new in Coleridge's criticism of Shakespeare. Between 1900 and 1930 a great deal had happened in the world of English letters to turn the tide of taste. Early in the century the influential T. E. Hulme attacked 'romanticism', which he labelled 'damp', and predicted a return to what he called 'dry' and 'hard' classicism. The cause of classicism was championed by no less influential critics, men of the calibre of Irving Babbitt and T. S. Eliot. Particularly in literary criticism, the word 'romantic' came to acquire an unsavoury flavour: people began to write about such topics as 'The Decline and Fall of the Romantic Ideal'. And although we can safely say that the campaign against romantic criticism is now over, it was not so long ago that a certain critic, who is also a distinguished Oxford scholar, wrote: 'Romantic poetry died of old age many years ago, and it is more than time that Romantic criticism also received its decent and final interment.'

The general reaction against the romantic critics was clearly visible in Shakespearean criticism as well: Emile Legouis wrote about it as early as 1928 (in *Essays and Studies*, XIII). For better or for worse the name of Coleridge is always linked with the word 'romantic'. Consequently, as a critic of Shakespeare, Coleridge suffered at the hands of professed anti-romantic critics and

1

scholars. On the whole the nineteenth century venerated Coleridge, and regarded him where Shakespeare is concerned almost as an infallible oracle – an oracle, however, whose advice was not scrupulously followed all the time. In the twentieth century a return to something like Dr Johnson's position was, for a time at any rate, claimed to be the orthodoxy; and by reacting against the nineteenth-century tradition, the twentieth attempted to reject much of what it stood for. An authoritative critic once hinted that the criticism of Coleridge on a particular Shakespearean play was not really an honest enquiry, but an attempt to present Coleridge himself in an attractive costume. Another critic claimed that Coleridge's critical work 'tells us nothing of what poetry is itself'. More recently a historian of criticism wrote that his remarks on the plays and characters of Shakespeare are often 'either trite or moralizing or, when ingenious, unconvincing', and denied that they are 'in any way integrated into a theory or even into a unified conception of a play'. This is not the place to consider these statements: I mention them only to show that an impartial evaluation of Coleridge's Shakespearean criticism seems to be overdue. We can now ask ourselves calmly: Was there after all any valuable contribution in Coleridge's criticism of Shakespeare? Or was the bulk of his critical writings, marginal notes and lectures on the great poet and dramatist merely, as Dr Babcock suggests, a summarization, or at best, an intelligent elaboration of current or past opinions – the thing which one can quite safely say of Dr Johnson's *Preface*?

In claiming that an evaluation of Coleridge's Shakespearean criticism is overdue I am aware that the past two decades have witnessed a remarkable resurgence of academic interest in Coleridge. This is revealed in the launching of the ambitious scheme for the publication of the *Collected Coleridge* under the general editorship of Kathleen Coburn, and in the appearance of more than a score of full-length studies (not to mention whole books devoted to him in other languages: French, German, Italian and even Arabic). These books, however, are mostly either general all-round studies or else they are about the poet, the thinker, the philosopher and theologian, the critic of society or of politics. The ones that profess to discuss his literary criticism – with the exception of J. V. Baker's *The Sacred River: Coleridge's Theory of the Imagination* (1958) and R. H. Fogle's slim volume *The Idea of Coleridge's Criticism* (1962) – do so only tangentially. Both J. A. Appleyard in *Coleridge's Philosophy of Literature* (1965) and J. R. de J. Jackson in *Method and Imagination in Coleridge's Criticism* (1969) are primarily interested in Coleridge's philosophical and theological thought and only secondarily in his literary criticism. Considering the limited amount of literary criticism proper which they contain, it is not surprising that the space allotted to Coleridge's Shakespearean criticism in these books is very small indeed. Jackson admits that in discussing Coleridge's criticism of Shakespeare he does not 'try to consider its place in the history of Shakespearean criticism' (p. 123), assuming that that has been settled. Despite the proliferation of books on Coleridge then, there is no full-length study of his criticism of Shakespeare, which is a curious omission, since we are often told by the Coleridge enthusiasts that he, the greatest English critic, produced his finest criticism when writing or lecturing on Shakespeare. Time and time again we read that he was the 'greatest of Shakespearean critics'.

The object of the present study is twofold: first, to attempt to understand the critical methods and assumptions in Coleridge's writings on Shakespeare, and, secondly to define the nature of his contribution to the criticism of Shakespeare in England. But in order to arrive at a just appraisal of his contribution it is necessary to have some idea of the development of Shakespearean criticism before his time. I have therefore devoted the first chapter to a background discussion of basic problems in Shakespearean criticism before Coleridge. This can only be a very brief account of a large and complicated subject, my aim being only to summarize my views which I have set out in some detail elsewhere.[1] If in my summing up I sometimes sound categorical I can only beg the reader's forbearance and refer him to the much fuller treatment with all the necessary supporting evidence in my forthcoming book on the subject. As far as serious literary criticism, and not vague rapturous writing is concerned – a distinction which Babcock and others do not always make – eighteenth-century criticism of Shakespeare, however varied it

[1] In my forthcoming book *Attitudes and Assumptions in Eighteenth Century Shakespearean Criticism*.

may appear in its interests, and whatever the stages of development into which historians may have divided it, constitutes one main tradition. I set out on this study with the commonly accepted view that Coleridge's criticism of Shakespeare has its roots in the criticism of the third or last quarter of the eighteenth century. But having examined closely the critical works of that period, I came to the conclusion that their main assumptions look backwards to earlier writing rather than forwards. With few exceptions, far from embodying, or even pointing forward to, what is basically Coleridge's approach, these works are to be understood as based on much earlier criticism. Indeed, some of their premises are to be searched for in the writings of Dryden and his contemporaries. What happened in the last third of the eighteenth century was not so much a basic change, as is generally thought, as an accentuation of elements in earlier criticism – an accentuation which made the disintegration of the organic unity of Shakespearean drama an indisputable fact of criticism. What I offer in my first chapter is not so much a bare historical survey as an interpretation which raises several questions. In the subsequent chapters of the book I discuss Coleridge's answers to these questions.

Coleridge was not merely an impressionist critic; nor was he a man in whom the reality principle was sadly deficient, but who was gifted with occasional flashes of psychological insight. On the contrary, it is my strong conviction that, at least in Shakespearean criticism, what sets off his criticism from that of his predecessors is its profoundly systematic nature. Coleridge had a theory of poetry which calls for serious analysis, and is not to be dismissed as mere rhetoric, as it has been by some critics. I therefore start with an attempt to relate his aesthetic theory to his actual practice as a Shakespearean critic. My conclusion is that while he inherited much from his eighteenth-century predecessors, Coleridge contributed both in theory and in practice something new and significant to English Shakespearean criticism. It is no exaggeration to say that the critical principles underlying his new approach to Shakespeare are the principles we now use ourselves. By going to the roots of problems, and by questioning basic assumptions in poetry and drama, Coleridge raised questions that are still alive – so much so that it has

4

sometimes been difficult to resist the temptation to place him among living critics, discussing him in relation to them and even defending his position against theirs.

Finally, there are one or two things which this study does *not* attempt to do. First, it does not deal with the hazardous question of Coleridge's direct debts, except on one or two occasions, and even then only indirectly. It does not offer any new evidence of, or clues to, Coleridge's acquaintance with his immediate predecessors. Of an omnivorous reader like Coleridge, it is extremely difficult to say for certain that he did not read this writer or that (although we may mention in passing that there is not a single reference in his writings to critics like Whately or Morgann or Richardson). The omission of a discussion of Coleridge's direct debts is really dictated by the nature of this work. For this is primarily a study in critical method; and here Coleridge's approach to Shakespearean drama is radically different from that of the eighteenth-century critics. Even if it were proved (which is by no means the case) that he owed this remark or that to an eighteenth-century critic, the remarks together would never add up to a system, but would remain a collection of disjointed comments. Coleridge's critical remarks, on the other hand, clearly form an integral part of a whole approach. It is because of this quality of 'wholeness' in Coleridge's criticism that the question of indebtedness, in spite of its interest, seems to me to be of decidedly secondary importance. This applies to his German sources no less than to his English ones.

Secondly, this is not a plea for 'romantic' criticism. In fact, I have tried to avoid, as far as possible, the use of the terms 'romantic' and 'classic'. The terms are misleading in a study of serious Shakespearean criticism, which is to some extent distinct from the history of ideas. Of course, the 'discovery' of Shakespeare was a major factor in the development of the romantic or pre-romantic consciousness. But this is not so much the case in England as on the continent, where for several reasons the effect of the introduction of his plays on the literary scene presents a relatively neat and tidy picture that can be traced by the literary historian.[1] In England Shakespeare was always admired, even

---

[1] It has been done systematically by Paul van Tieghem, *Le Préromantisme, la Découverte de Shakespeare sur le Continent* (1947).

5

in the days when the influence of the French theatre was at its highest – although naturally not always for the same reasons. And when we stop to consider what Shakespeare meant to his late eighteenth-century enthusiasts on the continent we shall find that it was largely freedom of expression, superiority and intractability to rules – what I have preferred to call primitivism – a primitivism which no doubt arose in England itself in the latter part of the century, and which is best expressed in Edward Young's *Conjectures on Original Composition*, a book which had a revolutionary effect in Germany.[1] We know where the *Sturm und Drang* school laid the emphasis.[2] As for the French romantics, Henri Fluchère tells us that when they cried '*Shakespeare avec nous!*' in the beginning of the nineteenth century, they 'could hardly bring out a reasonably valuable estimate of Shakespeare's genius'. What mattered to them '*was* the genius, and what it stood for', and his name meant to them nothing more than 'liberty of expression, repudiation of the unities, *mélange des genres* and poetry'.[3] But this was not what Shakespeare meant to Coleridge. As the reader will see, Coleridge did not share any of these excesses of the primitivists. On the contrary, in his theory of the imagination he clearly distinguished between the *order* of a work of art and the chaos of experience.

To show that my attempt to dispense with the words 'classic' and 'romantic' here does not stem from a facile and once fashionable dismissal of accepted critical terms, I will provide one or two of the numberless examples in which the neat distinction between 'classic' and 'romantic' breaks down in our study of English Shakespearean critics. If classicism means the apotheosis of the 'general' and romanticism that of the 'particular', then we can without much hesitation call Dr Johnson a classicist and Hazlitt a romantic. Did not Johnson proclaim that a Shakespearean character is always a species and did not Hazlitt take him to task because of that very assertion? But under which

[1] See J. R. Robertson, *Lessing's Dramatic Theory* (1939), p. 34, and M. H. Abrams, *The Mirror and the Lamp: Romantic Theory and the Critical Tradition* (1953), pp. 201ff.
[2] See Paul van Tieghem, *Le Préromantisme*, pp. 179ff.; H. B. Garland, *Storm and Stress* (1952), pp. 12, 17, 20, 36.
[3] Henri Fluchère, 'Shakespeare in France: 1900–1948', *Shakespeare Survey*, No. 2 (1949), p. 115.

category can we put Coleridge, who explicitly stated that the virtue of a Shakespearean character is that it is both individual and general at one and the same time? If, on the other hand, the difference between the classical and romantic critics of Shakespeare lies in that the classicist often judges by reference to a system of rules and principles and the romantic is a mere impressionist, then we may be able to say that Johnson and Hazlitt are classical and romantic critics respectively. But then again, what of Coleridge who claims that serious criticism should always be based on valid principles? But perhaps classical Shakespearean criticism should be taken to mean simply that which measures the plays of Shakespeare by the rules of antiquity as interpreted and applied in French drama, and romantic criticism that which does not take the rules to be absolute criteria. In that case we could easily dispose of Rymer or a later Gildon as classicist; but would we really be justified if we put Farquhar, Dr Johnson, Kames, and Coleridge in the same category? It is to avoid this kind of confusion that I have tried to do without these slippery terms in the following discussion. My plea is then not for Coleridge the romantic critic, whatever that may mean, but for Coleridge, the critic of Shakespeare.

Basic problems in Shakespearean criticism before Coleridge

I

It is generally accepted that by Dryden's time much of the Elizabethan tradition and outlook was lost, that the world of the Renaissance, to which Shakespeare belongs, bears a closer affinity to the medieval world than people at one time thought, and that its difference from the rational, scientific, secular and urban bourgeois civilization, which roughly coincided with the Restoration, is radical. The change had its effect on literary criticism no less than on other aspects of intellectual life. In the Shakespearean criticism of this period, what was significantly new was not so much the insistence upon classical rules (Sidney and Jonson had insisted upon them before), as the spirit in which that insistence was made, the spirit which dominated Shakespearean criticisim of the eighteenth century, and which was there all the time, even when critics reacted against the rules. Rationalism had created a craving for verisimilitude. Hence, in spite of his famous encomium on Shakespeare, which both Dr Johnson and Hazlitt admired, in 1672 Dryden disposed of plays like *The Winter's Tale*, *Love's Labour's Lost* and *Measure for Measure* as being 'grounded on impossibilities'. Likewise in 1710 Charles Gildon found the plot of *The Merchant of Venice* 'unnatural' and wanting in 'the Probability and Verisimilitude which is absolutely necessary to all the Representations on the Stage'.[1]

How far the rationalist attitude can go in the process of draining Shakespeare of tragic significance can be seen in Thomas Rymer's commonsense and literal-minded criticism of *Othello*. Of course, Rymer was not fully representative, and his view was rejected even by his contemporaries. Yet in its basic assumptions

---

[1] *Ker*, i, 165; Charles Gildon, *An Essay on the Art, Rise and Progress of the Stage* (1714), p. v.

8

his criticism is no different from that of the eighteenth-century rationalist commonsense tradition. Rymer represents the logical conclusion of an attitude, which, like that of Dr Johnson, regards 'the stage as only a stage' and 'the players as only players'.[1] It is not sufficiently realized how much of Rymer's influence remained throughout the eighteenth century, though the tone which characterizes his criticism may have disappeared. Even Dr Johnson was not free from it; he was quite serious when he found in *Othello* an admonition against 'disproportionate marriages'.[2] Echoing Rymer, who claimed that Shakespeare's genius 'lay for comedy and humour', and that in tragedy 'he appears out of his element', Johnson found Shakespeare's tragedy to be 'skill' and his comedy to be 'instinct', and he actually preferred Tate's version of *King Lear* to Shakespeare's play. Similarly Edward Malone preferred Shakespeare's comedies to his tragedies. But it is in Francis Gentleman, the author of *The Dramatic Censor* (1770), particularly in his strictures on the plot of *Hamlet*, that Rymer's tradition appears most conspicuously.[3]

Rymer's inability to appreciate Shakespeare's 'rhetoric' made him condemn as frenzy and nonsense Cassio's speech on Desdemona's safe landing.[4] Subsequent critics were never again so extreme in their denunciation of Shakespeare's style. But the charge of turgidity, inflation and false sublime remained a commonplace of eighteenth-century criticism of Shakespeare.

II

The question of the dramatic unities was one of the things which lay behind Rymer's attack on Shakespeare. The modern reader may find it surprising that so much importance was attached to this question. But by the beginning of the eighteenth century the unities had acquired a rational basis. Science had discovered a mechanical order in the physical universe, and an attempt in the same direction was being made, in response to Newton's own suggestion, in the sphere of morals and subsequently in

[1] *Raleigh*, p. 27. [2] *Ibid.* p. 198.

[3] Thomas Rymer, *A Short View of Tragedy* (1693), p. 156; *Raleigh*, p. 19; Francis Gentleman, *The Dramatic Censor* (1770), I, 52–5.

[4] Rymer, *Short View of Tragedy*, p. 110.

aesthetics. With the earlier critics of the century the rules of art came to represent order in nature, and for a man like John Dennis in his essay *The Grounds of Criticism in Poetry* (1704) the order in a work of art had a religious significance.[1] Shakespeare, the critics were aware, does not observe the rules of art, which have a rational basis, and yet he evinces formidable power to move us. To get out of this embarrassing dilemma they were driven to attribute this power to a wild, irregular and incomprehensible force which they called 'nature' and which, in a mysterious way, had control over the poet. Rowe wrote:

Perhaps we are not to look for his beginnings, like those of other authors, among their least perfect writings; art had so little, and nature so large a share in what he did, that for aught I know, the performances of his youth, as they were the most vigorous, and had the most fire and strength of imagination in them were the best.[2]

Such an absurd notion was rightly condemned by Johnson who attacked the unities of time and place.[3] His criteria for rejecting them, however, were the same as those of his predecessors, namely reason and commonsense: the spectator believes from the first act to the last that the stage is only a stage. In fact, nearly all his arguments were foreshadowed more than fifty years earlier in George Farquhar's *Discourse upon Comedy* (1702). In any case the rigidly formal criticism of the early part of the century was beginning to give way by Johnson's time, particularly against the background of the rise of the historical method and the growth of scholarship. But we must realize that the principles which had made that criticism acceptable were still held as the touchstone of criticism. And we hardly need to point out that the complex nature of the problem of the so-called dramatic illusion, could not be derived from a purely common-sense rational approach. Moreover, the implicit assumptions of verisimilitude, which Johnson had set out to remove, did not entirely disappear. Johnson, it must be remembered, allowed the violation of the unities only between the acts.[4]

On the need to observe the unity of action critics were unanimously agreed. Apart from Aristotle's sanction, it came to have a rational basis. Addison objected to the double plot on the

---

[1] *Hooker*, I, 336.   [2] *Smith*, p. 4.   [3] *Raleigh*, p. 37.   [4] *Ibid.* p. 27.

ground that 'it breaks the Tide of sorrow by throwing it into different channels', and towards the end of the century we find critics like Blair using the same argument. Johnson regarded the unity of action as 'more fixed and obligatory' than the other unities, and Kames found it 'conformable to the natural course of our ideas', since it reveals the law of association which he considered to be a fundamental law of the human mind.[1] But on tragi-comedy critics ranged themselves in two camps, with each trying to establish its view upon the authority of nature. Johnson, for instance, used the commonsense 'naturalistic' argument that Shakespeare's plays exhibit 'the real state of sublunary nature', and that 'drama pretends to be the mirror of life'.[2] Although he satirized the Dick Minims (*The Idler*, No. 60), there is a note of apology in his defence (particularly in *The Rambler*, No. 156), which reveals the conflict in the critic between his rationalized rule and his emotional response. It was not surprising that this conflict in a man of Johnson's integrity eventually led to a declaration of what amounts to the bankruptcy of the 'rules of criticism' as applied to Shakespeare: 'That this is a practice contrary to the rules of criticism will be readily allowed; but there is always an appeal open from criticism to nature.' It is difficult to see what purpose the rules of criticism serve if they do not primarily clarify and assist our genuine responses to works of art. Johnson's argument was substantially reproduced by most later critics. The old law of decorum, however, did not disappear. Not only Addison and Rowe but Kames, Cooke, and Richardson condemned the *mélange des genres*.[3]

III

Although the unities of time and place had been generally rejected by the time of Johnson, the antithesis between art and nature in Shakespearean criticism persisted. It lay behind various apparently unrelated problems which were the preoccupations of

1 *The Spectator*, No. 40; Hugh Blair, *Lectures on Rhetoric and Belles Lettres* (1783), III, 312; *The Rambler*, No. 156; Henry Home, Lord Kames, *Elements of Criticism* (1774), I, 27.
2 *Raleigh*, p. 15.
3 *The Spectator*, No. 40; *Smith*, p. 27; William Cooke, *The Elements of Dramatic Criticism* (1775), pp. 119ff.; Richardson, pp. 417ff.

many Shakespearean critics during the rest of the century. One early attempt to resolve this opposition between art and nature was to impute Shakespeare's lack of art to the barbarous taste of the times. Dryden's opinion that the 'times were ignorant' in which he lived was to be repeated by every succeeding critic for over half a century (for instance, Shaftesbury, Rowe, Pope, Theobald and Hanmer). And for the rest of the century critics like Johnson, Mrs Montagu and Gentleman generally introduced only variations on this main theme.[1]

By thus exculpating Shakespeare on the one hand and by following the Longinus cult on the other, it was not difficult for critics to justify to themselves their enjoyment of Shakespeare. Addison at the beginning of the century (*The Spectator*, No. 291), had expressed his preference, with Longinus, for the 'productions of a great genius, with many lapses and inadvertencies' to those of 'an inferior kind of author, which are scrupulously exact, and conformable to all the rules of correct writing', and this idea was to be repeated throughout the century (for instance, by Pope, Theobald, Johnson, Burke and Mrs Griffith among others). Shakespeare's works were likened to Gothic architecture or a forest, and contrasted with a neat modern building or an orderly pleasure garden. Their 'rudeness' or 'uncouthness' and irregularity were even sometimes thought to contribute to their 'sublime' effect.[2]

But with the elaborate theories of taste pouring from every direction in the second half of the eighteenth century, the baffling opposition between art and nature in Shakespeare's writings inevitably received a more sophisticated treatment at the hands of some critics. Burke, in his empirical *Philosophical Enquiry into the Origin of our Ideas of the Sublime and Beautiful* (1759), attributes wrong and bad taste to weakness of judgement and not to sensibility. It is precisely this point on which,

[1] *Ker*, I, 165; Anthony, Earl of Shaftesbury, *Characteristics*, ed. M. Robertson (1900), I, 141; *Smith*, pp. 32, 73, 94; *Raleigh*, p. 31; Mrs Montagu, *An Essay on the Writings and Genius of Shakespeare* (6th edn., 1810), p. xvii; Gentleman, *The Dramatic Censor*, I, 80, 139, and *Bell's Edition of Shakespeare's Plays* (1774) I, 5.

[2] *Smith* pp. 62ff.; *Raleigh* p. 34; Edmund Burke, *A Philosophical Inquiry into the Origin of our Ideas of the Sublime and Beautiful* (4th edn., 1764), p. 139; Mrs Elizabeth Griffith, *The Morality of Shakespeare's Drama Illustrated* (1775), p. 25.

towards the end of the century (1784) Richardson, the author of a *Philosophical Analysis and Illustration of Shakespeare's Characters*, bases his argument in the chapter on Shakespeare's faults. Richardson finds that Shakespeare's faults are caused by his lack of perfect taste, more especially by his weak discernment and want of knowledge, but never by want of feeling. Shakespeare, we are told, had 'no perfect discernment proceeding from rational investigation of the true cause of beauty in poetical composition'.[1]

Shakespeare was still considered, therefore, to be deficient in taste, at least in the particular element of taste which implies conscious artistry: what was called judgement or discernment. Indeed, as R. W. Babcock claims, in the last third of the century some critics endowed Shakespeare with 'judgement'. But as a rule judgement was found in Shakespeare's delineation of character, a power which has never been doubted at any time. Once or twice the word was used to describe very briefly Shakespeare's mode of conducting the plot of a particular play.[2] Daniel Webb also used the word when he discussed Shakespeare's poetry in *Remarks on the Beauty of Poetry* (1762). But as far as I am aware, the word was never used with reference to Shakespeare's general design of his form, plot, character and poetry at once – except perhaps by implication by Maurice Morgann (an exception we have often to make).

However, nobody doubted that Shakespeare had genius, which reveals itself in his characterization and his creative imagination. Inquiries into the nature of his genius, and of genius in general, were made simultaneously with the appearance of treatises on taste and often by the same authors. The opposition between art and nature, which reached its climax during the predominance of the rationalized rules early in the century, resulted in the equation of Shakespeare with nature, in the sense of irregularity, wildness, artlessness or absence of deliberate design. And this was also what the early critics understood by his genius, which generally meant intractability to the

---

[1] Burke, *Philosophical Inquiry*, pp. 32ff.; *Richardson*, p. 413.
[2] R. W. Babcock, *The Genesis of Shakespeare Idolatry* (1931), pp. 128ff.; also see the preface to the anonymous translation, *The Novel from which the Play of the Merchant of Venice written by Shakespeare is taken* (1755).

rules of art, or irregularity, originality, free self-expression and lack of self-consciousness; the poet, in short, was not in control of his powers. It is precisely these qualities (but of course intensified) which formed the concept of Shakespeare's genius in the writings of Edward Young, William Duff, Alexander Gerard and others until the end of the century.[1] Under the growing influence of the mechanical associationist psychology the passivity of Shakespeare's genius is implied in most, if not in all the criticism, whether it is rhapsodical or carried out according to the psychological and philosophical principles of the time. Gerard writes, in significantly Newtonian terms, that in a genius imagination draws images together 'as a magnet selects, from a gravity of matter, the ferruginous particles which happen to be scattered through it'.[2] Even Walter Whiter, despite his apparent modernity, belongs to this tradition. Whiter's attitude to Shakespeare's imagery is based exclusively on the association principle and therefore implies the absolute passivity of the artist: in the heat of invention Shakespeare's 'wild imagination' was subject to laws of association.[3] If imagery has any significance for him, it is only as a manifestation of one aspect of Shakespeare's mind, of the order in which it worked in its receptivity. In his book, *A specimen of a Commentary on Shakespeare* (1794) there is an explicit assumption that the part played by Shakespeare in the imagery was wholly unconscious.

In all the eighteenth-century treatises on genius, 'imagination', sometimes 'creative imagination', is claimed to be 'indispensably necessary' in the 'composition of genius'.[4] But the conception of imagination was also determined by sensationalist psychology. Burke had defined it as the power of the mind to represent voluntarily the images of things in the order and manner in which they are received by the senses, or to combine them in a different order and manner,[5] and his definition re-

---

[1] Edward Young, *Conjectures on Original Composition* (1759), p. 31; William Duff, *An Essay on Original Genius* (1767), pp. 260ff.; Alexander Gerard, *An Essay on Taste*, 3rd edn. (1764), pp. 168ff.

[2] Gerard, *Essay on Taste*, pp. 168ff.

[3] Walter Whiter, *A Specimen of a Commentary on Shakespeare* (1794), pp. 71ff.

[4] Duff, *Essay on Original Genius*, p. 7.

[5] Burke, *Philosophical Inquiry*, pp. 15ff.

mained fundamentally valid during this period. The creative power of the imagination, limited as it is, is not entirely unmechanical: here Gerard's simile of the magnet is peculiarly appropriate. The phrase 'creative imagination' has therefore to be interpreted very carefully. As the eighteenth century understood it, it never meant the whole imaginative conception of a work of art, or, by implication, the serious business of reducing the chaos of experience to an artistic shape. When applied to Shakespeare the sense is even more specific: it invariably meant his ability to create supernatural characters, which was enthusiastically extolled by critics from Dryden, who coined the phrase 'the Fairy Way of Writing', to Rowe, Addison, Joseph Warton, Dodd, Duff, Colman, Mrs Montagu and Morgann. Irving Babbitt and the many scholars who followed him were very wrong indeed in claiming that 'the emergence of the phrase "creative imagination" marks a decisive step in the break with neoclassicism'.[1] For the significance of Shakespeare's 'creative imagination' remained the same throughout the eighteenth century, even when neoclassicism was at its strongest.

Yet, despite the excessive praise of Shakespeare's mastery in his treatment of the supernatural, it is not surprising that the dramatic significance of the element of the supernatural was not fully realised in a rational and empirical age. For instance, Francis Gentleman in *The Dramatic Censor* doubts whether ghosts should ever be represented on the stage since 'they play on our passions in flat contradiction to our reason'. He condemns Hamlet for his superstition. Richardson explains away the influence of the supernatural agency in *Macbeth*. Tom Davies suggests producing *Macbeth* 'without such ghostly aid' as the Witches, which were only acceptable to a 'rude audience'.[2] The rational view, in its zealous attempt to exorcise the supernatural from life, tends to lose sight of its significance in Shakespearean drama. The eighteenth-century universe is a universe occupied only by man and a predominently rational God. When not felt to be rather comical (as the Witches in *Macbeth* were found to be by large sections of the audience, according to Morgann and

---

[1] Irving Babbitt, *On Being Creative and Other Essays* (1932), p. 5.
[2] Gentleman, *The Dramatic Censor*, I, 9, 44; *Richardson*, p. 28; Thomas Davies, *Dramatic Miscellanies* (1784), II, 165.

Davies)[1] the supernatural was relegated to the realm of fantasy and reverie. On this level Shakespeare's supernatural characters, like the supernatural element in Spenser, appealed to the growing primitivistic tendency in the eighteenth-century mind. In both cases the supernatural was robbed of any serious relevance to the human condition.

IV

Human nature is the object of dramatic imitation, but the eighteenth-century conception of imitation was that of direct copying. That drama is meant to be a copy of life is a principle on which Shaftesbury, Burke, Johnson, Kames, Hume, Gerard, Blair and Beattie, in fact all who wrote on the subject in the eighteenth century, were agreed. The pleasure we derive from drama was thought to be due either to our mistaking it for reality (hence our sense of security in the experience of tragedy, according to Addison) or to our consciousness that it is only a copy and, therefore, to our appreciation of the author's skill in imitation, and our delight in imitation as such. Those who, like Johnson, denied the reality of the representation desired realism no less than those who believed in 'delusion'. As for Kames, who in his theory of 'ideal presence' held a middle position between the two, he claimed that the state of waking dream into which the theatrical audience is thrown can only be brought about by a close and detailed copy of life.[2]

The assumption that drama is a copy of life is responsible for the attitude which we find accentuated later in the century, and which regards characters in Shakespearean drama as replicas of human beings, and even sometimes, as Morgann admits, as historic beings. Of course, there is a change in the treatment of these characters – a change from the general remarks on them to a more particular type of criticism, which analyses their actions, motives, sentiments and passions in great detail. But the attitude

[1] Davies, *Dramatic Miscellanies*, II, 23; Maurice Morgann, *Essay on the Dramatic Character of Sir John Falstaff*, ed. W. A. Gill (1912), p. 74n.
[2] Shaftesbury, *Characteristics*, I, 6, 129; Burke, *Philosophical Inquiry*, pp. 20, 80, 333; *Raleigh*, p. 28; Gerard, *Essay on Taste*, pp. 53ff.; Kames, *Elements of Criticism*, II, 398; I, 90–6; Blair, *Lectures on Rhetoric*, III, 329ff.; James Beattie, *Essays on Poetry and Music as they affect the Mind*, 3rd edn. (1779), pp. 33, 36, 45, 87; David Hume, *Essays and Treatises on Several Subjects* (1822), I, 204.

to imitation had not fundamentally changed. Even in the heyday of neoclassicism, with its high regard for the ideal of generality we find a critic like Pope maintaining (in the preface to his edition) that Shakespeare's characters are 'Draughts of Nature', or that they are 'so much nature herself, that 'tis an act of injury to call them by so distant a name as copies of her'.

This claim was never contested throughout this long period; on the contrary, against the background of the development of the novel, it was more emphatically reiterated as the century moved slowly under the influence of sensationalism from the ideal of the general to that of the particular and as the advance in psychology contributed towards the analysis of the inner life. Champions of the 'general' like Johnson or Richardson, who believed in selective imitation, no less than those of the 'particular', like Joseph Warton, Kames, Morgann or Whately, assumed with Mrs Montagu, that the characters 'speak with human voices; are actuated by human passions' and 'are of the same nature as ourselves'.[1] Pope had said in his preface that 'every single character in Shakespeare is as much an individual as those in life itself' and 'it is impossible to find any two alike, and such as from their relation or affinity, in any respect appear to be Twins, will upon comparison be found remarkably distinct'. What Thomas Whately did in his book *Remarks on some of the Characters of Shakespeare* (1785 – but written before 1772) was only to prove this point in detail with respect to Macbeth and Richard III. The attitude that regarded Shakespeare's characters as human beings had therefore been implicit from the beginning. But it was not so pronounced as it came to be in the latter part of the century – which has led scholars to assume that it was born then. And by their insistence on the novelty of their criticism, critics such as Morgann, Whately and Richardson helped to foster this misunderstanding.

Early in the eighteenth century, under the influence of Dennis and the newly discovered Longinus, critics began to analyse the emotions connected with the sublime, with the result that their attention was diverted from formal criticism to the psychological element in the aesthetic experience. By the middle of the century psychology was rapidly becoming the basis of aesthetics. The

[1] Mrs Montagu, *Writings and Genius of Shakespeare*, p. 60.

analysis of passions – an analysis conducted on the basis of the associational psychology of the time – came to be regarded as fundamental in criticism. This is clear in the work of Burke and Kames, to mention two examples. The assumption that the ability to paint passion is 'a prerequisite of genius' was accepted generally and not only by primitivist critics like Young and Blair.[1] Shakespeare's power of depicting the passions had been recognized as far back as Dryden's time. But with the intensive interest in passion and psychology, critics began to direct their attention to the analysis of passions in individual characters. There is a direct line of descent to be traced from the more general observations of people like John Upton through the more detailed remarks of Joseph Warton to the sophisticated analysis of Kames and finally Richardson.

Kames believes that in Shakespeare's characters we find a lively 'imitation' and not a cold 'description' of passions as in Corneille. As Shakespeare is 'superior to all other writers in delineating passions' and 'excels all the ancients and moderns in knowledge of human nature' Kames turns to his plays for most of the illustrations in the course of his analysis. Kames' method is further developed by Richardson who is primarily a moralist and psychologist. His intention, he admits, is 'to make poetry subservient to philosophy and to employ it in tracing the principles of human conduct'.[2] Because they are easier to study than living human beings he chooses Shakespeare's characters as objects of his empirical enquiry. What Richardson actually does in his successive essays is to analyse Shakespeare's characters in the light of the theory of the ruling passion, one of the most popular theories of psychology at the time.

The theory can, of course, be traced back to the medieval theory of humours or earlier still; but its wide popularity in the eighteenth century reveals a rational tendency to reduce the complex personality to a point under which every other point and trait can be subsumed. It is, in a sense, a Newtonian attempt to transport the order of the physical to the moral universe and to bring the apparent chaos of the inner cosmos to some neat and

---

1 Burke, *Philosophical Inquiry*, pp. 87ff.; Young, *Conjectures on Original Composition*, p. 88; Blair, *Lectures on Rhetoric*, iii, 338.
2 Kames, *Elements of Criticism*, i, 501ff.; *Richardson*, p. 33.

comforting pattern. Similarly, in order to evade the embarrassing problem of the irrational in life, the rational critic insisted upon adequate motives in characters, and where Shakespeare did not provide any, the critic either complained of the author's faults or else hunted for 'hidden motives'. Antonio's absence of motive in *The Tempest* is lamented, and Iago is provided by the critic with adequate motives. To make his villainy wholly justifiable Richard Hole claims that 'Iago's character before the play had been good, that Iago had reason to believe that Othello had seduced Emilia, that he suspected Cassio of the same crime and was jealous of Cassio's promotion'. The only exception, in fact, to this general tendency to extrapolate the law of causality in the physical world was Morgann, who raised his voice in protest against excessive rationalism: 'we are by no means so rational in all points as we could wish', he remarked.[1]

Thus Shakespeare's characters are wrenched from their context, analysed, and taken either as examples of certain human truths (which was the method of Kames) or analysed as if they were human beings, with the object of discovering human truths (which is the professed method of William Richardson). Morgann himself is no less guilty than Richard Hole of isolating character from its dramatic context and speculating on aspects of character which Shakespeare had no concern to show us. Starting from the opposite premise that in dramatic composition the 'impression' is the 'fact', Morgann has no difficulty in reconciling his response to Shakespearean drama with his judgement, and can therefore say of it that 'all the incidents, all the parts, look like chance, whilst we feel, and are sensible that the whole is design'.[2]

As we have seen, he attacks the rational view; yet he shares some of its assumptions. Although fully aware of the distinction between a dramatic character and a historic one, he chooses to treat Falstaff as a historic being. His essay on Falstaff embodies a fresher vision of Shakespeare than any we encounter in the whole of the century, but it is marred by the naturalistic assumption that because of its roundness and integrity, the character can

[1] *The Gentleman's Magazine*, No. 42 (December 1772), 576; Babcock, *Genesis of Idolatry*, p. 141; Morgann, *Falstaff*, p. 8.
[2] Morgann, *Falstaff*, pp. 71ff.

be abstracted from the formal pattern which alone gives it life, and treated as a human being.

The psychological analysis of Shakespeare's characters proved to be so fascinating that the attention of critics was diverted from the other component parts of drama. Character came to be regarded as the 'most essential part of the Drama', to use George Colman's words. Richardson wrote that character drawing was considered to require 'the highest exertion of poetical talents', and that the 'two essential powers of Dramatic invention', are 'that of forming characters and that of imitating the passions and affections of which they are composed'. In fact the 'unity of character' as it was termed in the latter part of the century, which was considered to be the prerogative of the 'moderns', gradually usurped the place of the old unities in the writings of critics. Both in theory and in practice character criticism soon became the highest object of Shakespearean criticism. Thomas Whately, for example, wrote that character criticism was 'more worthy of attention than the common topics of discussion'.[1]

V

Because Shakespeare's characters were treated as human beings, it was natural that their actions were related to moral standards, particularly in the age of the great moralists. From the very beginning the question of poetic justice had occupied the minds of critics, and it remained an object of discussion throughout the century. Shakespeare was censured for failing to observe it, both by Dennis and Johnson, and by Mrs Montagu and Gentleman. On the stage Shakespeare's plays were badly mutilated in order to square with the prevalent moral doctrine and promote the cause of virtue. Even Morgann tried to find in the final rejection of Falstaff an act of poetic justice. And although, in his time, Addison formed a single exception in attacking this doctrine and preferring Shakespeare's *Lear* to Tate's version of it, he still approached the work from the point of view of the moralist. The moral approach in this period is closely related to the rational

---

[1] George Colman, *Critical Reflections on the Old English Dramatic Writers* (1761), p. 17; *Richardson*, pp. 437, 33; Thomas Whately, *Remarks on Some of the Characters of Shakespeare*, 2nd edn. (1808), p. 2.

view of life. The point of poetic justice, like that of psychological motivation, is largely an outcome of the late seventeenth-century and early eighteenth-century belief in reason. The optimistic *Weltanschauung* which found a supreme order achieved by a rational god in the universe, the moral no less than the physical, demanded of drama, as Dennis writes, that it should show such an order in its ideal form.

Dramatic poetry, we are told, must express universal moral truths, but the moral has to be explicit. To Shaftesbury *Hamlet* is 'almost one continued moral'. Dr Johnson writes that in *Macbeth* the 'danger of ambition is well described'. The moral that Gentleman can deduce from *Hamlet* is that 'murder cannot lie hid'; in *Romeo and Juliet* he finds 'some very instructive lessons' such as the danger of disobedience in children, and of family quarrels. Richardson, who admits that he is primarily a moralist, never fails to point a moral at the end of his sophisticated analysis of every character, and so on. 'The moral to be drawn from this play is . . .' is the usual formula in the writings of eighteenth-century critics. Johnson blames Shakespeare because 'he seems to write without any moral purpose' and condemns him because his 'precepts and axioms drop casually from him', in other words, because he does not explicitly state his moral. Eighteenth-century critics generally could not conceive that literature can have a moral effect without professing an obvious moral purpose, without employing the crude machinery of morality.[1]

The *reductio ad absurdum* of the eighteenth century demand for explicit moral is to be found in Mrs Griffith's book *The Morality of Shakespeare's Drama Illustrated* (1775), which is typical of the general craving in other critics. In fact, her book was so popular that it was printed serially in *The Universal Magazine*. In it Mrs Griffith collected together from the plays, irrespective of their dramatic context, all the morals she could find; and whenever a play did not yield easily a moral to her, she simply forced one upon it. Thus we get this type of comment (which was occasioned by Iago's speech to Roderigo beginning with "'Tis in ourselves that we are thus or thus') : 'I wish that whenever my

[1] Shaftesbury, *Characteristics*, I, 180; *Raleigh*, pp. 20ff.; Gentleman, *The Dramatic Censor*, I, 59, 188.

reader remembers this particular speech he could contrive to forget the speaker.'[1] With that, together with the method of collecting the 'Beauties of Shakespeare', the process of the disintegration of the unity of Shakespeare's drama is completed.

VI

The 'Beauties of Shakespeare' is a complex phenomenon which grew naturally out of certain prevalent critical ideas and attitudes. The great change in the world picture which rationalism had brought about was naturally enough accompanied by a change in the attitude to language and poetry. Practically every writer in this period wishes us to believe that a process of purification and refinement had come over English civilization. The rise of the middle class, with its belief in the *status quo*, a belief sanctioned by such philosophies as Shaftesbury's, which finds this to be the best of all possible worlds, contributed to the enforcement of the idea of refinement. Hence the patronizing attitude towards Shakespeare and the Elizabethans in general which we encounter in Shakespearean critics, even during the last decades of the century, and in most of those who admired Shakespeare this side idolatry.

Dryden, significantly enough, was one of the first to tell us about the occurrence of this refinement; others were soon to follow suit. Addison and Warburton tried to find excuses for Shakespeare's faults of style by reference to the barbarous taste of the Elizabethans, who, according to Addison, obscured their great and just thoughts by 'sounding phrases and hard metaphors'. Shaftesbury's attack on the puns and other alleged barbarities of Shakespeare's style is notorious. Johnson, both in his *Preface* and in his *Lives of the Poets*, reminds us of the refinement of our 'numbers' achieved since the Elizabethan time. Gentleman, Mrs Montagu, Blair and others found Elizabethan taste in poetry rude and barbarous. Their ignorance of Elizabethan literature was not wholly responsible for their attitude. The gradual rise of scholarship with the advance of the century may have clarified some points; but it certainly did not make it much easier to recognize the function of some 'objectionable' elements in the style of Shakespeare. The patronizing attitude can be seen

[1] Mrs Griffith, *Morality of Shakespeare's Drama*, p. 521.

in Thomas Warton, the author of the *History of English Poetry*. Like Johnson, he believed that the progress of English poetry towards an ideal of perfection was begun by Waller. Other, and perhaps deeper, factors than the mere ignorance of critics, are therefore apparently involved.[1]

Clearly, what the eighteenth-century critics found unpalatable in Shakespeare's style was precisely what is now regarded as one of the sources of his greatness, namely, his amazing command of metaphor. Eighteenth-century criticism did not preach the exclusion of all metaphor, but its conception of metaphor limited its possibilities and levelled out its complexity. Cartesian rationalism and the attitude of the Royal Society insisted upon clarity above any other quality. 'Perspicuity,' Addison tells us (*The Spectator*, No. 285), 'is the first and most necessary qualification in any stile.' But the ideal of clarity demands that metaphor, if it is essential to the main tenor of writing, should have an illustrative function. Otherwise, it becomes simply an embellishment or an added grace. (Illustration or aggrandisement are the functions of 'metaphors' and 'similes' in Dr Johnson's definition in his *Dictionary*.) Shakespeare's metaphors are far more complex, and it was the failure to recognize this complexity that instigated the universal attacks on Shakespeare's style in the eighteenth century.

From the time of Dryden onwards the highly figurative style of Shakespeare had been a constant source of trouble to the critics. Dryden's complaint was reiterated in substance by succeeding critics: Shaftesbury, Addison, Pope, Rowe, Dennis, Warburton, Upton, Johnson, Mrs Montagu, Gentleman, Blair, Whately and so forth. As late as 1789 Robert Potter wrote in *The Art of Criticism as Exemplified in Dr Johnson's Lives*, that 'a figure of speech' is only 'the adoption of one ambiguity to explain another'.[2] Mixed metaphors were regarded as particularly vicious because they seem to divert the attention of the reader from the content and render it more obscure. They were universally condemned, even by champions of the 'particular'

[1] Shaftesbury, *Characteristics*, II, 244; Johnson, *Lives of the Poets*, ed. Birkbeck Hill (1905), I, 75.
[2] Robert Potter, *The Art of Criticism as Exemplified in Dr Johnson's Lives* (1789), p. 92; cf. Oliver Goldsmith, *The Collected Works*, ed. A. Friedman (1966), II, 145.

like Kames and Blair.[1] Here it would be illuminating (if only we had the space) to consider, for example, the anxiety of critics and editors over what they regarded as the 'mixed' metaphor in Hamlet's words:

> To take arms against a sea of troubles

and their various suggested emendations which were really meant to simplify it and make the point of likeness rationally clear.

Clarity and distinction, to which figures and mixed metaphors are inimical, are, in fact, the properties of abstract thought. Language was judged advanced or primitive, according to the degree of its clarity, and its capacity to express abstract ideas. A clear and lucid style was therefore thought to mark an advanced stage of civilization. The age of Queen Anne was regarded by Joseph Warton and Goldsmith, among others, as the heyday of English letters. The patronizing attitude to Shakespeare's metaphorical style was then established upon a widely held theory of the development of language, which considered the rise from the figurative and the concrete to the abstract and general as undoubted progress in the human mind. The condemnation of metaphors also arises from some distrust of the emotions; for this theory assumes that under emotional stress, primitive man expresses himself in a figurative manner, being unable to think clearly and subjugate his emotions to his reason. (A highly coloured description of this process is to be found particularly in Blair's 'Critical Dissertation on the Poems of Ossian', which turns so-called 'primitive' people into a giant race of unconscious poets.)

Figurative language, primitivism, wild imagination and passions are therefore mysteriously bound up in the eighteenth-century mind. But all these elements are in fact embodied in the concept of the 'sublime and the pathetic', and are likewise considered essential qualities of 'original genius'. It now becomes clear how, in eighteenth-century criticism of Shakespeare's poetry, all these elements are strangely combined. Shakespeare's poetry is described as incorrect but sublime and pathetic, in contradistinction to the correct and civilized type of writing.

---

[1] Kames, *Elements of Criticism*, ii, 285ff.; Blair, *Lectures on Rhetoric*. i, 360.

Both Shakespeare and Pope existed in the eighteenth century, each in his own right, in spite of the fact that the one violates the rules observed by the other. This polarity of interest in poetry, already to be found in Dryden and more especially in Addison, was maintained by most eighteenth-century critics of Shakespeare. As the century advanced, however, there was a growing tendency in certain quarters to equate one of these two conceptions of poetry (with all its faults and excellences) with true greatness and to relegate the other to a lower rank. But for these enthusiastic critics, such as Duff, Webb and Joseph Warton, the appeal of Shakespeare's metaphors was largely visual,[1] which was probably due to the impact of sensationalist psychology and philosophy.

The ideal of correctness was obviously an expression of an order of civilization which believed in 'good form'. The refinement which, Dryden tells us, had taken place since the Elizabethans was as much *social* as it was rational. Thus ladies and gentlemen of his time 'speak more wit' than the Elizabethan and Jacobean poets had been able to write. In the various adaptations of Shakespeare's plays the original texts were mangled in order that the diction, amongst other things, might be made to conform to the critical criteria of the time, for Shakespeare did not respect eighteenth-century canons of decorum or class distinctions in words. Johnson complained that before Dryden there was 'no poetical diction, no system of words at once refined from the grossness of domestick use, and free from the harshness of terms appropriated to particular arts'. Hence his attack on Lady Macbeth's invocation to the night 'Come, thick night . . .' because it contains such words as 'dun' and 'knife' (which are mean and vulgar) and his inability to 'check his risibility' at the thought of Heaven 'peeping through a blanket'. Before him Pope had in his edition of Shakespeare relegated to footnotes what he thought were mean images. But such examples are legion in the writings of eighteenth-century critics.[2] Equally common are the attacks on Shakespeare's 'rhetoric' (or his

[1] Duff, *Essay on Original Genius*, pp. 143ff.; Daniel Webb, *Remarks on the Beauties of Poetry* (1762), p. 79; Joseph Warton, *An Essay on the Writings and Genius of Pope*, 5th edn. (1806), I, 99.

[2] Johnson, *Lives*, I, 420; *The Rambler*, No. 168. See also George C. Branam, *Eighteenth Century Adaptations of Shakespearean Tragedy* (1956), ch. 3.

deliberately heightened style), which were perhaps exceeded only by the attacks on his puns.

Because Shakespeare was regarded as an uneven and incorrect poet it became necessary to separate his beauties from his 'false sublime'. The movement began with the early and limited attempts of critics such as Rowe, who enumerated the beauties of *The Tempest*, and Pope, who marked in his edition what he considered to be the most shining passages by commas in the margin, and prefixed a star to a scene, if the whole of it happened to conform to his idea of good poetry. It culminated in the work of William Dodd who by collecting the beauties together in his book *The Beauties of Shakespeare* (1752) initiated a tradition which continued to flourish for several generations after him.

The tendency to collect the beauties of Shakespeare was therefore the natural result of the prevalent attitudes towards language and poetry. It was also an expression of a certain assumption about Shakespearean drama. Although eighteenth-century critics (like Kames or Mrs Montagu)[1] sometimes talked of the organic unity of drama, in their treatment of Shakespeare they showed little awareness of such a unity. Otherwise, neither the adaptations nor the 'beauties' would have seen the light of day. As is to be expected, the passages included in the beauties are chosen not for their 'dramatic' value (which would make them integral parts of their context), but because they contain either a good description or a moral truth.

Very few critics claimed that Shakespeare's poetry reveals uniform conscious artistry and substantiated their claim by their practice. Webb, who did emphasize Shakespeare's conscious artistry, dealt with him as a poet, but hardly as a *dramatic* poet. With the character-critics, on the other hand, Shakespeare's poetry is often passed over in silence. We have seen how Richardson made poetry, which he regarded as a mere embellishment, completely 'subservient to philosophy'.

It is now clear that the rational, scientific and empirical attitude led to the splitting-up of the organic unity of the plays. The plot is long dead and lies buried; the poetry is dissociated from the drama, and its merits and demerits are discussed *in*

[1] Kames, *Elements of Criticism*, i, 27; Mrs Montagu, *Writings and Genius of Shakespeare*, pp. xff.

vacuo, without relation to the character and to the whole. The character moves in the foreground unrelated to either, with the psychological critics busy excavating in it for their truths. The particular vision of human existence realized in the plays and expressed as dramatic poetry seems to have been seriously impaired. The resolution of the 'soul' of a play, as it were, into its constituent parts is paralleled by Hume's reduction of 'self' or 'substance' in philosophy to a mere 'bundle or collection of different perceptions which are in a perpetual flux and movement',[1] and the two events are related to the mechanical view of the physical universe formulated by Newton and popularized throughout the eighteenth century.

Of course, in the study of each particular element (with the exception of plot) critics have made no small progress; but they have not fully realized the mutual relationships of these elements. For that realization, of course, what was needed was a fundamentally different attitude to Shakespearean drama, an attitude which regarded the plays with all their constituent elements, plot, character and poetry alike, in practice no less than in theory, as forming a truly organic whole, and as the work of a fully conscious artist. Of all the eighteenth-century critics only Maurice Morgann came close to achieving this. He is in many respects the exception that proves the rule, and it is no wonder that his *Essay on the Dramatic Character of Sir John Falstaff* (1777) did not have a fraction of the popularity of the more typical work of Richardson or Mrs Griffith. Yet, though clearly the most original of eighteenth-century Shakespearean critics, in some of his assumptions and attitudes Morgann still belonged very much to his age.

As for the numerous and indefatigable scholars of the period, like most scholars, they tended to be rather conservative people, and Dryden's tradition persisted among them much more strongly than is commonly realized. Indeed their contribution to the future developments of the study of Shakespeare was immense, but they generally seemed not to be fully aware of the aesthetic implications of their findings, and their interest was largely antiquarian. It was left to future generations to make a sound 'critical' use of the knowledge they acquired on the

[1] David Hume, *A Treatise on Human Nature* (1949), I, 239.

indigenous origin of English drama (and therefore of the form of Shakespeare's plays), on Elizabethan stage conditions, on Shakespeare's sources, on his idiom and his place in relation to his contemporaries and predecessors. Although we should extol the abilities of late eighteenth-century Shakespearean scholars as scholars, and appreciate the immense strides they took towards the restoration of Shakespeare's text and even praise them for initiating the genetic method in studying Shakespeare's plays, we must not be blind to the fact that as critics they were very much influenced by the common assumptions of the age, from which not even the great Malone was free.

2

The relation between Coleridge's Shakespearean criticism and his theory of poetry

When we turn from the main bulk of eighteenth-century Shakespearean criticism to that of Coleridge, we realize immediately that we are undergoing a radically different experience. His writings are at once alive and life-giving. We feel more akin to Coleridge even though we may disagree with some of his critical utterances, and that is not solely because we are closer to him in time. In the writings of most of those tireless and voluminous eighteenth-century critics and scholars we wade through a morass of pages in the hope that we may come across some illuminating remark or an important fact to encourage us to proceed on our laborious journey. But it is different with Coleridge. He may not give us the important fact, and as a rule he rarely does; yet we are amply rewarded in other ways.

The need for principles

The strength of Coleridge's Shakespearean criticism, fragmentary as it is, lies in its profoundly systematic nature, in the fine balance achieved in it between guiding principle and spontaneous response; and it is precisely in this quality that eighteenth-century criticism is painfully lacking. Here we encounter a vigorous mind playing freely, and a keen but disciplined sensibility. The reader's impression, true enough, is the starting point, just as it was in the case of Morgann; but it is usually translated into an intelligible statement, which in turn is referred back to some basic principle. In other words, Coleridge's strength as a critic consists in his being a 'philosophic' critic. Not content with simply recording his impressions, as the worst of the romantic critics do, or with forcing a work to fit in with a rigid, preconceived formula, as eighteenth-century critics often try to do, he arranges his various impressions into some sort of system – a system that has its place in a larger system of mind.

Opinions may vary as to whether the study of philosophy killed the poet in Coleridge; but there is no doubt that his philosophical preoccupation helped to make him the critic he was. One has to admit that, even if one may dismiss a great part of the philosophy itself.

To be able to see more clearly the systematic nature of Coleridge's criticism of Shakespeare it is necessary to make allowance for some important facts. With very few exceptions Coleridge did not publish his criticism himself; but the great bulk of it has reached us in the form of lecture notes, marginalia, and other fragments. He left us no formally complete interpretation of any of Shakespeare's works, a fact much to be regretted; it is absurd to try to explain it, as one over-enthusiastic scholar has recently done, by saying that Coleridge omitted to do so on purpose.[1] The limitations imposed by the form of lecturing, often improvised lecturing which in the opinion of Godwin, Robinson and others, fell infinitely short of his conversation in private company, have also to be taken into consideration. Given that repetition and digressiveness are among Coleridge's mental habits, still a considerable part of the digressions and repetitions may be excused on this score. Likewise his failure to acknowledge at least some of his debts may be due to the inconvenience of so doing in a public lecture room in the presence of a mixed audience of varying intellectual standards and backgrounds.

Yet some critics have suggested that in his practical criticism, or at least in his best criticism, Coleridge disregards his own principles, as if his criticism had no bearing upon his aesthetic theory, which is to be dismissed with the rest of his philosophizing as incoherent, obscure, and sometimes confused. It is strange to accuse a man, who at all times emphasized the need to return to fundamental principles, of taking little notice of such principles himself. The underlying theme of *The Friend*, *Biographia Literaria*, even *Aids to Reflection*, is a plea for a re-examination of contemporary basic principles in morality, politics, philosophy

---

1 Richard Harter Fogle, *The Idea of Coleridge's Criticism* (1962), p. 124. To claim as Fogle does that Coleridge deliberately left us no formally complete interpretations of individual plays by Shakespeare because of 'his conviction that literal completness of interpretation was death, mere copy rather than creative imitation', is silly.

and criticism, and an attempt to base all of them upon secure foundations. In almost everything he wrote, Coleridge felt the need to refer to basic principles, and that in spite of his obscurities which are frequently not unjustly complained of. Or perhaps it is because of his incessant desire to go back to such principles, which with him becomes almost an obsession, that he is often tortuous, involuted and obscure.

Biographia Literaria, rambling as it is, stresses the value of principles in literary criticism. In it one of Coleridge's main aims is to point to the chaos in critical writings, both in literary reviews and elsewhere, and the dangers of 'the substitution of assertion for argument', and to advocate a kind of 'philosophical criticism' which sets out by defining its principles. Before he embarked upon the actual criticism of Wordsworth's poetry he thought it wise to explain what he meant by philosophical criticism. I quote the passage in full, for it is important.

I should call that investigation fair and philosophical, in which the critic announces and endeavours to establish the principles, which he holds for the foundation of poetry in general, with the specification of these in their application to the different *classes* of poetry. Having thus prepared his canons of criticism for praise and condemnation, he would proceed to particularize the most striking passages to which he deems them applicable, faithfully noticing the frequent or infrequent recurrence of similar merits or defects, and as faithfully distinguishing what is characteristic from what is accidental, or a mere flagging of the wing. Then if his premises be rational, his deductions legitimate, and his conclusions justly applied, the reader, and possibly the poet himself, may adopt his judgement and in the independence of free-agency. If he has erred, he presents his errors in a definite place and tangible form, and holds the torch and guides the way to their detection.[1]

This is the method which Coleridge follows in his criticism of Shakespeare as well. But it is important to realize that Coleridge applies his principles with tact, revealing his awareness that they are not hard and fast rules, but useful tools to guide and clarify his responses to every individual work. First principles of criticism, he says, 'can indeed neither create a Taste

[1] *BL*, II, 90, 85. Cf. Letter to Byron, *CL*, IV, 598: 'My object [in *BL*] [is] to reduce criticism to a system.' On this point cf. George Watson, *The Literary Critics* (1962), p. 114.

nor supply the want of it but yet may conduce effectively to its cultivation and are perhaps indispensable in securing it from the aberrations of caprice and fashion'.[1] The critic is not one who voices his own personal 'opinions', which 'weigh for nothing'; he writes about a work 'in such a form, as is calculated either to effect a fundamental conviction, or to receive a fundamental confutation'.[2] As early as 1802 we find him writing to Sotheby: 'Be minute, and assign your reasons often, and your first impressions always, and then blame or praise, I care not which, I shall be satisfied.'[3] No doubt it is this quality of Coleridge's criticism that Hazlitt had in mind when in his essay 'On criticism' (in his *Table Talk*) – in part an indirect attack on Coleridge – he objected to the 'modern or metaphysical system of criticism' which 'supposes the question *Why?* to be repeated at the end of every decision'. As an impressionist Hazlitt believed that 'genuine criticism should reflect the colours, the light and shade, the soul and body of a work'.[4] The result is that, unlike Coleridge, Hazlitt often provides us with a genre of rhapsodical writing which tells us more about the critic than about the work.

Far from being desultory and impressionistic in his critical pronouncements on Shakespeare, Coleridge in practically every course of lectures on the subject is careful to begin by defining his principles. Some of these principles are involved in his definition of poetry, to which he often devotes the two initial lectures. This is significant. It is not explained away by reference to Coleridge's habit of repeating himself. Nor would it be convincing to say that the impecunious Coleridge found it easy to fill up two lectures with matter which became so familiar to him that it no longer required fresh preparation or previous labour. In the courses of lectures he gave he often had more material than he could dispose of in the allotted number of lectures announced, and on occasions he found it necessary to add one or more free of charge to the number originally planned. It is more probable, and more in keeping with his habits of thought, that Coleridge started his courses on Shakespeare with the discourse on the definition of poetry because of the importance of such a definition, and because of its immediate relevance to the

[1] Kathleen Coburn (ed.), *Inquiring Spirit* (1951), p. 156.
[2] *BL*, I, 65. [3] *CL*, II, 459. [4] *Hazlitt*, VIII, 214–15, 217.

subject in hand. His interest in his principles, and his belief in the intimate relation between them and the main subject of his lectures were such that occasionally one feels that his object in discoursing on Shakespeare was primarily to illustrate his theory of poetry and principles of criticism. This is not altogether un- justified, since he himself explicitly states in the prospectus to the 1811–12 course that the lectures would be given 'in illustra- tion of the Principles of Poetry'. In one of the lectures he admits that his object is 'not so much to illustrate the character of Shakespeare as to illustrate the principles of poetry'.[1] Any study of Coleridge's Shakespearean criticism must start with an examination of his definition – just as Coleridge himself thought that his study of Shakespeare ought to begin with a definition of poetry. And in order to know the exact nature of Coleridge's contribution to the subject we must study the relation of that definition to previous critical theory.

The pleasure principle

In a sense Coleridge was writing in the English critical tradition when he maintained, as he often did, that the end of poetry is pleasure. Poetry, he said, is opposed to science. 'The proper and immediate object of science is the acquirement, or communica- tion of, truth; the proper and immediate object of poetry is the communication of immediate pleasure.'[2] Bacon, in his essay 'Of Truth' had claimed that poets 'make lies for pleasure', although in *The Advancement of Learning* he had warned us that 'it is not good to stay too long in the theatre', philosophy, human and natural, being a far superior occupation to poetry. As we know, Bacon believed that the proper method of searching for truth is that which 'derives axioms from the senses and particulars'.[3] By setting a high value on the senses he became the originator of English sensationalism, and from him Hobbes, Locke, Hume, and Hartley derive a direct descent. Hobbes held that 'there is no conception in a man's mind' which cannot be traced back to 'the organs of sense', that imagination is only 'decaying sense'

[1] *SC*, ii, 26, 90. [2] *SC*, i, 163ff.; cf. ii, 66–8, 75–6.
[3] Francis Bacon, *Essays*, ed. A. S. West (1914), p. 1; *The Advancement of Learning*, ed. W. A. Wright (1869), pp. 104ff.; *Novum Organum*, tr. Ellis and Spedding (n.d.), bk. i, Aphorism xix.

and in no way differs from memory.[1] His 'simple' and 'compounded' imagination passed over to Locke and were renamed 'primary' and 'secondary' 'ideas', while sense was called 'impression'. Locke's impressions and ideas had a greater influence in the field of literary theory and practice than one would at first suppose. It is to the influence of sensationalism, much more than any other factor, that the rise of the naturalistic theory of literature can ultimately be attributed.[2]

In the early years of the eighteenth century we can easily detect Addison's debt to Hobbes and Locke in his papers on the Pleasures of the Imagination. Equally early, emotionalism became a force in English criticism, particularly in the writings of John Dennis, who regarded the 'pathetic', or the ability to arouse strong emotions, as a fundamental factor in the 'sublime'. Even before this time Dryden had said that he was satisfied as long as his poetry succeeded in exciting pleasure in the reader. Hume thought that the 'very essence' of beauty consists in its power of producing pleasure. In his analysis the pleasure arises from our realization of the object's conformity either to what pleases the primary constitution of our nature, meaning of course our physical nature (which is the physicalist view expounded at length in the greater part of Burke's treatise on the sublime and the beautiful), or to what by custom or caprice gives us pleasure (which is the basis of associationist aesthetics). By drawing a broad distinction between Taste, the faculty that gives us pleasure or pain, and Reason, which conveys the knowledge of truth or falsehood, Hume laid the basis for the opposition between poetry and science.[3]

With the advent of the once influential Dr Hartley, the eighteenth-century behaviourist who attempted an all-embracing explanation of all the departments of knowledge, sensationalism became truly popular and its immediate repercussions were felt everywhere. It is not irrelevant here to remember that about this time Garrick was gaining the applause of all theatre-goers by his deliberately naturalistic acting of Shakespeare. Of his per-

1 Thomas Hobbes, *Leviathan*, part I, chs. i, ii.
2 Cf. W. J. Bate's *From Classic to Romantic* (1946), where the author establishes a close connection between empiricism and the movement from the general to the particular.
3 David Hume, *The Philosophical Works* (1826), IV, 208ff.; II, 31ff.; IV, 375ff.

formance of the character of Richard III at Goodman's Fields in 1741 Murphy writes:

The moment he entered the scene, the character he assumed was visible in his countenance; the power of his imagination was such, that he transformed himself into the very man; the passions rose in rapid succession, and before he uttered a word, were legible in every feature of that various face. His look, his voice, his attitude changed with every sentiment . . . Everything he discovered was almost reality . . . In all this, the audience saw an exact imitation.

More particularly it was in Lear's madness, Murphy goes on, that 'Garrick's genius was remarkably distinguished'. Murphy is careful to point out that Garrick 'acquired the hint that guided him' from a friend of his who went mad over the loss of a beloved daughter of two, whom he dropped while fondling her at his dining room window. Garrick used to say therefore: 'I copied nature.'[1]

Sensationalism and the scientific spirit of rationality, with its emphasis on literal truth and verisimilitude in drama, had already determined the age's view of imitation quite early in the eighteenth century. Drama was considered a copy of life by early critics like Shaftesbury and Addison no less than by Blair, Beattie, or Mrs Montagu. But the belief in decorum and the criterion of generality, for some strange reason, remained unshaken. As the century proceeded, the uncomfortable contradiction became less striking, although it never quite disappeared until Coleridge attempted some kind of reconciliation between the general and the particular. Whenever the critic was left to his own individual responses to Shakespeare, there is no doubt what he would say, but as soon as he recalled his literary education and training he would fly over to the ideal of generality. The striking example here is William Richardson, whose case, though late in the century, is nonetheless typical. Richardson felt that Shakespeare's characters are so 'particular' and life-like, that he analysed them with the professed object of arriving at moral and psychological truths. Yet while praising Shakespeare for his knowledge of the human heart and his ability to portray passions, in the chapter he devotes to a discussion of

[1] Arthur Murphy, *The Life of David Garrick, Esq.* (1801), I, 22ff., 27ff.

Shakespeare's faults, he complains that Shakespeare imitated nature too closely, and even in his 'display of character' he finds him guilty of 'undeviating attachment to real appearance', of failure to observe decorum or produce 'the uniform and consistent conduct' of types.[1] But on the whole, the contradiction became less noticeable in the second half of the eighteenth century. It was then that an emotionalistic conception of poetry and a sensationalist psychology and philosophy combined to produce a naturalistic view of poetry and drama.

This took place about the time of Hartley, and can best be studied in the work of those critics who were heavily influenced by his book, *Observations on Man* (1749). Hartley himself, in the chapter dealing with poetry in his book, had written that since the pleasure received from poetry 'arises from the things themselves described or represented':

The chief art is to copy nature so well, and to be so exact in all the principal circumstances relating to actions, passions, etc., i.e. to real life, that the reader may be insensibly betrayed into a half belief of the truth and reality of the scene.[2]

But for a detailed application of Hartley's principles to literary criticism we may conveniently go to his disciple, Joseph Priestley, another popular writer of the time.

In his book, *A Course of Lectures on Oratory and Criticism*, Priestley writes that the end of poetry is to give pleasure. His crude associationist psychology, derived from Hartley, led him to the belief that the intellectual pleasure which poetry excites in us, like all our intellectual pleasures 'consists of nothing but the simple pleasures of sense combined together'. The pleasures of the imagination or the more delicate sensations which we feel when we read poetry, says Priestley, following his Hartley faithfully, are 'nothing more than a congeries or combination of ideas and sensations, separately indistinguishable, but which were formerly associated either with the idea itself that excites them, or with some other idea, or circumstance, attending the introduction of them'. By reducing the end of poetry to pleasure, the emotion it arouses in the recipient, and by interpreting pleasure in these terms Priestley concludes quite rightly that our

[1] *Richardson*, p. 425.   [2] David Hartley, *Observations on Man* (1771), I, 431.

passions are engaged 'in proportion to the *vividness of our ideas* of those objects and circumstances which contribute to excite them'. He gives us the best illustration of the naturalistic theory in his words:

With regard to the conduct of the passions, to represent things to the life, in order thoroughly to affect and interest the reader in the perusal of a composition, it is of singular advantage to be very *circumstantial*, and to introduce as many *sensible images* as possible.

The power of art has no other means of exciting our passions than by representing such scenes as are found to excite them in real life. Now in nature and real life, we see nothing but *particulars*, and to these ideas alone are strongest sensations and emotions annexed.

The poet should introduce 'the proper names of persons and things, which have a more immediate connection with scenes of real life'. The mention of time, place and person 'excites more determinate ideas; and the more precise and vivid are our ideas, with the greater strength do they excite all the emotions and passions that depend upon them. The mention of these particulars makes a relation to resemble real and active life'. Consequently Shakespeare is praised because, more than any other dramatic poet, he arouses the reader's passions, because he 'copies nature and real life in this respect more closely than most others'.[1] Under such 'despotism' of the senses, to use a Coleridgean expression,[2] the production of Shakespeare on the stage could only be naturalistic, with every minute detail reproduced faithfully in the stage decor. Commenting on the current state of stage productions a contributor to the periodical *The World* wrote (No. vi, 8 February 1753, p. 32):

The only preference that I shall pretend to give to the modern stage over Greece and Rome relates to . . . the daily progress we make towards nature . . . I did not hint at the representation of either persons or characters. The improvement of nature, which I had in view, alluded to those excellent exhibitions of the animal or inanimate parts of the creation, which are furnished by our worthy philosophers Rich and Garrick; the latter of whom has refined on his competitor; and having perceived that art was become so perfect that it was necessary to mimick it by nature, he has happily introduced a cascade of real water.

[1] Joseph Priestley, *A Course of Lectures on Oratory and Criticism* (1777), pp. 137, 73, 84ff.   [2] *BL*, I, 74.

37

It was in the middle of the eighteenth century, and not in Victorian England, that elaborate naturalistic stage productions of Shakespeare were born.

The belief that poetry has pleasure for its aim – and all that the belief involves – soon became predominant. It invaded even strictly rationalist circles. Beattie who was once a staunch advocate of the immutability of Truth, himself had no doubt that one end of poetry is 'TO GIVE PLEASURE'. The Horatian *utile et dulce* causes him to waver for a moment, but he soon waives the difficulty, maintaining that pleasure is still 'undoubtedly the immediate aim' of poetry. It is not altogether fanciful to suggest that Coleridge, who entertained a high opinion of Beattie, owes, perhaps unconsciously, something to this discussion. We remember that meeting with a similar difficulty in *Biographia Literaria* Coleridge ends his discussion by asserting that pleasure is at least 'the immediate end' of poetry. However, Beattie goes on to say emphatically: 'let this therefore be established as a truth in criticism, that the end of poetry is TO PLEASE.' In order that poetry may please, it must be naturalistic, it must 'exhibit real matter of fact, or something like it; that is in other words, must be either according to truth, or according to verisimilitude'. Beattie even goes as far as to declare that 'to a poem mere morality is not as essential as accurate description'. Not only poetry, but every art 'whose end is to please must be natural'.[1] This is what Beattie wrote in 1762. By 1783 he had been won over (or almost) to the opposite camp of Hartley. In *Dissertations Moral and Critical* he could lose himself in absurd irrelevancies like any thoroughgoing associationist when he attempted the task of analysing certain objects taken to be beautiful. To point out such irrelevancies is not my object; what I wish to make clear is the intimate connection between the rise of sensationalist philosophy and psychology and the spread of naturalism in art, and consequently in the discussion of Shakespearean drama. I do not imply that there is any logical relation between sensationalism and naturalism; but there was a historical connection between them.

Subsequent writers on the subject among Coleridge's con-

[1] James Beattie, *Essays on Poetry and Music as they affect the Mind* (1779), pp. 7, 27, 33, 23; *BL*, II, 9–10.

temporaries or near contemporaries adopted both sensationalism and the pleasure principle. The main concern of Archibald Alison's book *Essays on the Nature and Principles of Taste* (1790). is what he called 'the emotion of taste' which is an 'emotion of pleasure'. Likewise in *Analytical Enquiry into the Principles of Taste* (1805), Richard Payne Knight was certain that 'the first and most essential merit of poetry is to be pleasing'. In these studies of taste the principle of association assumes an overwhelming importance. For Knight 'all the pleasures of intellect arise from the association of ideas'; consequently, the pleasure which it is the object of poetry to produce is enhanced in proportion to the increase in 'the materials of association'. Naturalism went together with this attitude. Alison's conception of the 'emotion of taste' is such that naturalistic representation of objects becomes all-important. Knight's view of poetry is more explicitly naturalistic. Truth, he writes, 'is naturally circumstantial, especially in matters that interest the feelings; for that which has been strongly impressed upon the mind, naturally leaves precise and determinate ideas'. Exact detail he therefore praises as a virtue in poetry. Similarly in drama naturalism demands accuracy of detail in the human characters presented on the stage. Since its birth was connected with a passive view of the mind, naturalism makes it its aim to render everything on the stage as *sensible* as possible. There is not enough room left for the *creative* imagination of the audience: 'In dramatic representations there can be nothing left indeterminate for the imagination to work upon.' Consequently symbolic or non-human characters in Shakespearean drama, which cannot anyhow be represented naturalistically, lose their effect for a naturalistically minded spectator. For Knight the Witches in *Macbeth* lose 'totally their grandeur' by being exhibited on the stage. On the stage what is needed is 'a detailed adherence to the peculiarities of a common individual nature' and the most 'affecting' tragedies are found to be those 'taken from the events of common life'.[1]

Coleridge's view that poetry has pleasure for its end thus has

[1] Archibald Alison, *Essays on the Nature and Principles of Taste* (1790), p. vii; Richard Payne Knight, *Analytical Enquiry into the Principles of Taste* (1805), pp. 117, 139, 227, 291, 304.

a long history behind it. We need not agree with Raysor that he derived it from the article by 'The Enquirer' in the *Monthly Magazine*, since it was a view commonly held at the time. Besides, the author of the article was really interested in the question whether or not rhyme is essential to poetry, his thesis being that the distinction between prose and poetry is ill-grounded. The reply to this article written by 'Philo-Rhythmus' in the following number, which maintains that the distinction between poetry and prose should be made 'as clear and distinct as possible', shows where the real point of the article lies. It blurs the issue Coleridge was concerned with to relate his definition to this article, instead of placing it in the larger context of critical opinion. After all 'The Enquirer' himself was influenced by Blair, another emotionalist critic, and the distinction he drew between poetry and philosophy was made on the assumption that the proper office of the poet is to 'amuse', and that of the philosopher is to 'instruct', the world[1] – the very assumption we have been considering. The opposition between poetry and science in Coleridge's definition is the product of eighteenth-century poetics, which equated poetry with pleasure.

In Coleridge's critical theory the pleasure principle was accompanied by its corollary in eighteenth-century criticism, namely the tendency towards naturalism (although in his case it is more often than not successfully counteracted by his less crude conception of 'pleasure' and, more importantly, by his theory of the imagination). In his practical criticism Coleridge was sometimes inclined to look upon Shakespeare's characters as living human beings. In Shakespeare's plays, he said, 'you meet people who meet and speak to you as in real life'; they are 'flesh and blood individuals'. This is no different from Mrs Montagu writing about Shakespeare's characters:

They speak with human voices, are actuated by human passions, and are engaged in the common affairs of human life. We are interested in what they do or say by feeling every moment, that they are of the same nature as ourselves

or from Morgann:

If the characters of Shakespeare are thus *whole*, and as it were original,

---

[1] *SC*, i, 163n.; *The Monthly Magazine*, ii (1796), 453–6; 533.

while those of almost all other writers are mere imitation, it may be fit
to consider them rather as Historic than Dramatic Beings.[1]

When Coleridge came to defend Shakespeare's tragi-comedies
one of his arguments was as naturalistic as that of the eighteenth-
century critics: 'Shakespeare is the Poet of Nature, portraying
things as they exist.' Before him Dr Johnson had said that
Shakespeare's plays exhibit 'the real state of sublunary nature'
and that 'drama pretends only to be the mirror of life'. Beattie,
to mention but one other example, also said, 'Nature everywhere presents a similar mixture of tragedy and comedy, of joy
and sorrow, of laughter and solemnity, in the common affairs of
life.'[2]

But this is only half the story. And to think that Coleridge's
conception of poetry is all included in this definition, which is
based upon the opposition between truth and pleasure, is to mis-
understand him completely. Because Bronowski saw only this
half of the story, he could write:

Coleridge believes that man answers every question when he understands the pleasures which he takes in himself. The study of these
pleasures was Coleridge's step in psychology. In making it, Coleridge
did able and pioneer work in this social science. He did as able pioneer
work in seeing that poetry was a good field for experiments in this
science. But his work tells us nothing of what poetry is itself.[3]

Besides, as we shall see presently, the principles underlying this
definition are impossible to reconcile with those upon which
Coleridge's more valuable theory of imagination is founded.
Poetic imagination he conceived primarily not as a pleasure-
giving faculty, but as one which provides a mode of apprehending
reality. But in order to realize the inadequacy of Coleridge's
definition (and his own sense of this inadequacy) we must
analyse the definition in some detail.

Having attempted the distinction between poetry and science
on the grounds of the pleasure–truth opposition, Coleridge
realized that his definition would include all manner of writing

---

[1] SC, ii, 315; i, 13; Mrs Montagu, *Writings and Genius of Shakespeare*, p. 60;
Morgann, *Falstaff*, p. 62n.
[2] SC, ii, 313; i, 194; *Raleigh*, p. 16; Beattie, *Essays on Poetry and Music*, pp. 189ff.
[3] J. Bronowski, *The Poet's Defence* (1939), pp. 162–3.

which does not have truth for its object. He therefore tried to distinguish between poetry and prose by reference to a quantitative and a relational scale of pleasure more in keeping with the eighteenth-century mind than with his own philosophical position. Poetry, we are told, permits 'a pleasure from the whole consistent with a consciousness of pleasure from the component parts'; perfect poetry communicates 'from each part the greatest immediate pleasure compatible with the largest sum of pleasure in the whole'.[1] Supposing that pleasure is the criterion, why this should not apply equally to a well-written novel or prose drama is not clear. Coleridge seems to be thinking here of metre as the element responsible for the pleasure we derive from the parts, but surely, metre exists in good as well as bad verse and in the latter we feel no more pleasure in the parts than in the whole. As he himself says on another occasion, 'rhymes and finger-metre' 'renders poor flat prose ludicrous, rather than tend to elevate it, or even to hide its nakedness'.[2] But he half realizes that he has been trapped by his premise. In *Biographia Literaria*, when he comes to discuss the same point, suddenly the whole discussion collapses and he undermines his own grounds when he declares that 'poetry of the highest kind may exist without metre, and even without the contra-distinguishing objects of a poem',[3] meaning, of course, that poetry may exist in writings which do not propose pleasure for their object. And verysoon he shifts the argument from the point of view of the reader and recipient to that of the poet. For, he tells us, after all what distinguishes poetry is not the pleasure we feel in reading it, but 'that peculiar state and degree of excitement, which arises in the poet himself in the act of composition'. The 'most general and distinctive character of a poem', he says, 'originates in the poetic genius itself'.[4] 'What is poetry?' he writes in the same discussion in *Biographia Literaria*, 'is so nearly the same question with, what is a poet? that the answer to the one is involved in the solution of the other.' Once the argument is shifted from the point of view of the reader to that of the author, however, and Coleridge concentrates on an analysis of the poet's mind during the creative process, we detect elements other than pleasure

---

[1] *SC*, I, 164ff.; cf. II, 66ff.   [2] *MC*, p. 183.   [3] *BL*, II, 11ff.
[4] *SC*, I, 163–6; cf. II, 77.

surreptitiously intruding into the argument and in fact directing
it.

Theory of imagination

In order to understand the nature of the excitement the poet
suffers during the act of creation, which is after all that which
distinguishes what is poetry from what is not, Coleridge seems
to ask the reader to put himself in the poet's place, and to try to
recreate for himself what the poet actually undergoes. He must
first of all possess 'more than common sensibility'. By that is
meant that he must feel 'a more than common sympathy with
the objects, emotions, or incidents' which form the subject of
the poem. In other words, whatever object may happen to be the
subject-matter of a poem must obviously *mean* something to the
poet. Secondly, he must possess 'a more than ordinary activity
of the mind in respect of the fancy and imagination', which
means, in plainer language, that the field of the poet's experience
must be broad and inclusive (fancy being the aggregative and
collective power) but however widely disparate the component
parts of the experience may be, they must be reduced to a real
unity of some sort, a unity of vision or interest as Coleridge
prefers to call it (imagination being the unifying power).[1]
What then results from the coupling of more than usual sympathy with objects and more than ordinary activity of fancy and
imagination? A 'more vivid reflection of the truths of nature
and of the human heart', which is due to the working of sympathy (for sympathy from the latter part of the eighteenth
century onwards becomes a means of recreating the objects
upon which it is directed).[2] These 'truths of nature and of the
human heart', however, are not reproduced objectively as they
exist in the world of everyday life, but they are rather 'modified
and corrected' by the poet's activity of fancy and imagination,
sympathy, as it were, directing the poet's fancy to collect and
reproduce the material, and imagination reducing the collected
material to a unified and organic shape. Coleridge, indeed, in this
particular context does not state that it is the poet's imagination

---

[1] See, e.g., *CL*, II, 865–6; 'Fancy or the aggregating faculty of the mind, not
imagination or the *modifying* and *coadunating* faculty.'
[2] On 'sympathy' see Bate, *From Classic to Romantic*, pp. 132ff.

which modifies the truths, but rather says that the truths are modified by 'that sort of pleasurable emotion which the exertion of all our faculties gives in a certain degree'. But from his frequent utterances on the role of imagination there can be no doubt as to what it is that accomplishes the modification. Besides, the pleasurable emotion is only the result of the 'exertion of all our faculties', of the full working of sympathy, fancy and imagination, and it only takes place after all these powers of the mind have done their job in altering the objective world.

This brief analysis indicates that 'pleasure' is only a catch-word which confuses the aim of poetry with its result, or what attends the fulfiment of its function. Poetry is primarily a passionate apprehension of reality. Its object is to recreate human experience imaginatively, to set forth 'values', 'the truths of nature and of the human heart' not as they are in the flux of the world, but reduced to a unified and meaningful pattern. Coleridge himself is aware of this when he forgets about his pleasure principle. There is no stronger proof of the truth of that than his own theory of the imagination. It will be re-membered that in the famous formal definition in *Biographia Literaria* (ch. 13) the secondary imagination, i.e. the poetic, is described as 'identical with the primary in the kind of its agency'. The primary is stated to be 'the prime Agent of all human perception'. Now whatever meaning we may attach to the primary imagination, one thing is certain in the mind of Coleridge, and that is the importance of imaginative activity in human perception, whether the role of the activity is limited to imposing a pattern on the manifold of sensations making of them one concrete unified whole, according to the Kantian system, or is assigned itself the supreme importance in the act of percep-tion, as Schelling claims. By making the poetic imagination not only identical with, but even higher than, the primary, Cole-ridge bestows on poetry an overwhelming importance. Far from being trivial, as Bacon thought, or mere play, as some of Cole-ridge's contemporaries, such as Schiller, saw it, the poetic imagination is related by Coleridge to the serious business of life. The function of imaginative poetry is to create a unified and significant pattern of the chaos and welter of experience. That is precisely why, as Coleridge says, the whole personality of the

44

poet is engaged in the imaginative process. In imagination, we remember, the moral will is concerned, whereas in fancy it is only what Coleridge calls 'choice', which in his terminology, is something very different from the moral will.[1] Whereas imagination, therefore, is a serious activity, fancy is mere play: it 'plays with counters'.

Of the unsatisfactory definition in *Biographia Literaria* Shawcross complains, saying that 'instead of reaching a clear definition of poetry he contents himself with a description of the *poet*, which in its turn resolves itself into an enumeration of the characteristics of Imagination'.[2] But this is exactly the point about Coleridge's theory of poetry. While he would not abandon the eighteenth-century conception of poetry as having pleasure for its object, somehow at the back of his mind he feels the inadequacy of the conception, and so he always ends his definition by giving a description of the poet in terms of his theory of poetic imagination. We must believe Coleridge when he writes in the same work that his own 'conclusions on the nature of poetry, in the strictest use of the word, have been in part anticipated in the preceding disquisition on the fancy and imagination'. But it is remarkable that Coleridge did not realize that what he said about imagination is incompatible with the view that poetry is opposed to science in having pleasure and not truth for its object. Indeed M. H. Abrams once said that it was Coleridge's own intention to act 'the arbitrator between the old school and the new school' in criticism, and that he was a 'deliberate moderator between the old and the new'.[3] But it must be admitted that there is not the slightest indication that Coleridge was aware of any incompatibility or contradiction between these two aspects of his critical thought.

When we turn to the more strictly aesthetic essays, we find that I. A. Richards is understating when he diagnoses only 'some lack of confidence' in Coleridge about the equation of the end of poetry with pleasure.[4] In the first essay on the Principles of Genial Criticism he writes that 'the common essence of all [the

---

[1] *BL*, I, 193f.   [2] *Ibid*. II, 268, 12.

[3] M. H. Abrams, 'Wordsworth and Coleridge on Diction and Figures', in Kathleen Coburn (ed.), *Coleridge, a Collection of Critical Essays* (1967), pp. 126, 134.

[4] I. A. Richards, *Coleridge on Imagination* (1950), p. 115.

45

fine arts] consists in the excitement of emotion for the immediate purpose of pleasure through the medium of beauty'. Here we find a new element introduced in the discussion, namely beauty. And unless 'beauty' could be reduced in the last analysis to that which arouses pleasure (as was done by Hume), pleasure would cease to be the real differentia of the fine arts. Coleridge makes his position clear in the second essay when he tells us that 'the Apollo Belvedere is not beautiful because it pleases, but it pleases because it is beautiful'.[1] Beauty, therefore, and not pleasure is the real differentia of the fine arts, beauty which, he says, 'may be present in a disagreeable object'.[2] Pleasure is only what accompanies the perception of beauty, for 'the Beautiful not originating in the sensations, must belong to the intellect'. And 'when we declare an object beautiful, the contemplation or intuition of its beauty precedes the *feeling* of complacency, in order of nature at least'. Not only that, but the pleasure itself is an accidental accompaniment dependent upon a variety of contingent and fugitive factors: 'in great depression of spirits [the contemplation of beauty] may even exist without sensibly producing it [i.e. pleasure]'.[3] No one knew that better than the author of the *Dejection Ode*. Conversely, a good deal of the pleasure occasioned by a work of art may not be caused by the work of art itself, but may arise from purely personal associations. Again nobody realized that more forcibly than the great opponent of associationism: 'So far is the Beautiful from depending wholly on association, that it is frequently produced by the mere removal of associations.'[4]

In Coleridge's analysis of beauty the discussion, we notice, veers significantly towards his conception of the secondary imagination. 'The Beautiful, contemplated in its essentials, is that in which the *many*, still seen as many, becomes one.' The general definition of beauty is 'Multeity in unity',[5] it is the reconciliation of the one and the many; it is essentially 'Harmony': 'The Beautiful arises from the perceived harmony of an object, whether sight or sound, with the inborn and constitutive rules of the judgment and imagination: and it is always intuitive.' So he writes at the conclusion of his essays on the Principles of

---

[1] *BL*, II, 221, 224.   [2] *Ibid*. II, 257.   [3] *Ibid*. II, 241–2.   [4] *Ibid*. II, 232–3.
[5] *Loc. cit.*

Genial Criticism. It is interesting to note that pleasure is not mentioned as an essential in this recapitulation of his thoughts on the subject, but only as an attendant on that perception: 'As light to the eye, even such is beauty to the mind, which cannot but have complacency in whatever is perceived as pre-configured to its living faculties.'[1] And the faculty of taste in his treatment at this stage becomes very close indeed to that of imagination: 'Taste is the intermediate faculty which connects the active with the passive powers of our mind, the intellect with the senses.'[2] As Coleridge's thoughts on the subject develop, and as he comes under the influence of Schelling, the unity of the manifold, which has constituted his conception of beauty, becomes essentially an *organic* unity, the kind of unity which it is the privilege of imagination alone to create. Art stamps the elements it combines into unity 'in the mould of a moral idea'. The 'common definition of the fine arts' then becomes: 'that they all, like poetry, are to express intellectual purposes, thoughts, conceptions, and sentiments which have their origin in the human mind', and 'a work of art will be just in proportion as it adequately conveys the thought, and rich in proportion to the variety of parts which it holds in unity'.[3] At this moment we cease to hear of pleasure altogether.

Of course, Coleridge's conception of pleasure is not as crude as that of the eighteenth-century literary theorists. The empiricist and associationist idea of pleasure was fraught with all kinds of foreign matter. Even Hume could not see the distinction between art and utility. And as late as Coleridge's own time the confusion still persisted. It is to be found in Alison, Dugald Stewart, Richard Payne Knight, and Jeffrey, the editor of the *Edinburgh Review*. Coleridge, on the other hand, tried to point out the disinterested nature of poetic pleasure. In this respect his pleasure is more strictly aesthetic and closer to Kant's conception than to Hartley's. Following the *Critique of Judgment* he went to great pains to distinguish between the beautiful, the agreeable, and the useful. At times indeed, in his treatment, pleasure became a feeling of spiritual joy, almost the reverse of what the empiricists and associationists understood by it. In *Biographia Literaria* he expressed his dissatisfaction with the use

[1] *Ibid.* ii, 243.   [2] *Ibid.* ii, 227.   [3] *Ibid.* ii, 253–5.

of the word 'pleasure' in this context: 'The term, pleasure, is unfortunately so comprehensive, as frequently to become equivocal.'[1]

But still the definition suffers from making the end of poetry an emotion, although in his search for a criterion of excellence in poetry Coleridge is continually referring to what is beyond pleasure or mere emotion. Faced with an unsophisticated and straightforward presentation of his theory in George Dyer's preface to his own *Poems*, namely, that 'the immediate object of poetry is to please', he indignantly exclaims in a marginal note: 'Damned nonsense!' and writes, 'The poet *must* always aim at pleasure as his specific *means*; but surely Milton did; and all ought to aim at something nobler as their end.' And in a MS note we read: 'Not the mere quantity of pleasure received can be any criterion, for that is endlessly dependent on accidents of the Subject receiving it, his age, sensibility, moral habits, &c.– but the worth, the permanence, and comparative Independence of the Sources, from which the Pleasure has been derived'.[2] The sources turn out to be none other than reason, arbitrement, judgement, fancy, imagination and sensations all operating 'in due proportion and harmony'. Parts of Collins's *Ode on the Poetical Character* 'inspired and whirled' him 'along with greater agitations of enthusiasm than any of the most *impassioned* Scene in Schiller or Shakespeare', and yet he regarded the latter as the 'more valuable' poetry, and it is not really clear why he should think so, if he assumed that pleasure was the criterion. Gray's poem, *The Bard*, once 'intoxicated' him, but that is no proof that it is a good poem: in fact he later came to think it is positively a poor piece of writing. Pleasure therefore is no criterion of poetic excellence. To a mature mind, if it takes place at all, it arises only as an attendant on the understanding of a poem. On the other hand, to a 'mind in its simplicity' the pleasure is greatest when poetry is 'only generally and not perfectly understood', when, in other words, the reader's response is made up more of his own imagining than of what a poem has to offer. As Coleridge himself said, as early as 1796, poetry, even that which deals with abstract truths, is 'deemed *impassioned*, by him who reads it with impassioned feelings'.[3]

[1] *Ibid.* II, 224. [2] *MC*, pp. 320–1. See Humphry House, *Coleridge* (1953), p. 150.
[3] *CL*, I, 279; Kathleen Coburn, *Inquiring Spirit*, p. 156.

Coleridge realized that the end of poetic drama is something more than an emotion. Poetic drama is first and foremost a 'kind' of *poetry*, and as such it has not for its end the mere arousing of emotions. In fact he blames contemporary dramatists precisely for being satisfied with the excitement of emotions in their spectators, without considering whether their works should or should not embody a philosophy of life or a vision of existence. The ancient dramatists both in England and in France, he writes in *The Friend*, considered both comedy and tragedy as 'kinds of poetry'. Their excellence is that 'they excite the minds of the spectators to active thought and to a striving after ideal excellence. The soul is not stupefied into mere sensations by a worthless sympathy with our own ordinary sufferings, or an empty curiosity for the surprising, undignified by the language or the situations which awe and delight the imagination.' The moderns, on the other hand, 'sought in comedy to make us laugh merely' and in tragedy condescended 'to wheedle away the applause of the spectators, by representing before them facsimiles of their own mean selves in all their existing meanness, or to work on the sluggish sympathies by a pathos not a whit more respectable than the maudlin tears of drunkenness.'[1]

Mere laughter and tears are not the ends, or the criteria of comedy and tragedy respectively. Coleridge's spirited attack in chapter 23 of *Biographia Literaria* on Maturin's popular tragedy, *Bertram*, is directed against its emotionalism, no less than its immorality and subversion of the natural order of things. To Klopstock's remark that the criterion of a good tragedy is 'its power of exciting tears' Coleridge replied that 'nothing was easier than to deluge an audience, that it was done every day by the meanest writers'.[2] Of that criticism of his own tragedy, *The Remorse*, which arraigned it because of its lack of pathos, he wrote to Robert Southey: 'As to the out-cry that the Remorse is not pathetic (meaning such pathos as convulses in Isabella or The Gamester) the answer is easy. True! the poet never meant that it should be.'[3] It is because he saw that the end of poetry is not an emotion that he rejected Garrick's version of *Romeo and Juliet*. Garrick

---

[1] *BL*, ii, 33n., 158.   [2] *Ibid.* ii, 179.   [3] *CL*, iii, 434.

had altered the catastrophe of Shakespeare's play, and made Juliet awake the very moment Romeo has taken the poison. In his surprise Romeo forgets what he has done, and transported with joy both he and Juliet 'break out in a strain of rapture'. But their bliss does not last long for soon the poison works on him and he dies at her feet. The 'scene of bliss is changed to grief and anguish' and Juliet soon stabs herself to death. In his criticism of this alteration Coleridge says that 'a narrative is one thing and a drama another, and that Shakespeare's judgement revolted at such situations on the stage'. If the end of tragedy were purely emotional, what difference would there be, he asks, between a tragedy and a blunt razor, which can equally produce tears by 'shaving the upper lip'?[1] Against such a verdict it may be illuminating to set a typical emotionalist comment. Arthur Murphy regrets that Shakespeare had not seen this version of Bandello, for otherwise 'he would have known how to make the best use of these extraordinary circumstances'. By his alteration, Murphy believes, Garrick 'rouses a variety of passions: we are transported with joy, surprise, and rapture, and by a rapid change, we are suddenly overwhelmed with despair, and grief and pity. Every word pierces to the heart, and the catastrophe, as it now stands, is the most affecting in the whole compass of the drama.'[2]

Coleridge's attitude in this respect may also be usefully contrasted with that of Hazlitt. Hazlitt's emotionalism is such that he believes that in a tragedy the human soul is, or should be, absolutely crushed. Sophocles, in his opinion, did not write real tragedies: in his dramas 'the mind is not shaken to its centre, the whole being is not crushed or broken down'. Unlike modern tragedians, he does not present to us heroes whose souls are 'utterly subdued, or even convulsed and overthrown' by misfortune and passion. According to Hazlitt we go to see tragedies 'for the same reason' as we read newspaper accounts of 'dreadful fires and shocking murders' and 'frequent executions and trials', and that is 'because there is a natural tendency in the mind to a strong excitement, a desire to have its faculties aroused and stimulated to the utmost'.[3] This crude account of the paradox

---

[1] *SC*, ii, 35.   [2] Murphy, *Garrick*, i, 151–2.

[3] Elizabeth Schneider, *The Aesthetics of William Hazlitt* (1933), p. 134; *Hazlitt*, v, 213. Cf. Mrs Montagu, *Writings and Genius of Shakespeare*, p. 12.

of tragic pleasure is similar to that given by many an eighteenth-century critic.

According to Coleridge, great drama undoubtedly should arouse our emotions; but it should do so 'in union with the activity both of our understanding and imagination'. Immediately the understanding and the imagination are introduced we realize that it is not merely a matter of producing an emotional attitude. Coleridge's view of the origin of metre, we must remember, is that although metre demands passion as the stuff and raw material of the experience it also arises from the need to impose order upon that passion. He once described music as 'Poetry in its grand sense', because in it we get not only passion, but 'passion and order' at once; and in hyperbolic language he called poets 'Gods of Love who tame the Chaos'. 'All other men's worlds are the poet's chaos', he said on another occasion.[1] Poetry then is not just the expression of, nor does it result in, mere emotion. It primarily consists in imposing a meaningful pattern upon the flux and chaos of the emotions. In Coleridge's view great poetry is not just 'interesting' or 'entertaining'. Indeed the reporter of his 1811 lectures put it well when he wrote of his treatment of poetry: 'To those who consider poetry in no other light than as a most *entertaining* species of composition, this gentleman's mode of inquiring into its principles may want attraction.'[2] Without a 'most profound, energetic and philosophical mind', Shakespeare might have become a 'very delightful poet, but not the great dramatic poet'.[3] In *Biographia Literaria* we are told that without 'depth and energy of thought' poetic powers 'could scarce exist in a high degree'.[4] In the verses from *Orchestra*, in which Coleridge finds an analogy to the working of poetic genius, the final destination of the activity is not the 'senses' but the 'mind': poetry, as it were, in Coleridge's own words, 'steals access through our senses to our minds'.[5]

Coleridge's definition of poetry on the ground of the truth–pleasure opposition has, however, been once more emphasized in recent years by Humphry House, who made a special plea for

[1] *CN*, ii, 3231, 2355; *Miscellanies, Aesthetic and Literary*, ed. T. Ashe (1892), p. 347.
[2] *SC*, ii, 199. Cf. *ibid*. ii, 18, and *MC*, p. 160n.   [3] *SC*, i, 214. Cf. i, 228–30.
[4] *BL*, ii, 18ff.   [5] *SC*, i, 167 and nf.

the reinstatement of the emotional element in Coleridge's theory. As a reminder that the modern trend which insists upon nothing but meaning can go too far, his attempt is laudable, although it must be pointed out that he forces Coleridge's distinction between imagination and fancy to yield him the emotional element which, at least in theory, he is looking for.[1] But even apart from its historical association with naturalism, the opposition between science and poetry on the grounds of truth is a false and misleading one, and is based on an outmoded view of science. For, fundamentally it is a question of relationship or attitude. One and the same object can no doubt be treated scientifically as well as poetically, and unless we confuse categories it is difficult to see how the scientific explanation can be 'truer' than the poetic interpretation. Kierkegaard was much nearer the mark when, writing of science, he said: 'Science, fully as much as poetry and art, assumes a mood both on the part of the producer and on the part of the recipient, that an error in modulation is just as disturbing as an error in the exposition of thought'.[2]

Poetic faith and dramatic illusion

Coleridge's celebrated phrase 'the willing suspension of disbelief' suggests something similar to Kierkegaard's observation about the adoption of the right 'mood'. We suspend our disbelief for the sake of poetic faith. Coleridge's use of the words 'disbelief' and 'faith' in this connection is indeed telling. Coleridge did not say the suspension of disbelief for the sake of poetic *belief*. And unless I am very much mistaken the word 'faith' here implies something different from 'belief' or 'disbelief'. In any case, we are told that Coleridge 'used very frequently to insist upon the distinction between belief and faith'.[3] Disbelief is essentially an intellectual matter, whereas in 'faith' the question of values and the whole personality of man (his total faculties with their relative worth and dignity) enters. In *Biographia Literaria* he tells us that this poetic faith is an 'Analogon' of religious faith.[4] I cannot object, as some Coleridge scholars

1 Humphry House, *Coleridge*, p. 148.
2 Søren Kierkegaard, *The Concept of Dread*, tr. Lowrie (1944), p. 13n.
3 *TT*, 28 July 1832. Coleridge defines 'faith' as 'a collective energy, a total act of the whole moral being' (*BL*, I, 84). See also 'Essay on Faith' in *AR*, p. 349.
4 *BL*, II, 107.

have done, to the use of the word 'willing' in this context. Far from being an unhappy choice, in my opinion, it has an important function to fulfil. To read poetry as it should be read one must adopt the right attitude, one must assume the proper 'mood', to use Kierkegaard's term. We could, if we wished, read parts of *Paradise Lost* as if it were a treatise on astronomy. Coleridge himself, actuated by assumptions about 'pleasure', did read parts of Wordsworth's *Immortality Ode* with the wrong attitude. He chose not to suspend his disbelief for the sake of poetic faith. The suspension of disbelief is therefore an act of will.

Besides there is a historical justification for Coleridge's use of the word 'willing'. 'Willing' is necessary to distinguish the type of activity an ideal recipient is engaged in, according to Coleridge, from the mere passive reading of literature to which associationism leads. In *Elements of Criticism* for instance, Kames had assumed that there was a middle state between complete delusion and total incredulity which he called 'ideal presence', to distinguish it from real presence, and defined it as a 'waking dream' because it disappears the moment we reflect upon it. Based ultimately upon sensationalism and associationism, the theory assumes the power of ideas to raise perceptions, of 'language to raise emotions'. The reader's or spectator's emotions are not aroused, however, unless he falls into that state of 'ideal presence, till he be thrown into a kind of reverie, in which state, forgetting that he is reading, he conceives every incident as passing in his presence precisely as if he were an eye witness'. Of all the means of producing ideal presence, Kames considered 'theatrical representation the most powerful'.[1] But by stressing the element of choice Coleridge seems to be saying that while we are suspending our disbelief we are not mere 'lazy lookers on' on the world that is revealed to us in poetry. We are not 'ideally present' as Kames's sensationalism would have us believe, nor are we indeed dreaming or even half-dreaming as Coleridge himself suggests at times.[2] Just as the poet himself, while composing, reveals 'judgement ever awake and steady self-possession', so does the ideal reader.

The suspension does not at all imply divorcing poetry from

---

[1] Kames, *Elements of Criticism*, I, 90–6.　　[2] *SC*, I, 129, 202. See below, pp. 60–4.

life. On the contrary. It only means that we adopt a specific attitude to human experience – an attitude other than that of science. Our starting point is always human experience. And although the experience itself is transmuted in the creative process into something else, something purer, deeper and more lasting as a pattern than the flux of individual experiences – yet it is with the affirmation of some human value that we always end. As we shall see later, the values that are affirmed in Shakespearean drama are shown by Coleridge to be in some broad sense moral values, related to man's spiritual life, his joy and suffering, the dignity and grandeur of the human soul, 'the power of destiny and the controlling might of heaven, which seems to elevate the characters which sink beneath its irresistible blow'.[1] That is why it will not do to hold either the naïve assumption that what we see on the stage is something as close as possible to a real event (i.e. complete delusion) or at the opposite extreme, the hard, commonsense assumption that we believe all the time while passing through, for instance, the harrowing experience of *Lear*, that it is nothing but fiction – the two views prevalent in the eighteenth century. The first confuses art with reality, and ignores the vast difference between our responses to a tragedy and our responses to a catastrophic event in everyday life. The latter view suffers from the application of the scientific attitude to what lies outside the realm of science, from a confusion of 'moods'.

Does Coleridge, then, describe adequately the nature of our involvement in drama when he discusses the question of dramatic illusion, or when he deals with the cognate problem of imitation? Does he advance the discussion of the subject a step further than his predecessors? As regards the problem of imitation we have seen that the question of the unities as a means of producing verisimilitude had already been settled in the eighteenth century both on historical and 'rational' commonsense grounds by Kames, Dr Johnson and others. That drama aims at perfect illusion is an opinion, which, Coleridge feels, needs 'no fresh confutation'.[2] But in combating the theory of verisimilitude Johnson in particular moved to the opposite extreme, denying all dramatic illusion. This Coleridge found to be an equally erroneous view.

[1] *BL*, ii, 163. [2] *SC*, i, 128.

The truth of the matter, he maintains, lies somewhere between the two positions.

Coleridge follows his predecessors in holding imitation to be the end of drama. But he differs radically from them in his conception of imitation. In the eighteenth century the Aristotelian *mimesis* acquired the sense of direct copying.[1] Strengthened by scientific influence, this meaning, which held ground throughout the century, was in a large measure responsible for the direction taken by Shakespearean criticism, particularly later in the period. We have seen the effect of rationalism in the insistence upon literal truth and verisimilitude in drama and of commonsense in the denial of dramatic illusion. Drama was considered by all the critics to be a copy of human life, and the enjoyment the spectator obtains from it to be derived either from this delusion, that is, from his mistaking it for reality, or from his consciousness that it is only a copy of it. The 'truth' of the copy to the original was never doubted, although the nature of this truth was not always interpreted in the same way. Even those critics who insisted upon generality as the criterion of good character drawing, still did not deviate from their conception of imitation as copying, which is a strange position indeed. Imitation could be selective in eighteenth-century aesthetics, but it was never understood to mean creation in accordance with an idea. It never ceased to be copying, even if it was only copying certain features and dropping others, preserving what is common to all and omitting what is singular and unique. In Richardson's theory of selective imitation the idea of copying is naturally implicit. The poet simply intensifies or diminishes some points in his original; he 'veils infirmities', 'softens and conceals harsh and unbending features', and at best adds from 'the store-house of fancy and observation' what will make a character more pleasing.[2] Dr Johnson, who probably more than any other eighteenth-century critic preached the ideal of generality, gave no meaning in his dictionary that would show a right understanding of the Aristotelian *mimesis*. On the contrary, his argument in defence of Shakespeare's *mélange des genres*, as we have seen is naturalistic. According to the eighteenth-century view of generality the

---

[1] See J. W. Draper, 'Aristotelian Mimesis in Eighteenth Century England', *PMLA*, xxxvi (1921), 375. [2] *Richardson*, p. 421.

creative process consists in observation and abstraction. Dryden himself had said of Falstaff that he is 'a miscellany of humours or images drawn from so many several men'.[1] In Gerard's opinion the Greek artists were 'not contented with imitating the most perfect *individual* they could meet with; but collecting the perfections of many they formed one *general* idea more complete than could be drawn from any single real existence'.[2] In the same way Beattie said that 'it seems to be from observation of many things of the same or similar kinds, that we acquire the talent of forming ideas more perfect than the real objects that lie immediately around us'.[3] It is as if Shakespeare created his characters by a process of induction.

Coleridge, on the other hand, believed that imitation is not a copy, and the difference between the two consists in a certain degree of difference in the former from the objects imitated. That is why a completely naturalistic view of the characters would be inconsistent at least with Coleridge's principle of imitation. In the discussion of imitation in drama with special reference to Shakespeare, Coleridge shows that he is somewhat aware of the conventionality of Shakespearean drama – though the discussion itself in many parts is far from satisfactory. The copy, he tells us, arouses disgust, whereas a successful imitation causes delight. So far so good. But when he goes on to explain that the quantum of difference that we find in imitation is 'an indispensable condition and cause of the pleasure we derive from it', and almost in the same breath he tells us that while watching a play 'our sense of probability' is in 'slumber'[4] we suspect that the argument is breaking down, particularly as elsewhere, when he comes to analyse the state of dramatic illusion, he tells us that our power of judgement or comparison is suspended. For how can we obtain the pleasure of imitation, i.e. the pleasure arising from the perception of the quantum of difference between imitation and imitated, unless we are in possession of the power of judgement by means of which we can compare the two? 'In all imitation,' says Coleridge, 'two elements must exist, and not only exist but must be *perceived* as existent.'[5] He further compli-

[1] *Ker*, i, 84.   [2] Gerard, *Essay on Taste*, p. 50.
[3] Beattie, *Essays on Poetry and Music*, pp. 55–8.   [4] *SC.* i. 128.
[5] *MC*, p. 208; the italics are mine.

cates matters by on the one hand likening the state of dramatic illusion to that of a dream, the explanation given by some eighteenth-century English (as well as German) critical theorists, which is compatible with a passive view of the mind,[1] and on the other hand introducing the Kantian view that the moment we exclaim of a work 'How natural!' we perceive in it a high degree of art.[2]

But in the hope of throwing some light on the question, let us shift our focus for a moment from the recipient to the poet. Raysor remarks justly that 'the distinction of copy and imitation, as applied to the product of art, has a close connection with the distinction of observation and meditation, as applied to the artistic process'.[3] Perhaps the analogy can explain more precisely what Coleridge means by his theory of illusion. If observation can only lead to a copy and meditation to an imitation the difference between a copy and an imitation can perhaps be put in this way. In a copy we only meet with the external appearance of the world in which the artist does not enter; whereas in an imitation we get not so much the external world as it appears 'objectively', but rather a vision of the world experienced and felt by the individual poet. The difference therefore between a copy and an imitation is not a difference in degree: in Shakespearean drama we do not get a picture of the world recorded by observation, in which some elements are suppressed and others superadded, as was understood by eighteenth-century critics. It is a difference in kind. It is, in fact, the difference between the 'primary' and 'secondary' imagination. The world of Shakespearean drama is other than the world of everyday reality. It is an experience of it seen from a particular point of view; it is essentially a world of the spirit, an expression of the value and the meaning the external world held for the poet. That is precisely what we do not obtain from a copy.

Subjective indeed it is, but because the experience does not touch the poet's petty personal self, but arises from the very depths of his being, from 'the unfathomable depths of his own oceanic mind', it has a universal significance:

[1] On the German ancestry of the dream analogy see Dorothy I. Morrill, 'Coleridge's Theory of Dramatic Illusion', *MLN*, XLII (November 1927), 7.
[2] *SC*, I, 204.   [3] *Ibid.*, I, 200n.

Shakespeare shaped his characters out of the nature within; but we cannot so safely say, out of *his own* nature, as an *individual person*. No! this latter is itself but a *natura naturata*, an effect, a product, not a *power* . . . Shakespeare in composing had no *I* but the *I* representative.[1]

Coleridge again and again points out the impersonal nature of this subjective experience. It is an essential mark of a true genius, he says, that 'its sensibility is excited by any other cause more powerfully than by its own personal interests'. The choice of subjects 'very remote' from personal self is considered by him to be 'a promise of genius'. What he finds of specific excellence in *Venus and Adonis* is 'the utter *aloofness* of the poet's own feelings from those of which he is at once the painter and the analyst'.[2] The same thought he expresses in his letters:

It is easy to clothe Imaginary Beings with our own Thoughts and Feelings, but to send ourselves out of ourselves, to *think* ourselves in to the Thoughts and Feelings of Beings in circumstances wholly and strangely different from our own *hoc labor hoc opus* and who has achieved it? Perhaps only Shakespeare.[3]

One could in fact produce a powerful catena of quotations to prove Coleridge's insistence on the impersonality of great art, particularly as exhibited in Shakespeare. It is therefore not quite accurate to say, as Middleton Murry does, that he had 'a marked tendency to regard the writer who gave immediate expression to his mode of experience – the personal writer – as the type and norm of the creative artist in literature', or that he 'made the mistake of regarding – in his more abstract considerations at all events – the personal writer as superior to the objective writer'.[4] Coleridge always believed that the greatest artist in literature was Shakespeare, whose impersonal art no other critic pointed out with greater clarity or consistency. As to his critical theory Coleridge's position is sufficiently clear. This complete detachment and negation of self (what Keats calls 'negative capability'), this complete absence of personal interest, may help to explain Coleridge's emphasis on the relation between poetic genius and deep morality. In his *Philosophical Lectures* he

[1] *TT*, 15 March 1834; *MC*, pp. 43–4.   [2] *BL*, I, 30; II, 14, 16.   [3] *CL*, II, 810.
[4] John Middleton Murry, *The Problem of Style* (1949), p. 40.

says that 'to have a genius is to live in the universal'; meaning that during the act of creation the poet's individuality is 'lost' and with it 'his little unthinking contemptible self'.[1] The morality of a great poet, in Coleridge's view, does not, therefore, consist, as F. L. Lucas claims, in upholding 'prudish moral standards', nor has it anything to do with conduct or whatever lies outside the moment of creation.

From his other writings, particularly from his 'Essay on Method', we know the significance Coleridge attached to the distinction between observation and meditation. In observation the mind is a passive recorder of the impressions of the outside world, and is, as it were, a mirror which cannot but produce a copy. Meditation, contrariwise, is an inward recoiling of the mind upon itself: in it the mind is essentially active and imposes its forms on the passive gleanings of the senses, making of them meaning and sense. It is by meditation and not by observation that 'ideas' are born. Truth 'in whatever science', Coleridge believed, originates in the mind. Hence his emphasis on the subjective element in the creative experience: 'For in all that truly merits the name of poetry in its most comprehensive sense, there is a necessary predominance of the ideas (i.e. of that which originates in the artist himself), and a comparative indifference of the materials.'[2] This explains why, in his treatment of Shakespeare, Coleridge's attention is wholly absorbed by an analysis of what is essentially Shakespearean, to a degree such that he tends to isolate him from his age and contemporaries. In the creative act meditation always comes first in the order of importance, and then observation. It is well known that in his approach to Shakespeare's plays Coleridge disregards, nay distrusts, scholarship completely. But it is not sufficiently realized that he does so, as it were, on principle. The scholarly approach which pointed out sources and hunted for analogues to the plays represented to him the view that regarded artistic creation as a passive act of 'observation', and which in giving its attention to the parts tended to lose sight of the 'idea' or the unifying principle of the whole, which is simply the product of the poet's own mind:

[1] *PhL*, p. 179; F. L. Lucas, *The Decline and Fall of the Romantic Ideal* (1937), p. 188. See especially *CL*, II, 810 and *TT*, 20 August, 1833.
[2] *The Friend*, ed. Barbara E. Rooke (1969), I, 459, 464.

It has escaped some critics, that in the Fine Arts the Mental initiative must necessarily proceed from within. Hence we find them giving, as it were, recipes to form a Poet, by placing him in certain directions and positions; as if they thought that every deer-stealer might, if he pleased, become a Shakespeare, or that Shakespeare's mind was made up of the shreds and patches of the books of his day, which by good fortune he happened to read in such an order that they successively fitted into the scenes of *Macbeth, Othello, The Tempest, As You Like It,* etc.[1]

Whereas observation leads to a mere artificial form, by meditation a poet achieves a real organic unity in his work. Meditation in art is in fact Coleridge's description of that activity of the mind during the creative process which must include the imaginative act in the strictly Coleridgean sense. In Beaumont and Fletcher's works where the power of meditation is lacking, there is an artificial form hiding 'an inward impossibility': 'just as a man might fit together a quarter of an orange, a quarter of an apple, and the like of a lemon and of a pomegranate, and make it look like one round diverse coloured fruit.' Meditation, on the other hand, creates a genuine object with a life of its own. By meditation Shakespeare 'evolves the germ from within by the imaginative power according to an idea', with the result that his works give the impression that 'the thing said not only might have been said, but that nothing else could be substituted to excite the same sense of its exquisite propriety'.[2] The 'ideas' which are arrived at by meditation, and of which the works of art are the embodiment, are the 'values' which poetic genius reveals in a world 'of which, for the common view, custom had bedimmed all the lustre, had dried up the sparkle and the dewdrops'.[3] The values themselves constitute the poet's interpretation of the human condition: the mind of a genius feels 'the Riddle of the World' and 'may help to unravel it'.[4]

The dream analogy

If we consider the question of imitation and dramatic illusion from this angle, and Coleridge's theory of imagination invites us to do so, we realize how the 'dream' analogy which Coleridge suggests at times[5] is not only unhappy but misleading. Instead of

[1] *Method*, p. 62.   [2] *MC*, pp. 42ff.   [3] *BL*, I, 59.   [4] *CN*, I, 1622.
[5] *SC*, I, 129, 202.

stressing their 'poetic truth', i.e. the values of which they are the expression, it links the plays to harmful and aberrational forms of self-indulgence, like daydreams or reveries, which Coleridge tirelessly condemns.[1] The fact that the whole state of 'dramatic illusion' depends upon the will ('we choose to be deceived', says Coleridge) should alone be sufficient to make it something qualitatively different from dreaming and to refute the assertion that a dream-like experience is 'the highest degree' of the aesthetic state. But Coleridge seems to be influenced here by sensationalist psychology and the pleasure principle. If the object of poetry is to give us pleasure, then we must do all we can to obtain that pleasure. We must blind our judgement and willingly deceive ourselves. But this will not do. We are not mere passive spectators bewitched or lulled into a state of semi-sleep by a series of events unfolding before our eyes. On the contrary, as Coleridge himself recommends, we respond actively to a play with the whole of our personality engaged – only we do not approach it with the improper attitude, e.g. the attitude of science. If our judgement is suspended it is only suspended in one field or on one level. We do not indeed ask ourselves whether Hamlet is really Garrick declaiming a set of fine speeches, or whether Gertrude is really Mrs Pritchard cleverly simulating death by poison – not because we are in a state of 'a waking dream', or because we are absolutely suspending our judgement, but because such questions would be irrelevant, because our attention is wholly absorbed by a certain event which demands from us a certain attitude. It is not that we willingly deceive ourselves, but we willingly adopt a certain 'mood', to use Kierkegaard's term again. Such moods we continuously adopt in our daily life, for practical considerations, otherwise our life would be a chaos. If we do not judge whether or not the action and events in a play are real in the sense that our presence in the theatre is, we can still judge whether one

1 See, e.g. *BL*, I, 34: 'day-dreaming, during which the mind of the dreamer furnishes for itself nothing but laziness, and a little mawkish sensibility, etc.' See also his warning against making a habit of the passive reading of contemporary novels because it 'occasions in time the entire destruction of the powers of the mind', and 'produces no improvement of the intellect, but fills the mind with a mawkish and morbid sensibility, which is directly hostile to the cultivation, invigoration, and enlargement of the nobler faculties of the understanding' (*SC*, II, 57).

part of the play is in keeping with another and harmonizes with the whole pattern. We can still ask ourselves such questions as 'What is the meaning of the whole play?' In fact, while watching a play we are in a state of complete vigilance and mental alertness. An apparently insignificant incident, a little remark dropped casually by one of the characters, will perhaps determine our whole response to the play. This is not done completely unconsciously on our part. Without our readiness to interpret, the incident or remark may pass unnoticed, and its significance may be lost on us. That is why in an ideal recipient the exercise of judgement and a state of mental awareness are indispensable. For instance, irony, a sharp and effective tool in the hands of a master dramatist, would cease to produce the required effect without that state of awareness. When we respond to a play rightly we judge and interpret all the time, even though a great deal of our interpretation we do almost unwittingly. Is it too much to say that a sensationalist psychology which has led to the belief that we are completely passive spectators, has also contributed towards blinding the critics to the presence of tragic irony in Shakespearean drama?[1]

Nothing in fact can be more misleading about the nature of drama than this dream analogy. By stressing the element of 'unreality' it suggests a divorce between poetry and life. Once a dream or reverie is over and we apply the reality principle, we forget completely about it. But in the case of our experience of drama, because it brings our whole personality into action, many a good play has altered in some subtle ways one's outlook on the serious business of life. The relation between art and life is an intimate one at all points, and art cannot be divorced from life except to its own detriment. As Coleridge himself says, in good reading we should not judge of books by books, but rather we should refer what we have read to our own experience.[2] Any theory that deprives literature of the exercise of its noble function in life must therefore be discouraged, at least on the grounds that it is not true to experience.

Coleridge himself is not always satisfied with this description of our experience of drama in terms of a dream, in which we suspend our judgement. When he breaks loose from the

---

[1] See below, ch. 3. [2] *SC*, i, 206.

eighteenth-century sensationalist critical tradition he tells us a different and more convincing story. The experience then becomes, as he describes it, very far indeed from the sickly self-indulgence in pleasant unrealities. Although we do not apply everyday life criteria, no delusion of any kind enters into it, however 'innocent' it may be.[1] The 'delightful dream of our inner nature' is 'in truth more than a dream'.[2] Similarly, at times, he realizes the inadequacy of his assumption that we suspend our judgement, and fumbles for a more satisfactory explanation: 'I admit the prerogative of poetic feeling, and poetic faith; but I cannot suspend the judgement even for a moment.'[3] He finds that, despite all the poetic faith in the world, he cannot accept as a good poem one in which there is a purely arbitrary interpretation of life, in which the poet simply 'makes things so and so'. The experience then becomes something like the loss of our narrow personal self into an experience larger and purer than our own. The pleasure, or rather, the deep inward joy, we feel is what accompanies 'the being innocently – shall I say, deluded? – no! but drawn away from ourselves into the music of noblest thoughts in harmonizing sounds'.[4] The great poet is one 'who makes me forget my *specific* class, character, and circumstances' and who 'raises me into the universal man'.[5] That is why Coleridge thinks that the effect of poetry resembles in some respects that of religion. Like religion, poetry has for its 'object':

to generalize our notion; to prevent men from confining their attention solely, or chiefly, to their own narrow sphere of action, and to their own individual circumstances. By placing them in certain awful relations it merges the individual man in the whole species, and makes it impossible for any one man to think of his future lot, or indeed of his present condition, without at the same time comprising in his view his fellow-creatures.[6]

This indeed is a truer account of the state of aesthetic response than any dream image can be, for the so-called 'illusion' in drama is not something *sui generis*, but is exactly of the same nature as our experience of any other form of art. And when Coleridge writes about 'the spiritual vision' in *The Tempest*,[7] we

<hr />

[1] *Ibid.* I, 204.   [2] *Ibid.* II, 110.   [3] *MC*, p. 162.   [4] *SC*, I, 79.   [5] *MC*, p. 293.
[6] *SC*, II, 147.   [7] *Ibid.* I, 132.

see that the dramatic world is no longer conceived of either as a dream world of illusion or the world of everyday life, but essentially as a world of the spirit. As he himself says elsewhere, in accordance with his theory of the imagination, poetry is 'ideal'; it is not 'the mere copy of things, but the contemplation of mind upon things'.[1] 'High poetry is the translation of reality into the ideal'.[2]

Because Coleridge realizes that the dramatic world is neither the one world nor the other he is driven to the middle state which he styles 'illusion' – a word unfortunate for its association with deception. And in order to describe this state in more intelligible terms, he has to fall back upon the dream analogy, which is the product of the eighteenth-century critical tradition with its passive conception of mind and art and its tendency to relegate poetry, as contra-distinguished from science, to the realm of pleasing dreams and fancies.[3] The result is that instead of clarifying the discussion, the analogy makes it only more muddled and throws it into violent contradiction with Coleridge's other and more valuable principles which are revealed in his theory of imagination.

Relation of critical theory to practice

The question of dramatic illusion is not as purely theoretical as it may seem. In fact it has a direct bearing upon the practical criticism of drama. If the object of a dramatist is to produce as much delusion as possible, then his work will be judged by the degree of its resemblance to everyday life and considerations of form will be ignored. His job will be fulfilled if he manages to portray characters which are true to life. In this case the end of a Shakespearean critic will be only to analyse Shakespeare's characters with a view to pointing out their truth to life, measuring

---

[1] *SC*, ii, 81.   [2] *MC*, p. 162. Cf. *SC*, ii, 80–1.

[3] For the apparent influence of sensationalist philosophy upon Coleridge see, e.g., his MS note in the margin of volume i of Hartley's *Observations on Man* in the British Museum (on p. 81): 'Ideas may become as vivid and distinct and the feelings accompanying them as vivid as original impressions – and this may finally make a man independent of his senses. – One use of poetry.' The thought is essentially in keeping with the sensationalist associationist philosophy and psychology, although it is here given a characteristic Coleridgean twist. The substance, however, is that of the 'ideal presence' of Kames, and even the expression is reminiscent of a man like Priestley.

their actions and motives strictly by the moral and psychological criteria we apply in our dealings with our fellow human beings. This is precisely what we have seen eighteenth-century critics do. Coleridge, by denying delusion to drama and acknowledging the middle state, cannot be charged with the same fault. But because his conception of this middle state was in terms of the eighteenth-century views on the subject, he hovered somewhere between their position and a new position of his own. Since he conceived of the 'illusion' as a dream he tended sometimes to attach great value and significance to whatever conduced to this illusion and sustained the slumber. He would say, for instance, that all the 'excellencies of drama' such as 'unity of interest', 'distinctness and subordination of the characters', 'appropriateness of style', 'the charm of language and sentiment' are 'means to this chief end, that of producing and supporting this willing illusion'; but he would also say that 'it is not even always or of necessity an objection to them [i.e. all these excellencies] that they prevent it [i.e. the illusion] from rising to as great a height as it might otherwise have attained; it is enough, if they are compatible with as high a degree as is requisite',[1] or would demand only 'a human interest and a semblance of truth sufficient to procure for these shadows of imagination that willing suspension of disbelief for the moment, which constitutes poetic faith'.[2] Hence in his criticism of Shakespeare we find that he sometimes treats the Shakespearean character as a medium for value, and as a part of the meaning of the whole play as the poet's vision, and at other times, looking upon illusion as an end in itself, he is satisfied as long as a character is psychologically probable, or reveals psychological insight on the part of the poet, instead of considering psychological probability purely as a means. Here again, as in his definition of poetry, we have a mixture of what is the eighteenth-century heritage and what is Coleridge's own.

It is clear from the preceding discussion that Coleridge's Shakespearean criticism forms part and parcel of his general critical theory. The critical theory itself contains contradictory elements, the result of his attempt to combine what belongs to eighteenth-century sensationalism and what is essentially the product of his own dynamic and idealistic position. On the one

[1] *SC*, I, 130.   [2] *BL*, II, 6.

hand, we have the view that the object of poetry is to arouse an emotion of pleasure and all that this view entails, from the opposition it draws between science and poetry to the conception of poetry as a pleasant unreality to be willingly indulged in like reveries and daydreams. On the other, there is the theory of imagination, which regards poetry essentially as a mode of apprehending reality and as the poet's interpretation of existence. I. A. Richards, writing as 'a materialist trying to interpret the utterances of an extreme idealist', says that 'in the final theory' what Coleridge has learnt from Hartley and Kant 'came together'.[1] We can now see that it is difficult to take this coming together in Richards's sense. Far from being fused 'imaginatively' by Coleridge (how can they ever be?), the two elements were, so to speak, held loosely and separately. In his actual criticism Coleridge does not deviate from his theory, but he alternately applies now this set of principles, now the other. It is perhaps the failure to see this dichotomy that has led some critics to assert that his theory is one thing and his criticism is another. I hope that the preceding discussion has at least done something towards proving that such an approach to Coleridge's criticism is neither right nor fair.

The dichotomy or polarity in his critical position may explain – his constitutional failure to execute his innumerable projects apart – why Coleridge was unable to commit to paper his whole theory of poetry, except in fragments, for his ambitious book on poetry was never written. It is this dichotomy that may also help explain the baffling phenomenon in the history of criticism and ideas, namely the fact that several people representing diametrically opposite views have claimed allegiance to Coleridge, critics as widely different as Bradley, Herbert Read, and I. A. Richards, to say nothing of past thinkers like J. S. Mill and even Cardinal Newman. Since the theory of imagination is, as has been shown, the more valuable theory, I shall treat Coleridge's criticism of Shakespeare in the following chapters mainly from this point of view.

[1] Richards, *Coleridge on Imagination*, p. 16.

3

Form and meaning

Relation between content and form

That a Shakespearean play is essentially a dramatic and poetic vision of human existence is, as we have seen, a necessary conclusion from Coleridge's theory of the imagination. What it is concerned with are 'ideas', 'truths' or 'values', which constitute the poet's interpretation of life. This critical position, which represents a new departure in the history of Shakespearean criticism, is revealed even in Coleridge's general remarks on the characters of the plays, which at first sight may seem to belong to the eighteenth-century tradition. For example, a passage like the following:

The truth is, Shakespeare's characters are all *genera* intensely individualized; the results of meditation, of which observation supplied the drapery and the colours necessary to combine them with each other. He had virtually surveyed all the great component powers and impulses of human nature – had seen that their different combinations and subordinations were in fact the individualizers of men, and showed how their harmony was produced by reciprocal disproportions of excess or deficiency. The language in which these truths are expressed was not drawn from any set fashion, but from the profoundest depths of his moral being, and is therefore for all ages.[1]

This might be regarded by the hasty reader as evidence in support of the theory, put forward again recently by René Wellek (in *A History of Modern Criticism*, 1955), that Coleridge's criticism does not fundamentally differ from that of the eighteenth-century character-critics. And, indeed, unless we read his words with the care and attention they deserve, unless, that is, we are sufficiently aware of the precise significance of his terminology, we may be led to believe that Coleridge is saying here very much the same thing as, for instance, William Richardson in:

[1] *SC*, I, 137.

Shakespeare is most eminently distinguished by imitating the passion in all its aspects, by pursuing it through all its windings and labyrinths, by moderating or accelerating its impetuosity according to the influence of other principles and of external events, and finally by combining it in a judicious manner with other passions and propensities, or by setting it aptly in opposition.[1]

But a closer examination of these passages, especially in their wider contexts, will immediately bring out a basic difference between the two critics, and consequently set forth the nature of part of Coleridge's contribution. Richardson's Shakespeare 'imitates' the passion in all its aspects, and although by imitation Richardson means 'selective imitation', his conception of it remains what Coleridge designates 'observation'. On the other hand, a Shakespearean character is conceived by Coleridge as the embodiment of an 'idea', the product of his 'meditation' on the human condition. It is essentially the result of a subjective creative process, and a deep inner experience. Because of the profundity of the experience the 'idea' has a permanent relevance to human nature. The dictum 'Shakespeare's characters are all *genera* intensely individualized' means that the 'ideas' or 'truths' are only felt and realized in concrete human situations. Both critics are moralists, for to Coleridge these human 'truths' have ultimately a moral significance. But Richardson's morality is an explicit morality, which is essentially non-dramatic. Richardson's method is to choose a particular Shakespearean character which suffers from a moral flaw, analyse it in the light of his 'ruling passion' psychology, deducing from it a moral which he ends by exhorting the reader to follow. His truths about human behaviour he arrives at purely through an analysis of the story of the plays, and he would have been equally able to obtain them from a faithful prose rendering. The dramatic poetry, he admits, is only an embellishment. With Coleridge, however, it would seem that the 'truths' would be incomplete without the very expression. Shakespeare's language, he points out, is 'drawn from the profoundest depths of his moral being', the very source of 'meditation' by means of which the poet arrives at these 'truths'.

The relation between the thing said and the way it is said,

---

[1] *Richardson*, pp. 32ff.

between content and form, is, therefore, a subtle and intimate one. This is a critical commonplace now, but it was not so common before Coleridge's time: Blake was perhaps the only other English critic to be aware of it. The 'truths' which Coleridge finds in a Shakespearean play are not abstract notions, metaphysical or philosophical statements, or general rules of conduct, and it is only by an act of abstraction that they can be discussed at all in prose. Poetic truth, he says, is not abstract truth, and dramatic poetry 'must be poetry *hid* in thought and passion, not thought or passion disguised in the dress of poetry'.[1] Considerations of form, then, are not to be regarded as extraneous to the truths or ideas in Shakespearean drama. For, according to Coleridge, true poetic form is not a mould which is separate from the material, into which the material is poured. 'Could a rule be given from *without*,' he says in a well known statement in *Biographia Literaria* (ch. 18), 'poetry would cease to be poetry and sink into a mechanical art.' The question of the unities, to which great importance was attached in the eighteenth century, is, in fact, based upon an inadequate conception of poetic form. Whether a play observes the unities or not is neither a virtue nor a fault in its construction. What is vitally important, however, is the inner form, or as Coleridge sometimes calls it, 'dramatic interest'. If every part of a play, every scene, and almost every word in the poetry contribute towards the setting forth of the 'truths' embodied in the play, its meaning and its main theme and interest, then the form of a play is to be praised. Otherwise, the play is deficient in form. To Coleridge this complete interdependence of the constituent elements of a play is always, at least in theory, the criterion of dramatic excellence. In spite of his enthusiasm for *Romeo and Juliet* he still considers it an immature work compared with the great plays of Shakespeare. In it, he says, 'are to be found all the crude materials of future excellence. The poet, the great dramatic poet, is throughout seen, but,' he adds, 'the various parts of the composition are not blended with such harmony as in some of his after writings.'[2]

Coleridge's formal criticism

In this sense of form Coleridge offers a great deal of formal

[1] *MC*, p. 343. [2] *SC*, II, 127ff.

criticism of Shakespeare's plays. His observations on the dramatic preparation in the plays are well known. That Coleridge often dwelt in his criticism on first scenes and on dramatic preparation is, however, no accident. In Shakespearean drama, he writes, 'all is growth, evolution, γένεσις – each line, each word almost, begets the following – and the will of the writer is an interfusion, a continuous agency, no series of separate acts'.[1] Since the plays grow and develop, it is important, in order to know what they really are, that we should watch their development from the very beginning. In his criticism of the first scenes in *Romeo and Juliet* or in *Hamlet*, he is, as it were, trying to catch the 'germ' of the play, to use one of his own terms, and to define the nature of its growth and development. It is misleading to say, as R. W. Babcock does,[2] that the only possible contribution of Coleridge to Shakespearean criticism lies in his criticism of first scenes, implying, indeed stating, that in everything else his criticism of Shakespeare does not in any way differ from that of his eighteenth-century predecessors. Coleridge's criticism of first scenes is only one manifestation of what was then a new critical attitude to Shakespearean drama, an attitude of which one of the assumptions is that each play is an *organic* whole, a temporal development and not a static adding of one scene to another. Every individual scene has an implied past, a present and a future. That is what he means when he says that in Shakespearean drama we get 'expectation in preference to surprise'.[3]

When Coleridge praises Shakespeare's 'management of first scenes', it is important to note, he does not treat these scenes in isolation. What he is always careful to point out is 'the wonderful balance between the progressive action, and the immediate interest of the dialogue'.[4] There is perhaps no scene in the canon which won more consistent admiration throughout the eighteenth century than the Ghost scene in *Hamlet*. Coleridge also praises this scene. But the difference between the two modes of treatment is enormous. Of the remarks of the eighteenth-century critics, major and minor, from the time of Nicholas Rowe right down to that of Mrs Montagu and William Duff, the main theme is the wonderful power Shakespeare displays in presenting the

---

[1] *MC*, p. 89. [2] Babcock, *Genesis of Idolatry*, p. 226. [3] *SC*, I, 225.
[4] *Ibid*. I, 229.

supernatural convincingly, and the awe-inspiring nature of the Ghost. By them the scene is taken in isolation and praised, as if it were a picture revealing the truth of the remark on Shakespeare that in the realm of magic and the supernatural none dared walk but he. In Coleridge's treatment, on the other hand, the scene is extolled not simply because of its intrinsic merit, but also because of the valuable function it fulfils for the whole play. We are told that Shakespeare with great art attempted to make the Ghost convincing and important only to interest us the more in Hamlet himself. The great interest Shakespeare has gradually aroused in the appearance of the Ghost and its importance is all shifted to the hero when we are told by Horatio that Hamlet, whose name is mentioned at this point for the first time, must be informed of the strange appearance of the Ghost, who must have for him a message of serious import. Likewise, the subdued language with which the play opens, the dead silence, the cold, the welcome relief of the guard, the broken expressions – 'all excellently accord with and prepare for the after gradual rise into tragedy', a tragedy 'the interest of which is eminently *ad et apud intra*'.[1] What Coleridge admires is 'the judgement with which Shakespeare always in his first scenes prepares, and yet how naturally and with what a concealment of art, for the catastrophe'.[2] For example, in *Richard II* we see how he 'presents the *germ* of all the after events in Richard's insincerity, partiality, arbitrariness, favouritism, and in the proud, tempestuous temperament of his barons'.

This is his typical approach. In plays like *Macbeth* and *Twelfth Night* the first scenes 'strike at once the key note, give the predominant spirit of the play'. In 'the feuds and party spirit of the servants of the two houses' with which *Romeo and Juliet* opens, we have before us 'in one glance both the past and future in some effect which implies the continuance and full agency of its cause'. *The Tempest* is an example of another device employed by Shakespeare, which consists in starting at once 'the action so as to excite a curiosity for the explanation of the following scenes'. Here 'the storm of the wind, the waves, and the boatswain' arouse our curiosity, 'instead of anticipating it' as other first scenes do, and thus prepare us for the explanation

---

[1] *Ibid.* I, 20.   [2] *Ibid.* I, 153.

that follows. Yet because the tempest is in many ways symbolical of the meaning of the play the element of danger, 'the real horrors' of a storm are 'abstracted' from it.[1] In nearly all Coleridge's remarks on these first scenes a scene is judged by him valuable in proportion to its dramatic service to the other scenes, to its contribution towards the total effect of the whole play.

It is with the whole play or the total situation that Coleridge is usually concerned – only he does not conceive this situation statically or as a Chinese picture. His conception of drama is essentially dynamic. In his treatment there is always the implicit assumption that mere juxtaposition as such, effective as it may be, is not essentially dramatic. It becomes dramatic only when it is juxtaposition in motion, and when the relationship between the parts is a living one, and the elements opposed act and react upon one another, modifying, enhancing or subduing one another in the manner of the 'secondary imagination' described in his famous definition. For, after all, drama is growth and development. Thus at the masque scene in *Romeo and Juliet* Capulet's 'impetuosity' is at once 'contrasting, yet harmonized with, the young Tybalt's', and 'precipitation' is 'the character of the play'.[2] In *Lear* Edgar's assumed madness takes off 'part of the shock from the true madness' of Lear, as well as displaying 'the profound difference' between the two. The relationship between the Fool and Lear is another example already pointed out by one critic. Similarly, the blinding of Gloucester (with which Coleridge found fault at first) seen in this light, is a means of harmonizing the cruelty of Goneril and Regan to their father, making the latter more credible.[3] In *Othello* Iago's duping of Roderigo, with which the play opens, acts as a prelude to his more momentous and tragic ensnaring of Othello, both enhancing it and making it more convincing. Likewise, Iago rehearses on Roderigo 'his intentions on Othello' when he persuades him that Desdemona is in love with Cassio.[4] In the character of Prospero we are shown 'how completely anything that might have been disagreeable to us in the magician, is reconciled and

<hr />

[1] *SC*, 1, 41–2, 132.   [2] *Ibid*. 1, 8–9.
[3] *Ibid*. 1, 64–6. For Coleridge's earlier view on the blinding of Gloucester see *CN*, 1, 127.   [4] *SC*, 1, 52.

shaded in the humanity and natural feelings of the father'. Conversely, Miranda is 'never directly brought into comparison
with Ariel, lest the natural and human of the one and the supernatural of the other should tend to neutralize each other'.
Again, in the same play, the effect of the scene where Antonio
and Sebastian plot against the lives of Alonzo and Gonzalo is
'heightened by contrast with another counterpart of it in low
life', i.e. the scene in which Stephano, Trinculo, and Caliban plot
the murder of Prospero.[1] In a Shakespearean play the characters
are often 'connected, all by likeness or contrast'. For instance,
in *Richard II* York's 'boldness of words and feebleness in act'
is harmonized with Richard's '*wordy* courage that betrays the
inward impotence'. Bolingbroke's 'ambitious hope', calm and
'decorous and courtly checking of his anger in subservience to a
predetermined plan' after hearing the sentence of banishment
in the beginning of the play is 'beautifully contrasted' with
Mowbray's 'desolation' and 'unaffected lamentation'. This last
quarrel between Mowbray and Bolingbroke, and the contrast
between the two characters which it reveals 'seems introduced
for the purpose of showing by anticipation the characters of
Richard and Bolingbroke'.[2]

It is because Coleridge is not interested in character in isolation from the whole situation that he does not find the death of
Mercutio a forced machination on the part of the dramatist. In
spite of his enthusiastic appreciation of his character Coleridge
considers him only instrumental to the bringing about of the
catastrophe. 'By his loss,' he says, 'it was contrived that the
whole catastrophe of the tragedy should be brought about: it
endears him to Romeo and gives to the death of Mercutio an
importance which it could not otherwise have acquired.' Upon
his death, he continues, 'the whole catastrophe depends . . .
Had not Mercutio been rendered so amiable and so interesting,
we could not have felt so strongly the necessity for Romeo's
interference, connecting it immediately, and passionately, with
the future fortunes of the lover and his mistress.'[3] But there is
no end to the examples one might quote. For Coleridge was
highly sensitive to the orchestral movement of a play as a
whole. His criticism is rich in remarks on the interrelation of the

---

[1] *Ibid.* I, 133–6.   [2] *Ibid.* I, 154ff., 147ff.   [3] *Ibid.* II, 132ff.

parts, be they incidents, characters, images or odd phrases.[1]

When in tragedy the relation does not harmonize, but throws into relief the opposing nature of the elements, resulting in an extension of meaning, we get something like 'tragic irony'. As far as I am aware, Coleridge does not use the phrase. (According to *O.E.D.*, the phrase was first used by Bishop Thirlwall in his essay on Sophoclean drama in 1833; the date, incidentally, is significant.) The word 'irony', of course, occurs in Coleridge's Shakespearean criticism, as well as in his other writings, but he does not mean by it the same thing as we do when we use the word in its tragic context. Had F. L. Lucas noticed that he would never have sneered at what he described as Coleridge's insensitivity to tragic irony in *Macbeth*.[2] Coleridge used the word in the sense of deliberate equivocation, of saying one thing and meaning another, when, for instance, he talked about the 'irony' of Richard III. This seems to have been the only sense the word had in his time. (In 1828 Richard Whately defined 'irony' in *The Encyclopaedia Metropolitana* as 'saying the

---

[1] Examples of this kind of formal criticism, in the profound sense of the term, are scarce in the work of Coleridge's predecessors. One of them is provided by a critic, who was not primarily a literary critic, but significantly enough a critic of art, who could perhaps respond to the formal patterning of a work of art more sensitively than his contemporary literary critics. The scene in *Macbeth*, before Macbeth's castle, where Duncan and Banquo praise the very castle in which Duncan will meet his fate, Sir Joshua Reynolds describes as an instance of 'repose', a term borrowed from painting. The fine comment deserves to be quoted in full: 'Their conversation very naturally turns upon the beauty of its situation, and the pleasantness of the air: and Banquo, observing the martlets' nests in every recess of the cornice, remarks that where those birds most breed and haunt, the air is delicate. The subject of this quiet and easy conversation gives that repose so necessary to the mind after the tumultous bustle of the preceding scenes, and perfectly contrasts the scene of horror that immediately succeeds . . . This is frequently the practice of Homer, who from the midst of battles and horrors, relieves and refreshes the mind of the reader, by introducing some quiet rural image, or picture of familiar domestic life' (*The Literary Works of Sir Joshua Reynolds* (1870), I, 442ff.). There are also some brilliant, though brief and undeveloped remarks, which are worthy of the name of formal criticism, interspersed in Morgann's *Essay*. E.g. he notes that 'the real madness of Lear, the assumed wildness of Edgar, and the Professional *Fantasque* of the Fool' all operate 'to heighten and contrast each other' and that Caliban who is 'a compound of malice, servility and lust, *substantiated*, . . . is best shown in contrast with the lightness of Ariel, and the innocence of Miranda'. Morgann, *Falstaff*, p. 75n. Dr Johnson's defence of the functional nature of Mercutio's death is also to be remembered (*Raleigh*, p. 188).

[2] F. L. Lucas, *Decline and Fall of the Romantic Ideal*, p. 192n.

contrary to what is meant'.) But Coleridge also wrote of the 'natural irony of self-delusion', a sense which he seemed to have derived from Schlegel.[1] When Coleridge denied that there is any irony in *Macbeth*, he was apparently under the influence of Schlegel, and was using the word in Schlegel's sense. The latter's conception of irony in tragedy is limited to the half-conscious self-deception of the characters, and to the parodying of the main serious plot in the comic sub-plot. Schlegel also believed that 'whenever the proper tragic enters everything like irony immediately ceases', meaning presumably everything in the nature of a comic sub-plot. Following him, Coleridge thought that because *Macbeth* is wholly tragic, irony is completely absent from it. But when he freed himself from the shackles of Schlegel's influence, and relied upon his own response to the play, he pointed out, as we shall see later, the presence of irony even in Schlegel's sense (the sense of half-conscious self-deception) in the characters of Macbeth and Lady Macbeth, although he did not actually use the word. However, in spite of the fact that he had a different name for it, Coleridge's conception of tragic irony, which is implied in the examples to which he drew our attention, is essentially our own. It consists in a character giving expression to a thought truer than he would have dreamt, or in complete opposition to what the subsequent turn of events will reveal – and, by extension, in the whole pattern of action, which the very conception of tragedy involves, although it cannot be said that in his recorded criticism Coleridge ever discussed this wider implication of tragic irony. Coleridge's use of the word 'presentiment' does not differ materially in sense from the phrase 'tragic irony'.[2] The examples he offers of 'presentiment', of which, he says, Shakespeare is fond, are precisely those of what we now call tragic irony.

I have not been able to detect in the large body of Shakespearean criticism and commentary written before Coleridge any awareness of the presence of tragic irony in Shakespeare's plays. For instance, the only comment Dr Johnson makes, in his edition of Shakespeare's plays, on Iago's words to Othello:

She did deceive her father, marrying you (III. iii. 206)

[1] *MC*, p. 344; A. W. Schlegel, *A Course of Lectures on Dramatic Art and Literature*, tr. John Black (1861), pp. 369ff.   [2] See, e.g., *SC*, I, 70.

75

which, as we know, are strongly reminiscent of Brabantio's:

BRA.   Look to her, Moor, if thou hast eyes to see:
       She has deceived her father, and may thee.
OTH.   My life upon her faith (I. iii. 293–5)

and in which Coleridge points out the irony,[1] is the crude moral exhortation that 'this . . . ought to be deeply impressed on every reader. Deceit and falsehood, whatever convenience they may for a time promise or produce, are, in the sum of life, obstacles to happiness', and an admonition against 'disproportionate marriages'. This inability to see tragic irony is a symptom of a certain way of reading Shakespeare, a way which is both piecemeal and literal-minded. Coleridge, on the other hand, who was aware of the subtleties of the plays, and their wholeness, often pointed out the tragic irony in them. He was the first to draw our attention to Duncan's words on hearing the news of the death of the traitor, Cawdor:

There's no art
To find the mind's construction in the face;
He was a gentleman on whom I built
An absolute trust. (*Macbeth*, I. iv. 11–14)

'interrupted by the "worthiest cousin" on the entrance of the deeper traitor to whom Cawdor had made way'.[2] Coleridge was also the first to point out the ironic contrast between Macbeth's soliloquy before the murder and his remorseful utterance immediately after it.

That Coleridge was one of the first English critics, if not the first, to point out the frequency of tragic irony in Shakespearean drama need not surprise us. To be aware of tragic irony a critic must be able to hold in mind the *whole* of a play, to perceive the subtle meaning of one part in relation to another, as well as to the whole. No amount of detailed study, however painstaking, of every scene, as it were, in isolation can make us see irony. Besides, tragic irony, particularly verbal irony, has affinities with puns and ambiguities; it arises from the same, or similar mental habits. It is not an accident that the critic who perceived irony was the one who was himself passionately interested in

1 *SC*, I, 49.   2 *Ibid*. I, 70; cf. *MC*, p. 449.

76

puns and words in general, and who tirelessly defended Shakespeare's puns on functional grounds. There is also another aspect to the question, which bears a relation to Coleridge's 'secondary imagination'. Irony seems to be a perfect illustration of the type of organic unity it is the privilege of the secondary imagination alone to produce. As Empson once put it, irony 'gives one some means of understanding the view of a work of genius as a sort of miracle whose style carries its personality into every part of it, whose matter consists in microcosms of its form, and whose flesh has the character of the flesh of an organism'.[1]

Coleridge's subtlety enabled him to see art where previous critics could only find fault and negligence. Johnson, for instance, could not see the value of dramatic preparation in *Lear*, but, instead he found 'obscurity' or 'inaccuracy' in the first scene of the play. He could not understand how Lear 'has already divided his kingdom, and yet when he enters he examines his daughters, to discover in what proportions he should divide it'.[2] Coleridge, who was fully alive to the dramatic function and implication of preparatory scenes, did not dismiss the apparent incongruity here as the result of haste or negligence. To him it was not 'without forethought and it is not without its due significance' that Shakespeare deviated from his source in making Lear divide his kingdom already before summoning his daughters to hear their declaration of love before the assembled court. If the arrangement of the scene is regarded as deliberate on the part of Shakespeare, then the trial of professions becomes a mere trick in which the aging and capricious monarch indulges in order to satisfy a whim. The whim itself is important, because it forms a significant feature of Lear's character; it suggests the need for, and the length of his arduous and painful journey towards wisdom and self-knowledge, as well as reflecting the meaning of the whole play. In the opening of the play there is to be found, in retrospect, 'these facts, these passions, these moral verities on which the whole tragedy is founded'.[3] Lear indeed appears in the beginning of the play as 'irrational' as Goethe

---

[1] William Empson, *Seven Types of Ambiguity* (1957), pp. 44–5.
[2] *Raleigh*, p. 154.
[3] *SC*, I, 55ff. Cf. W. B. Ronnefeldt (tr.), *Criticisms, Reflections and Maxims of Goethe* (n.d.), p. 19.

noticed disparagingly; but Shakespeare intends to show him at that point with all the irrationality of folly on his head. As for the possible adverse effects of this initial folly and irrationality upon our response to his character, Shakespeare, Coleridge points out, circumvents them by a subtle dramatic method, which will be discussed in the next chapter. From his careful reading of the text Coleridge shows how the initial scene serves other purposes as well. In it we are first made aware of the difference between the characters of Albany and Cornwall, which will be developed and clarified in the course of the play. Also immediately after Lear, who is 'the *persona patiens* of the drama, and whose character, passions and sufferings' form its 'main subject matter', it introduces to us most judiciously the person who is second in importance in the play, and who will be responsible for much of its important action, i.e. Edmund. From the casual and natural conversation between Kent and Gloucester, we are given the circumstances of his birth, education and situation in life – all the details necessary for understanding his future actions.

Because of this remarkable power of reading one part with an eye on the whole, Coleridge could see relations and harmony where others could only find disjunction and heterogeneity. He sees the *mélange des genres*, which the eighteenth-century mind found repulsive and distracting, in practice if not in theory, as interfusion and functional interrelation. The comic scenes in Shakespeare's tragedies, unlike those in the works of Beaumont and Fletcher, 'react upon and finally fuse with the tragic interest'. In Beaumont and Fletcher, 'the comic scenes are rarely so interfused amidst the tragic as to produce a unity of the tragic on the whole, without which the intermixture is a fault. In Shakespeare this is always managed with transcendant skill.' But the plays of Beaumont and Fletcher are only 'aggregations without unity', while 'in the Shakespearean drama there is vitality which grows and evolves itself from within – a keynote which guides and controls the harmonies throughout'.[1] Accommodating himself 'to the taste and spirit of the times' in introducing fools and clowns in his serious plays to satisfy the demand of the Elizabethan audience, Shakespeare by no means sacrifices artistic considerations. In *Lear* the Fool constitutes an integral

[1] *MC*, pp. 78, 43; *TT*, 1 July 1833.

part of the whole, and in the other plays, Coleridge remarks in Lecture II of the 1811–12 course, 'though perhaps in a less degree, our great poet has evinced the same skill and felicity of the treatment'. Even the songs, as Shakespeare uses them, often have a dramatic function to fulfil. For example, they are 'often made characteristic of the person who has called for them', as in the case of Desdemona and of the Duke in *As You Like It*. Of a more complex nature is the relation of Ophelia's songs to the dramatic structure of the play.[1] It is not that Coleridge always pointed out in detail how the component parts of the plays form organic wholes, or that he was always right in the cases where he attempted such an analysis. This is not the point at issue. Our present concern is to show the extent of his formal criticism of these plays, something which is still not sufficiently realised.

Considering the amount of formal criticism with which his writings on Shakespeare abound, it scarcely seems just to accuse Coleridge of neglecting plot. As Barbara Hardy has complained, even T. M. Raysor, who has done much to make Coleridge's Shakespearean criticism available, joined the ranks of his accusers. Although scholars[2] are now beginning to realize the injustice of such accusations, the charges are still made, even in unlikely quarters. It is not surprising to find them repeated in the unsympathetic treatment furnished by René Wellek in his *History of Modern Criticism*; but one had hoped Raysor would modify his position in his new edition of the text in 1960. He disappoints us, and so does Alfred Harbage, whose recent sympathetic introduction to Terence Hawkes' selection of *Coleridge's Writings on Shakespeare* (1959) does not mention a word about Coleridge's criticism of form or structure. More recently J. A. Appleyard, in his book *Coleridge's Philosophy of Literature* (1965), asserted that 'the formal or structural aspects of dramatic art seem to have concerned him not at all'.[3] Yet Coleridge is the

1 *SC*, II, 73; I, 33, 226–7.
2 In fact the following seem to be the only voices that have been raised in protest: Barbara H. Hardy, 'A Smack of Hamlet', *Essays in Criticism*, VIII (1958); M. M. Badawi, 'Coleridge's Formal Criticism of Shakespeare's Plays', *Ibid*. x (1960); R. H. Fogle, *The Idea of Coleridge's Criticism* (1962), p. 113.
3 Wellek, *History of Modern Criticism*, II, 178–9; S. T. Coleridge, *Shakespearean Criticism*, ed. T. M. Raysor (1960), I, 182n; Terence Hawkes (ed.), *Coleridge's Writings on Shakespeare* (1959); J. A. Appleyard, *Coleridge's Philosophy of Literature* (1965), p. 146.

first English Shakespearean critic to write serious formal criticism of a number of plays. It is true that at one point he does not mention 'plot' among the constituent elements of poetic drama;[1] but this can hardly be taken seriously against him as a sign of neglect of 'plot or structure' in the teeth of the overwhelming evidence of his practical criticism. In the very fragment in which he sets down the constituents of poetic drama, Coleridge tells us that 'each part should be proportionate, tho' the whole perhaps impossible: at all events it should be compatible with a sound sense of logic in the mind of the poet himself' – which is nothing if not a criticism of structure. Raysor claims that Coleridge's criticism of Shakespeare is 'poetic rather than dramatic'. Yet, as we shall see (ch. 6), no critic insisted more strongly upon the distinction between poetry and *dramatic* poetry.

We must remember that by 'plot' Coleridge does not mean the artistic structure of a play, but rather the mere story or fable. This is clear from the imaginary conversation between himself and a defender of the contemporary melodrama, published in the second of Satyrane's letters in *Biographia Literaria*. There we are told that it is not the story that matters:

The greater part, if not all, of his [Shakespeare's] dramas were, as far as the names and the main incidents are concerned, already stock plays. All the *stories*, at least, on which they are built pre-existed in the chronicles, ballads, or translations of contemporary or preceding English writers.

It is 'the manner, the situations, the action and reaction of the passions' that matter. The story is only the 'canvas', so to speak, *on* which, and not *by* which a dramatist displays his 'appropriate excellence'. The manner and situations are Coleridge's words for 'plot' in the profound sense. In the fragment on 'The Characteristics of Shakespeare' he describes the function of plot in exactly the same terms as he does the story here. The plot, he says, 'is only the canvas'.[2] Coleridge is of course right when he stresses the 'subordination' of plot in the sense of the mere story and the external arrangement of incidents. Because he throws all the emphasis on the handling or treatment of the story rather than on the story itself, reading Coleridge is a

<hr>

[1] *SC*, I, 205–6.   [2] *BL*, II, 161ff.; *SC*, I, 226.

tonic against the excesses of any historical approach that sets too great a value on similarity in story or fable and stands in danger of regarding Shakespearean drama as a period piece.

Indeed in his practical criticism Coleridge did not write about the plots of Shakespeare's plays in the manner of the eighteenth-century critics. Unlike them, he did not make a facile application of Aristotle's rules for a beginning, a middle, and an end in fable, or the mechanical criticism of the unities. Such formal criticism, in the superficial sense of the word, finds no place in his work. With his deep sense of the organic form of Shakespearean drama, he considered the whole outward movement of a play as the embodiment of the vision it expresses. The 'fable' of a play in this view ceases to be important in itself, and becomes, as it were, a concrete symbol of the meaning of the play. 'The events themselves,' he writes, 'are immaterial, otherwise than as the clothing and manifestation of the spirit that is working within.'[1]

It is, of course, true that of the body of his criticism that has reached us in the form of lectures (but not of marginalia), criticism of character seems to take the lion's share; but this is no proof that Coleridge neglects plot or fails to see its importance. In the compact ninth lecture of the 1811–12 course, for example, we have a magnificent analysis of the plot of *The Tempest*, which was meant to prove the poet's superb judgement. 'The storm,' he is reported to have said, 'and all that precedes the tale, as well as the tale itself, serve to develop completely the main characters of the drama, as well as the design of Prospero.' The first scene:

was meant as a lively commencement of the story; the reader is prepared (by the bustle and excitement) for something that is to be developed, and in the next scene he brings forward Prospero and Miranda. How is this done? By giving to his favourite character, Miranda, a sentence which at once expresses the violence and fury of the storm, such as it might appear to a witness on the land, and at the same time displays the tenderness of her feelings.

The reader is finely prepared for what is to follow:

Prospero is introduced, first in his magic robe, which, with the assistance of his daughter, he lays aside, and we then know him to be a being

[1] *SC*, I, 139.

81

possessed of supernatural powers. He then instructs Miranda in the story of their arrival in the island, and this is conducted in such a manner, that the reader never conjectures the technical use the poet has made of the relation, by informing the auditor of what it is necessary for him to know.

The next step is the warning by Prospero, that he means, for particular purposes, to lull his daughter to sleep; and here he exhibits the earliest and mildest proof of magical power. In ordinary and vulgar plays we should have had some person brought upon the stage, whom nobody knows or cares anything about, to let the audience into the secret. Prospero having cast a sleep upon his daughter, by that sleep stops the narrative at the very moment when it was necessary to break it off, in order to excite curiosity, and yet to give the memory and understanding sufficient to carry on the progress of the history uninterruptedly . . .

The manner in which the heroine is charmed asleep fits us for what follows, goes beyond our ordinary belief, and gradually leads us to the appearance and disclosure of a being of the most fanciful and delicate texture, like Prospero, preternaturally gifted. In this way the entrance of Ariel, if not absolutely forethought by the reader, was foreshown by the writer.

Coleridge goes on commenting on the way Shakespeare introduces Ariel, Caliban, the lovers, the conspiracies, and so on, showing how 'the same judgment is observable in every scene, still preparing, still inviting and still gratifying, like a finished piece of music'. This is criticism of plot or structure in the best sense, criticism which enters imaginatively into the poet's workshop, but all the while taking into account the effect the work has on the recipient. 'Caliban is described in such a manner by Prospero, as to lead us to expect the appearance of a foul unnatural monster. He is not seen at once: his voice is heard; this is the preparation: he was too offensive to be seen first in all his deformity.' This kind of criticism of plot does not deal with the management of events only as such. It is rather an organic approach to plot, relating event and character, when the two illuminate each other and help to enforce the design of the whole. Ariel's reluctance 'to be under the command even of Prospero' (itself in keeping with his character) 'is kept up through the whole play, and in the exercise of his admirable judgment Shakespeare has availed himself of it, in order to give Ariel an interest in the event, looking forward to that moment when he was to gain his last and only reward – simple and eternal liberty'. As a reporter of one of his 1818–19 lectures said, 'criticism of this kind cannot be abridged'; and on that ground I hope that the preceding lengthy quotations may be excused.[1]

According to the syllabus of the 1812–13 lectures, the object of the seventh lecture was partly to give 'the proofs that a profound judgment in the construction of his Plays is equally the characteristic of Shakespeare'. One of the lectures given in Bristol (1813–14) was concerned with the analysis of the construction of the two tragedies, *Hamlet* and *Macbeth*. In the prospectus to his last course of lectures on Shakespeare (1818–19), the text of which is still missing, we are told that Coleridge intended to give:

a course of Six Lectures, each having for its subject some one play of Shakespeare's, scene by scene, for the purpose of illustrating the conduct of the plot, and the peculiar force, beauty and propriety, of the language, in the particular passages, as well as the intention of the great Philosophical Poet in the prominent characters of each play, and the unity of interest in the whole and in the apparent contrast of the component parts.

On every occasion Coleridge declared his conviction, stated in *Biographia Literaria* (ch. 2) that Shakespeare revealed 'consummate judgment not only in the general construction, but in all the detail, of his dramas'. But because Coleridge's criticism of plot is of the kind that 'cannot be abridged', and criticism of character is at any rate much easier to note down and remember, it may be that a great part of his criticism of structure, given in the lectures, has unfortunately failed to reach us.

The difference between Coleridge's conception of dramatic structure and that of his predecessors becomes even clearer when we consider his treatment of the unities. Coleridge realized how the particular conditions of the stage for which Shakespeare wrote determined the form of his plays. By his time the argument that Elizabethan drama, unlike that of Greece, did not observe the unities because it was intended for a different kind of stage had already become general knowledge. Like some of his

[1] *SC*, ii, 169–79, 322.

predecessors who had rejected the unities of time and place, Coleridge thought it necessary for a dramatist to observe the unity of action. This unity, however, Coleridge understood in a way which makes his position entirely different from that of his predecessors. Dr Johnson was perhaps the most powerful critic in the eighteenth century to advocate the unity of action as the only essential law of drama. But in Johnson's view the law affects only the external arrangement of events; it recommends neat causal relations between the various actions of a play. Coleridge, probably under the influence of Schlegel, as Raysor and Wellek suggest, preferred to call his law 'instead of unity of action' 'homogeneity, proportionateness, and totality of interest'. The difference is not simply one of nomenclature. Coleridge's amounts to a new law, and reveals a different attitude to drama. Whereas Johnson's law is concerned with the plot, in the sense of the surface and purely logical relation between the events, Coleridge's affects the whole form and structure of a play. The totality of interest is the totality of the vision the play expresses; it pervades plot, character, imagery and rhythm alike. This, Coleridge believed, is what only a genius can produce; for the work of a genius is 'effected by a single energy, modified *ab intra* in each component part'. Despite the shortcomings of *Romeo and Juliet* (he thought it is more of a poem than a poetic drama), he could still detect and trace the working of genius in it. He summed up the character of the play in the speeches of Romeo and Friar Laurence:

> ROM.   Do thou but close our hands with holy words,
> Then love-devouring death do what he dare,
> It is enough I may but call her mine.
> FR.L.   These violent delights have violent ends,
> And in their triumph die, like fire and powder
> Which as they kiss consume: (II. vi. 6–11)

His comment, substantiated later by Caroline Spurgeon's card index method, was that the speeches reveal clearly 'the precipitation which is the character of the play'. The precipitation is to be found not only in the love of Romeo and Juliet and their hasty marriage; it marks the heat of the family feud, which Coleridge takes to be one of the main themes of the play, and it is there in the 'impetuosity' of Tybalt and Capulet and in the latter's decision to bring Paris into wedlock so soon. The theme of the family feud is introduced with all its variations in a minor key in the opening of the play: 'With his accustomed judgment Shakespeare has begun by placing before us a lively picture of all the impulses of the play, like a prelude.' Human folly, in the shape of the family quarrel, is set before us first in 'the laughable absurdity of the evil in the contagion of the servants', then in its serious aspect, which is to be developed later on in the play, and the remainder of the scene is 'a motley dance of all ranks and ages to one tune'.[1]

Reinstatement of Shakespeare's conscious artistry

To refute the view that the plays are shapeless products, a new understanding of form was necessary. What was needed was a critical position, like Coleridge's, which both in theory and in practice insisted upon the sharp distinction between the organic and mechanical forms:

The form is mechanic when on any given material we impress a pre-determined form, not necessarily arising out of the properties of the material . . . The organic form, on the other hand, is innate; it shapes as it develops itself from within, and the fullness of its development is one and the same with the perfection of its outward form.[2]

Most probably, this view, with its clear differentiation between the two types of form, is ultimately not original. Coleridge may have borrowed it from Schlegel, Richter and Schelling. It does not really matter that Coleridge has borrowed it, since he has thoroughly assimilated it into his general critical position. The comparison between a Shakespearean play and an organism was not itself very new. Eighteenth-century critics and aestheticians, like Kames, Gerard, and even Mrs Montagu, sometimes introduced it in their writings.[3] But there it is referred to merely as an abstract principle, which is never applied in criticism of the individual plays. The only type of formal criticism we find in the

---

1 *Ibid.* I, 4ff. Cf. Wellek, *History of Modern Criticism*, II, 155n.
2 *SC*, I, 224. See also *MC*, p. 212 and n.1. For a detailed exposition of the distinction see *AR*, pp. 40–1, and *PhL*, pp. 354–5.
3 See, e.g., Kames, *Elements of Criticism*, I, 27, and Mrs Montagu, *Writings and Genius of Shakespeare*, pp. x–xi.

eighteenth century is that which deals with the unities, and, naturally enough, after the dethronement of the unities we virtually cease to find formal criticism altogether. Coleridge, however, having learnt the German distinction, spent the rest of his life expounding it in theory in England, and the large body of his actual criticism of Shakespeare's plays is an example of the application of the principle. That is why it ceases to matter whether or not he arrived at it himself. M. H. Abrams even tells us that in Coleridge's detailed application the principle became a speculative instrument of such power of insight that it 'had no peer among the German organic theorists', a view which has been recently reiterated by W. J. Bate.[1]

There are reasons why Coleridge felt at home in this application. Apart from any question of debt to others, the principle of the organic unity of a work of art seems to be a direct outcome of his theory of imagination. To those who assert that in his practical criticism Coleridge was oblivious of his theory, the answer is so simple that indeed it is a matter of wonder how it could have been missed. If one were to summarize the whole of Coleridge's contribution to Shakespearean criticism one could quite safely describe it as the application of the principle of the organic unity of the plays. Now a moderate study of Coleridge's theory of imagination will reveal that it is the function of the 'secondary imagination' to produce this kind of unity. (It is this idea which led him to the notorious false etymology of the German word *Einbildungskraft*.) Works which achieve this unity are always described by him as works of imagination, while others in which this unity is lacking are called works of fancy. As is often the case with Coleridge, what he borrows in the course of his reading he assimilates into his own system. The organic and mechanical forms become in his system the products of imagination and fancy respectively. Thus the plays of Shakespeare are often cited as examples of works of imagination while those of Beaumont and Fletcher are designated works of fancy. In the former, he claims, there is an organic unity; in the latter there is only a mechanical one. In *Biographia Literaria* (ch. 15) he says that 'the power of reducing multitude into unity of effect and modifying a series of

[1] M. H. Abrams, *The Mirror and the Lamp* (1953), p. 170; W. J. Bate, *Coleridge* (1969), pp. 147–8.

86

thoughts by some one predominant thought or feeling' is a gift of the imagination.

Because Coleridge believes that the form of Shakespeare's plays is both organic and considered, he regards it as one of his main functions as a critic to combat the popular erroneous notion that Shakespeare was 'a great dramatist by a sort of instinct', a 'pure child of nature', a great genius indeed, but 'wild', 'ir- regular' and devoid of 'taste or judgment'.[1] That this view was still popular can be clearly seen from, e.g. Jeffrey's reviews of Weber's edition of Ford's *Works*, or of *Wilhelm Meister*. As late as August 1811 Jeffrey could write in the *Edinburgh Review*:

If it be true that no other man has ever written so finely as Shakespeare has done in his happier passages, it is no less true that there is not a scribbler now alive who could possibly write worse than he has sometimes written – who could, on occasion, devise more contemptible ideas, or mis- place them so abominably, by the side of such incomparable excellence.

Or:

The notoriety of Shakespeare may seem to make it superfluous to speak of the peculiarities of those old dramatists, of whom he will be admitted to be so worthy a representative. Nor shall we venture to say anything of the confusion of their plots, the disorders of their chronology, their contempt of the unities, their imperfect discrimination between the provinces of Tragedy and Comedy.

Yet in his review of Hazlitt's *Characters of Shakespeare's Plays* Jeffrey called himself an idolator of Shakespeare. Coleridge is well aware that the criticism of the preceding century, especially that which rationalized the 'rules', had, paradoxically, ended in the supernaturalization of Shakespeare, in making him an in- explicable phenomenon. He deprecates this, and exposes its absurdity: 'To a thinking mind it cannot but be painful to find any excellence merely human, thrown out of all human analogy, and thereby leaving us neither rules for imitation, nor motives to imitate.' And he takes it upon himself to show that Shakespeare's judgement and conscious artistry are equal to his genius. He even gives much of his attention to the study of Shakespeare's early non-dramatic output – which had hardly any critical con- sideration prior to Coleridge's time, and which was summarily dismissed by Hazlitt as not worthy of criticism – in order to

[1] *SC*, I, 219ff.; cf. II, 164.

prove that Shakespeare 'appears from his poems alone, apart from his great works, to have possessed all the conditions of a true poet'. His conclusion in *Biographia Literaria* (ch. 15) is that Shakespeare was 'no automaton of genius, no passive vehicle of inspiration possessed by the spirit, not possessing it'.

In Coleridge's opinion genius cannot rightly be opposed to rules; these rules in any case are not imposed from without, and being only a means to an end they have no sanctity in themselves, but vary with every age and even with every individual work. He had read Lessing, whom he admired all his life, and whose biography he long contemplated writing, with sufficient attention to realize that the eighteenth-century conception of 'wild genius' is not tenable. Indeed an entry in one of his *Notebooks* (I. 1255) suggests that he had reached this conclusion independently quite early in his life. Coleridge did not belittle the role of inspiration, the unconscious element, in poetry; but he believed that no great art is made up of inspiration alone; there must be a balance between the conscious and the unconscious. Without judgement, he said, genius 'either cannot be, or cannot at least manifest itself'.[1] As Humphry House pointed out,[2] the belief that there must be a large conscious element in a work of art is a necessary corollary to Coleridge's theory of imagination, for without the coexistence of the conscious will with the secondary imagination we would inevitably get 'mania', 'which is the final state of the Imagination "if the check of the senses and the reason were withdrawn"'. Consequently, wherever possible Coleridge stresses the conscious and deliberate artistry of Shakespeare and expresses his doubt 'whether the judgment or the genius of the man has the stronger claim to our wonder'.[3] In the 'Essay on Method' he elaborates on the theme (expressed in chapter 1 of *Biographia Literaria*) that poetry has a logic of its own, 'no less severe' than that of science. What the critics find to be pure irregularity in Shakespeare's work, he says, is only a higher and 'more methodical sense of harmony' than they can understand. 'A very slight knowledge of music will enable any-

---

[1] *MC*, p. 101. On the role of the unconscious in Coleridge's view of the imagination see James Volant Baker, *The Sacred River: Coleridge's Theory of the Imagination* (1958). [2] Humphry House, *Coleridge*, p. 145.

[3] *Coleridge on Logic and Learning*, ed. A. D. Snyder (1929), p. 110.

one to detect discords in the exquisite harmonies of Haydn or Mozart', but will never reveal to him the superior judgment of the composer in introducing the minor note into the major key.[1]

Of course, for the reinstatement of Shakespeare's conscious artistry it was also necessary to realize that Shakespearean drama is a genre of its own, and that it is highly developed, not drama in its infancy. For that a certain amount of historical knowledge was needed. Despite his notorious lack of respect for Shakespeare scholars, Coleridge was not as ignorant of the historical background of Shakespearean drama as he is sometimes made to appear. Of its relation to the morality plays he was aware: he knew the affinity between the villain and the Devil, between the Clown and old Vice. He also knew the relation the plays bear to the romance tradition: he pointed it out, for instance, in his notes on *Love's Labour Lost*. He was also sufficiently familiar with the basic features of the Elizabethan stage. Indeed, in his preoccupation with the lasting element in Shakespeare's works, he sometimes went so far as to say that the stage Shakespeare wrote for is really 'that of the universal mind'.[2] But such a statement, because of the hyperbole it contains, should not be taken to mean that Coleridge did not recognize that Shakespeare wrote for a 'particular stage'. Coleridge undoubtedly knew the facts about Elizabethan stage conditions which had been unearthed by late-eighteenth-century scholars. Capell and Malone had already pointed to the relative bareness of Shakespeare's stage, and its freedom from the modern elaborate paraphernalia of scenery, as well as to the inference that the plays appealed mainly to the ear and the imagination. Coleridge may have tended to minimize the importance of the visual appeal of Elizabethan stage performances, but there is no doubt that he believed that the peculiar structure of the Elizabethan stage and the manner of Elizabethan acting emphasized the poetic nature of drama. It is not true to say, as M. C. Bradbook does, that he 'condemned Shakespeare's age and stage by implication'.[3] On the contrary, he objected to the contemporary naturalistic style of performance which treated Shakespeare's poetic drama as if it were the same kind of thing as the

[1] *SC*, II, 347f.   [2] *Ibid.* I, 4.
[3] M. C. Bradbrook, *Elizabethan Stage Conditions* (1932), p. 14.

contemporary realistic play. He explicitly said that if Shakespeare 'had lived in the present day and had seen one of his plays represented, he would the first moment have felt the shifting of the scenes' and 'he would have constructed them [his plays] no doubt on a different model'. But Coleridge was grateful that Shakespeare lived at a time when theatrical conditions were more favourable to poetic drama.[1]

What is most important here is that he entertained no misguided notions on the intellectual standard of the Elizabethan audience. They were not ignorant people whose barbaric taste was responsible for all the unhappy irregularities of Shakespeare's plays – the thing which we constantly hear in the eighteenth century, especially in its first half. Nor were they, as the late eighteenth-century primitivists thought, primitive and unenlightened people, who because they lived in an early stage of society, were gifted with a fiery imagination that made ghosts and other supernatural phenomena everyday realities, and who could speak a colourful language vitiated by an abundance of mixed metaphors. Just as he exploded the preposterous notion that Shakespeare was a wild and irregular genius Coleridge showed this view of the Elizabethan audience to be crude and unacceptable. The picture he painted of the intellectual standard of Shakespeare's times was, if anything, slightly idealized. The English court, he believed, 'was still the foster-mother of the state and the muses'; and 'the courtiers, and men of rank and fashion, affected a display of wit, point and sententious observation, that would be deemed intolerable at present'.[2] Against such a background a satire like *Love's Labour's Lost* becomes intelligible. But this may seem too like the picture of the Elizabethan court and society imagined by eighteenth-century critics, in which we are told that 'the public taste was in its infancy; and delighted (as it always does during that state) in the high and turgid', or that 'the professor quibbled in his chair, the judge quibbled on the bench, the prelate quibbled in the pulpit, the statesman quibbled at the council-board; nay, even majesty quibbled on the throne'.[3] Apart from taking word play

---

[1] *SC*, ii, 85; cf. 97, 278.   [2] *Ibid.* i, 93ff.

[3] William Warburton, 'Preface to Shakespeare', *Smith*, p. 104; Mrs Montagu, *Writings and Genuis of Shakespeare*, pp. xiii–xiv, 89.

as a sign of mental vigour, Coleridge knew well that the Elizabethan audience were highly trained in the art of language by eloquent sermons, political pamphlets and miscellaneous tracts:

A hundred years of controversy, involving every great political, and every dear domestic, interest, had trained all but the lowest classes to participate. Add to this the very style of the sermons of the time, and the eagerness of the Protestants to distinguish themselves by long and frequent preaching, and it will be found that, from the reign of Henry VIII to the abdication of James II no country ever received such a national education as England.[1]

When we know that Shakespeare's times were marked by what Coleridge described as 'a general energy of thinking', we cease to find it baffling or mysterious that Shakespeare's great dramas were possible and popular.

That Coleridge went too far in his attempt to reinstate Shakespeare's judgement hardly needs to be said now. Some of his pronouncements on Shakespeare are uncritical, and have been found unacceptable. He is guilty, with the eighteenth-century critics, of pure bardolatry; yet he wears his bardolatry with a difference. The origin of the bardolatry of his predecessors, with the possible exception of Morgann, is their belief that Shakespeare, in spite of faults, was a wonderful creator of characters. They regarded him almost with awe, as if he were a mysterious phenomenon; they could not explain how such a man, so ignorant of the rules of art and whose plays are so shapeless, could produce such an amazing gallery of living characters. What struck them most in him, especially as the century drew to its close, was his miraculous power of characterization. Coleridge's bardolatry is of a different brand. It was due to his realization that Shakespeare was not only an inspired creator of characters, but was also a fully conscious artist, who wrote plays which are 'perfect' in form.

The search for meaning

If Shakespeare was a fully conscious artist, who never wrote anything without design, the question then arises while reading

---

[1] *SC*, i, 94; cf. ii, 84, 86.

him: What was the design behind each particular play? What is the play's meaning? For instance, this is how Coleridge opens his discussion of *Hamlet* in the twelfth lecture of the 1811–12 series:

The first question we should ask ourselves is – What did Shakespeare mean when he drew the character of Hamlet? He never wrote any thing without design, and what was his design when he sat down to produce this tragedy?

In his search for the meaning of the plays the question of their form persistently presented itself to Coleridge's mind. After all, form and meaning are two facets of the same thing, distinguishable only for the sake of critical convenience. Coleridge found that Shakespeare's plays are divided roughly into two groups. In some plays, like *Hamlet*, the main interest lies in one or two 'indisputably prominent' characters, and the meaning of such plays is to be inferred from the nature of the experience these characters pass through. But this does not mean that such prominent characters should be disengaged completely from the artistic pattern of the whole. Coleridge's aversion to the performance of Shakespeare in his time was caused by the fact that plays were never acted in their original form, and by the prevailing habit of giving 'star performances', instead of harmonious productions of integral wholes. In Lecture iv of the 1811–12 course he deplores the practice of giving important roles to celebrated and gifted actors like Kemble and Mrs Siddons, and the minor parts to incompetents, who were incapable of reciting poetry, and 'who owed their very elevation to dexterity in snuffing candles'. The result was a distortion of the pattern of the plays, since Shakespeare 'shone no less conspicuously and brightly' in the minor characters. Coleridge also deprecates the habit of going to the theatre not 'to see a *play*, but to see Master Betty or Mr Kean, or some individual in some *one* part'.[1] In plays of this category, the importance of the main characters should be stressed, but not to the extent of distorting the whole design. In other plays, like *A Midsummer Night's Dream* and *As You Like It*, the interest is equally divided among the characters, and the total effect is produced 'not from the sub-

[1] *MC*, p. 339.

ordination of all to one, either as the prominent person or the principal object', but 'by a coordination of the characters, by a wreath of flowers'. The meaning of such plays resides in their total pattern, and in them 'one effect is produced by the spirit of the whole'. Here Coleridge points out that the titles of the plays are relevant to their meaning. Some plays derive their titles from the names of the main characters, suggesting that their main interest lies in these characters. Others are called *The Winter's Tale* or *As You Like It* because their meaning does not lie largely in the experience of any one of the characters, but all the component parts of the play have an equal importance. This is no more than a useful guide, and not an absolute rule. Coleridge knew that *Cymbeline*, for instance, belongs in fact to the second group.[1]

A Shakespearean play is not simply a structure of words and scenes that has pleasure for its object. It has a meaning and a moral significance. That is why Coleridge describes Shakespeare as a 'philosopher'. Coleridge does not mean that from the plays a system of moral philosophy can be abstracted, the thing which Dr Johnson suggested in his *Preface*, and which the Victorian critics wrote much about. Nor does he mean that the characters utter moral aphorisms to be detached from their dramatic context, and even from their speakers, and collected, as was done by Mrs Griffith in her book *The Morality of Shakespeare's Drama Illustrated* (1775). In his introduction to *The School of Shakespeare* (1774) William Kenrick said that much had been written on Shakespeare as a poet, and suggested that it was time that he should be discussed as a moral philosopher. But this unacceptable separation between the poetry and the philosophy, so common in the eighteenth century, was only possible when a theory of poetry existed that made it easy to isolate form from content in poetry. In Shakespearean drama the philosopher and the poet cannot be separated except to the detriment of both. In the immature poetry of Shakespeare, Coleridge writes in *Biographia Literaria* (ch. 15), the poet and philosopher are not quite one: 'Each with its excess seems to threaten the extinction of the other.' But 'at length in the drama they were reconciled, and fought each with its shield before the breast of the other'.

---

[1] *SC*, I, 41; cf. *MC*, p. 95.

What shape does this reconciliation take in the plays? Coleridge's criticism of an early play, *Love's Labour's Lost*, gives some idea of the reconciliation Shakespeare effected in the drama, and shows how Coleridge suggests that a Shakespearean play has meaning. Berowne's crucial speech on love and the relative values of learning and living (IV. iii. 324–65) Coleridge finds to be 'quite a study'. Here poetry and philosophy are at harmony – but because the poetry is predominantly rhetorical Coleridge describes the speech as 'logic clothed in rhetoric'. The phrase is not particularly happy, since it suggests that the philosophy is separable, and that it is merely sugar-coated, as it were. But, as Coleridge explains later, this is not the case. The 'profound truths' are only to be arrived at through the 'most lively images'. Further, they are not tacked on to the play: they do not form a gnomic passage to be detached and viewed in isolation. Since both the poetry and the philosophy are indissolubly wedded, the whole passage, the thought-expression, has its meaning only in the dramatic context of which it forms a part. It is 'faithful to the character supposed to utter the lines' and also constitutes 'a further development of that character'.[1]

Not that Coleridge failed to see that in some of Shakespeare's plays the speeches of some characters fulfil a function similar to that of the chorus in Greek drama. Coleridge knew that and pointed to it in his remarks on *Richard II*. There he also noted that such speeches are distinguished from others by their rhymes and formal quality, and that in them we get 'the *general* truths', as distinguished from the 'passions of the dialogue'. But the sacrifice of a fairly important character to the task of uttering 'general truths', was not regarded by Coleridge as good dramatic technique. Such 'general truths' must be conveyed obliquely and without any detriment to the character uttering them. In Shakespeare's mature works, he observed, this artistic defect disappears: the practice 'is infrequent in proportion to the excellence of Shakespeare's plays'.[2] In the mature plays 'the truths he teaches he told in character and with passion. They are the "sparks from heated iron".' Otherwise, the general moral reflections are 'put in the mouths of unimportant personages'

[1] *SC*, I, 93–7.   [2] *Ibid*. I, 146.

who act as chorus commenting on the action, and whose speeches are meant to guide our responses to the plays.[1]

Character, therefore, while remaining self-consistent, is at the same time a medium for the value and meaning in a play. Coleridge does not treat the matter in detail. Nor does he, in the manner of one writing a study of *Love's Labour's Lost*, analyse fully the particular meaning and values embodied in the play. As usual, he is content with dropping a hint or a suggestion. But the hint and suggestion, however fragmentary, reveal a sound method of approach. The play is a satire on pedantry; but it has a deeper meaning. This, Coleridge suggests, is to be found in Rosaline's final speech to Berowne, in which she dictates to him the penance he is to offer for having been 'a man replete with mocks, Full of comparisons and wounding flouts'. The play then deals with the education of the soul without which love's labour is lost, and the passage is indeed crucial to the whole conception of the play. A parallel punishment is dealt to the other lovers. Shakespeare cures his young men, who would set themselves against nature, by making them fall in love, thereby breaking their preposterous oaths to rise above nature and shun the company of women. Here, with an exquisitely comical effect, nature triumphs over unnaturalness and hypocrisy. But they have to be educated further; they have to lay aside their vanity and mockery, learn humility and be acquainted with human sorrow, in order to attain the goals of their love.

Perhaps a few instances of Coleridge's search for the meaning of Shakespeare's plays will make the method clearer. Coleridge found *Troilus and Cressida* difficult to understand: he 'scarcely knew what to say of it'; yet in some ways the judgement he attempted of it reveals his method best. It is neither vitiated by crude moralizing nor disturbed by insensitivity to form. He was not, like Dr Johnson, disgusted by the vicious characters; he did not find Cressida and Pandarus merely 'detested and condemned'. Nor was the play, in his opinion, as Hazlitt regarded it, 'one of the most loose and desultory of our author's plays'.[2] On the contrary, he thought it presents a precise grouping of characters representing certain values. In the foreground we have the lovers, each the embodiment of a different value. In

---

[1] *Ibid.* II, 17, 283.   [2] *Raleigh*, p. 184; *Hazlitt*, IV, 221.

Cressida Shakespeare has drawn 'the portrait of a vehement *passion* that, having its true origin and proper cause in warmth of temperament, fastens on, rather than fixes to, some one object by liking and temporary preference'. This is set against the 'profound affection represented in Troilus, and alone worthy the name of love; affection, passionate indeed... but still having a depth of calmer element in a will stronger than desire, more entire than choice, and which gives permanence to its own act by converting it into faith and duty'. But the contrast between the turbulence of passion and the profundity of moral life as expressed in the characters of Cressida and Troilus finds its place in a larger contrast between the group of characters representing the Greeks, and those representing the Trojans. Shakespeare has 'inwoven' with the two characters the theme of the opposition of 'the inferior civilization but purer morals of the Trojans to the refinements, deep policy, but duplicity and sensual corruptions of the Greeks'. The meaning Coleridge finds in the play is the superiority of the moral and spiritual to the worldly and calculating. There are also related themes (although Coleridge does not think the relation was stressed by Shakespeare): for example, in grouping Agamemnon, Nestor, Ulysses as opposed to Achilles, Ajax and Thersites Shakespeare seems to have meant the 'subservience and vassalage of strength and animal courage to intellect and policy'.[1]

We may find this interpretation of *Troilus and Cressida*, which has meant so much to the twentieth-century mind and which has been best analysed and perhaps understood by it, naïve and inadequate – although in 1930 G. Wilson Knight found in the play a meaning very like Coleridge's. But this is not the point. What is important is that in Coleridge's criticism we meet for the first time in English criticism an attempt to find the meaning of a Shakespearean play, not in terms of crude psychological truths or moral aphorisms, but in terms of values. Johnson, when not explicitly moral, was satisfied to remark on this play that Shakespeare 'has diversified his characters with great variety, and preserved them with great exactness'. Hazlitt, who wanted as much psychological realism in the characters as possible, complained that Troilus 'is no character: he is merely a common

---

[1] *SC*, I, 109ff.

lover', and praised the portraits of Cressida and Pandarus for being so true to life: they are 'hit off with proverbial truth'.[1] Different indeed from these approaches is Coleridge's, and what distinguishes his is the realization that the individual characters or group of characters are intended to mean something. He offers an interpretation which he arrives at after asking: What does every character or group of characters mean? What is the meaning of the whole? And it is a legitimate interpretation, in the sense that its truth or falsity can be tested, by its self-consistency and by reference to the text. We may disagree with Coleridge on this particular play or that, but in doing so we assume in our minds some other interpretation, which as an interpretation does not differ *in structure* from Coleridge's. Coleridge has given us the critical apparatus with which we can test his or anybody's criticism, or form our own. When we refute him we are using his tools. For intance, it follows from his interpretation of *Troilus and Cressida*, as a poetic and dramatic statement of the superiority of the moral or spiritual to the worldly or sensual, that the character of Thersites is 'the Caliban of demagogues' life – the admirable portrait of intellectual power deserted by all grace, all moral principle, all not momentary purpose'.[2] We may now find it difficult to accept this view of Thersites's character. We may regard him not as 'a mule, quarrelsome by the original discord of its nature' but as a chorus pointing to the meaning of the play. But then we do that because we may have a different interpretation of the play, which sees it as a 'Discord in the Spheres'. And we have arrived at this interpretation by fundamentally the same process as Coleridge's. Not content with considering how far a character is true to life as an end in itself, we have asked ourselves questions concerning its meaning and the meaning of its relation to other characters. Nowadays we ask questions regarding the meaning of other elements beside character – such as imagery – which Coleridge in this instance does not raise. But these, as we shall see elsewhere, he does not really neglect.

The tragedy of Macbeth, to choose another example, may be taken as that of a man suffering from a diseased will. But it is more than that. It is the tragedy of self-deception, just as

---

[1] *Raleigh*, p. 184; *Hazlitt*, iv, 221.   [2] *SC*, i, 111.

Othello has for its theme the enormity of human deception. Both Macbeth and Lady Macbeth are sadly ignorant of their own true selves. The case of Macbeth is the clearer of the two. Before he succumbs to the temptation of murdering Duncan he interprets 'the inward pangs and warnings of conscience' as *'prudential reasonings'*. After the murder he is 'ever mistaking the anguish of conscience for fears of selfishness, and thus, as a punishment of that selfishness, plunging deeper in guilt and ruin' – although sometimes 'conscience rushes in in her own person' undisguised, as when, immediately after the murder, he refuses to take back the dagger to the scene of murder, or when he wishes that the knocking at his castle gate could 'wake' Duncan. This last speech (II. ii. 73ff.) Coleridge asks us to contrast with his previous equivocal speech before the murder: 'If it were done. . .' In his vain endeavour to obtain peace of mind and get rid of the horrible dreams which shake him and his wife nightly, and which he wrongly attributes to his insecure position, Macbeth commits further atrocities, upsetting the whole order of nature: he 'tears himself live-asunder from nature'.[1] Trusting none, he causes everybody to mistrust him. Like him, all those who work under him are motivated by fear. Fear, therefore, is what haunts the universe of *Macbeth*; it is to be found in all the characters of the play. Coleridge puts the matter thus:

Macbeth mistranslates the recoilings and ominous whispers of conscience into prudential and selfish reasonings, and after the deed, the terrors of remorse into fear from external dangers – like delirious men that run away from the phantoms of their own brain, or, raised by terror to rage, stab the real object that is within their own reach.[2]

But towards the end we hear no more of his 'prudential prospective reasonings' and Shakespeare concentrates now on the 'inward'. Once Macbeth sees the truth of his situation there is nothing left for him but despair. On the speech he delivers when he hears of his wife's death Coleridge's remark is that 'despondency' is 'the final wretched heart-armour'. No less self-ignorant than Macbeth is Lady Macbeth. She has been living in a world of unreality and fantasy, and is no less deceived in herself than

[1] *SC*, I, 74–6. For a detailed discussion of Coleridge's interpretation of *Othello* see below, ch. 5.   [2] *Ibid*. I, 80.

her husband. In spite of her early conviction of her own heroic nature she soon loses the power to bear reality, and she gives way before her husband, who in her opinion was the weaker. When we last see her, before her mind is disordered in the sleep-walking scene, she is merely endeavouring 'to reconcile her husband and her own sinkings of heart by anticipation of the worst shapes and thoughts and affected bravado in confronting them'.[1] Coleridge sums up the character justly when he writes that:

Feeding herself with day-dreams of ambition, she mistakes the courage of fantasy for the power of bearing the consequences of the realities of guilt. Hers is the mock fortitude of a mind deluded by ambition; she shames her husband with a superhuman audacity of fancy which she cannot support, but sinks in the season of remorse, and dies in suicidal agony.[2]

The meaning Coleridge finds in *Hamlet* is only too well known. But it is important to realize that he reaches the conclusion that the meaning of the play resides mainly in the character of the Prince, as a consequence of his total response to the play and of his subsequent analysis of some of its dramatic features. We are shown, for instance, how the preparation leads to the dramatic building-up of the character of Hamlet. Shakespeare does not make Hamlet himself appear in the first exciting scene on the battlements, but introduces him later on at the royal court, and that still later than an important but subordinate character, Laertes. His object is to make the character of the hero – who also happens to be the chief organ of the meaning of the play – arouse as much interest as possible: 'How judicious that Hamlet should not have to take up the leavings of exhaustion.' The love theme in the play, important enough to be sure, is not made conspicuous, or presented directly to the audience. Rather, it is often to be inferred: for instance, Hamlet's 'spite to poor Polonius, whom he cannot let rest',[3] the audience are meant to understand, is in part caused by his love for Ophelia which has been frustrated by Polonius. If it had been otherwise presented the unity of interest might have been jeopardized. Shakespeare sees to it that nothing should deflect attention from

[1] *Ibid.* i, 80. [2] *Ibid.* i, 72. [3] *SC,* i, 22, 30.

the crux of the play, which is Hamlet's attitude to the duty of revenge laid upon his shoulders. In conformity to the theme and interest of the play the tempo of *Hamlet* is marked by the utmost slowness, as contrasted, for instance, with the breathless and crowded rapidity of *Macbeth*. The contrast between the two plays is not new: Schlegel had already pointed it out.[1] But, as we find in Lecture III of the 1813–14 course, Coleridge characteristically links it with his view of Hamlet's character. Thus the starting-point of his interpretation of *Hamlet* is not the character of the protagonist, but a dramatic consideration of the form and structure of the play, which leads to the character.

Or consider Coleridge's criticism of the history plays, scanty as it is.[2] Coleridge felt the epic breadth which characterizes them. He also knew that the problem which faced Shakespeare the artist was how to convert 'the epic into the dramatic': 'An historical drama is...a collection of events borrowed from history, but connected together in respect to cause and time poetically, by dramatic fiction.' Shakespeare, therefore, had to deviate from history; he had to emphasize the role of human will, and the significance of choice, without which no drama would be possible. He also had to introduce little concrete incidents in order to give the plays 'reality and individual life', thereby distinguishing them from mere history, as we find, for example, in the Gardener episode in *Richard II*, and in the comic scenes of low life in *Henry IV*, though the concrete incidents must be shown as organically related to the structure of the play they happen to form part of.

In his treatment of the history plays, Coleridge regarded every play as an autonomous individual work of art. But he still noted the continuity and the close connection between one play and another – a thing in which he found a decisive argument against the view that Shakespeare was no conscious artist. While writing the individual play, the pattern of the series seemed to have been taking shape in his mind. Coleridge admired the art by which Shakespeare 'makes one play introductory to another', and the way in which the character of Gloucester in *Henry VI* was portrayed 'evidently with a view to Richard III', how Bolingbroke in *Richard II* was a preparatory study for

[1] *SC*, II, 273.   [2] *Ibid*. I, 138–43, 152–6; II, 281–4.

Henry IV, and how casual questions dropped by him prepare for Prince Hal of the future play. But although Coleridge does not analyse in detail the epic quality of the history plays or any major theme that links the whole series together, in his view the plays are not devoid of meaning. They are the expression of the ethos of a people, and the poetic and dramatic statement of the value of patriotism and of harmony and order in the state.

A Shakespearean play, then, has a meaning; it discloses a particular vision of life, which is ultimately the poet's vision. But it is also an autonomous work of art, in which the poet does not speak his own thoughts crudely and directly, and nowhere does Coleridge try to trace the poet's personal convictions. As artist Shakespeare reveals an amazing power of detachment from his creations, a power which Coleridge detects and admires even in his earliest non-dramatic poetry. In *Venus and Adonis* he notes how the poet 'works exactly as if of another planet'.[1] It is precisely this quality of detachment which made Schiller complain in his well known essay *On Naïve and Sentimental Poetry* that there is an element of cruelty in Shakespeare's art. But Coleridge insists that impersonality is an indispensable feature of all art that merits the epithet 'great'. He therefore praises, for instance, 'the wonderful philosophic impartiality in Shakespeare's politics' which is displayed in *Coriolanus*: Shakespeare, he says, 'is quite peculiar. In other writers we find the particular opinions of the individual...but Shakespeare never promulgates any party tenets.'[2] In spite of the poet's sensitivity to the follies and absurdities of the mob, his treatment of it is impartial.

Such is the way Coleridge searches for meaning in Shakespeare's plays. But it cannot be said that this is always his approach. There are times when he lapses into eighteenth-century ways, letting the moralist in him dictate to the critic. On such occasions he tends to disengage the character from the whole fabric, and the moral judgements he passes are as crude and explicit as those of the eighteenth-century critics only too often are. Thus, concentrating on the character of Angelo in *Measure for Measure*, he fails to see the point of the play. To him Angelo represents only 'cruelty with lust and damnable

[1] *Ibid.* I, 89, 136.   [2] *Ibid.* I, 89.

baseness', and he therefore must not pass unpunished. Coleridge does not stop to ask himself, whether it is significant that Shakespeare disposed of him otherwise. Instead he concludes that Angelo's pardon and marriage 'not merely baffles the strong indignant claim of justice...but it is likewise degrading to the character of woman'. With his moral sense so wounded he complains that *Measure for Measure* is the 'most painful – say rather, the only painful – part of his genuine works', and he compares the marriage of Angelo and Marianne to that of Alathe and Algripe in the *Night-Walker*, the work of the morally irresponsible Beaumont and Fletcher.[1] That Coleridge made that judgement of a play which was for long considered a 'problem' play, and on which even now there is not much agreement among critics, may be understandable, but it cannot excuse the faulty method of criticism, which, against his better judgement and knowledge, he here pursues. But this brings us to considerations of character proper, which is the subject of the two following chapters.

[1] *SC*, I, 113–14.

4

Character and psychology

Psychological truth not an end in itself

Although as early as the beginning of the eighteenth century the Aristotelian *mimesis* was understood in the sense of direct copying, Shakespeare's characters were then generally considered as representative of classes. This attitude, which is obviously a reflection of the neoclassical belief in the ideal of generality, was best expressed by Dr Johnson, the last great critic of the early eighteenth-century tradition. Johnson, we remember, wrote in his *Preface* that in Shakespeare's writings, as contra-distinguished from those of other poets, a character is 'commonly a species'. But with the spread of empirical philosophy and psychology, the emphasis was gradually shifted, whether in theory or in practice, by Joseph Warton, Kames, Morgann, and Whately to the individual. Although the conflict between response and theory could be acute, by the last quarter of the century it was no longer surprising to find Shakespeare's characters openly treated as historic beings who have, imposed upon them by the critic, a past before the play starts. At the beginning of the nineteenth century this criterion of individuality assumed a much greater significance. The main butt of Hazlitt's attack in the preface to his *Characters of Shakespeare*, a book written apparently with Schlegel's lectures fresh in his mind, is the ideal of generality as represented in Johnson's *Preface*. Here Hazlitt censures Johnson for saying of Shakespeare, 'in contradiction to what Pope had observed, and to what everyone else feels, that each character is a species, instead of being an individual' – just as he elsewhere attacks Reynolds for expressing in his *Discourses* the same belief in the criterion of generality.[1] Hazlitt himself sets out in his book on Shakespeare's characters to point out as best he can 'the individual traits' in them which Johnson could not or would not find.

[1] *Hazlitt*, IV, 175ff.; VIII, 141.

In this long-standing feud between the general and the particular Coleridge sided with neither party. If anything, unlike Hazlitt, who complained that modern dramatists 'scout individuality as beneath the sublimity of their pretensions',[1] he blamed contemporary poets for making their characters 'as much as possible specific, individual, even to a degree of portraiture'.[2] He found that neither the concept of the general nor that of the particular alone fits the nature of the Shakespearean character. A Shakespearean character, he maintains, is both at once, and here is an example of the principle of the reconciliation of opposites which imagination embodies. The character is neither an individual nor a class alone, but, as it were, 'a class individualized'.[3] In *Biographia Literaria* he wrote that 'the ideal', which is the province of poetry, 'consists in the happy balance of the generic with the individual. The former makes the character representative and symbolical, therefore instructive... The latter gives it *living* interest; for nothing *lives* or is *real*, but as definite and individual.' To those who believe that Coleridge was a master of verbalism it may be necessary to point out that this is not just a verbal solution. The 'general' and the 'individual' represent two different approaches to Shakespeare's characters, or to any work of art for that matter; they give rise to two different types of practical criticism, although the distinction is somewhat blurred in the eighteenth century because of the age's narrow view of imitation. Whereas the belief in the general results primarily in a literary and moral type of criticism, the outcome of the belief in the individual is the psychological; its direct progeny is the Ernest Jones or Freudian variety. By reconciling both approaches Coleridge managed to write Shakespearean criticism which is both psychological and something else. Unlike the character critics of the late eighteenth century, Coleridge did not treat the psychological analysis of characters as the end of the critic; he went beyond it (without neglecting it or underrating its importance as some modern critics have done) and asked further questions about the 'meaning' of a character and of a whole play.

Indeed the spread, if not the rise, of the psychological school of Shakespearean criticism is often associated with Coleridge.

---

[1] *Hazlitt*, xii, 53.   [2] *BL*, ii, 21.   [3] *SC*, i, 72; ii, 33; *BL*, ii, 187.

Even William Walsh in his recent general study of Coleridge links his name to this movement.[1] Indeed, Coleridge's psychological criticism of character has been found by many, including his editor Raysor, to be his only valuable contribution. Other critics, reacting against the psychological criticism of character, have blamed him chiefly for lending his authority to an erroneous approach, and for diverting Shakespearean criticism into irrelevant channels. But the charge is exaggerated, if not groundless. There are indications that Coleridge, as a rule, does not treat psychological truth as an end in itself, that sometimes when he talks about the truths of the human heart he does not mean merely psychological truths, but broad human values, which it is the business of serious literature to concern itself with. In the version of the 'Essay on Method', which appeared in the *Encyclopedia Metropolitana*, he tells us that Shakespeare 'was pursuing two Methods at once; and besides the psychological Method he had also to attend to the poetical'.[2] The 'poetical method' itself, we are told in the same essay, involves the apprehension of deep moral values. In his practical criticism the psychological sometimes gives way to the poetical.

There is for instance a fragment of his otherwise missing criticism of *A Midsummer Night's Dream*, which is particularly significant. I am not concerned at present with the truth or falsity of the criticism, but with the method and assumptions the fragment reveals. Helena's behaviour in betraying her friend Hermia (I. i) Coleridge finds to be in accordance with the truths of psychology as he understands it. 'The act,' he writes, 'is very natural; the resolve so to act is, I fear, likewise too true a picture of the lax hold that principles have on the female heart, when opposed to, or even separated from passion and inclination.' But it is not enough for a dramatic character to be psychologically true. It has to fulfil other requirements which a work of art entails – requirements which vary from one work to another according to the meaning, mood and emotional level of every particular work: 'But still, however just [the act may be psychologically] the representation is not poetical; we shrink from it

---

[1] William Walsh, *Coleridge, the Work and the Relevance* (1967), p. 57.
[2] *SC*, II, 348.

and cannot harmonize it with the ideal.'[1] Similarly in *The Winter's Tale* (IV. iii. 29–30) Autolycus's speech is, according to Coleridge, marred by the words 'for the life to come, I sleep out the thought of it', although the utterance itself is in keeping with the character. It is 'delicately characteristic of one who had lived and been reared in the best society, and had been precipitated from it by "die and drab"'. So far Coleridge is saying what in substance is Dr Johnson's verdict: 'the character of *Autolycus* is very naturally conceived, and strongly represented.' But it is not sufficient that a character should say what is consistent with itself: what it says should also harmonize with the predominant tone of the whole. In this particular instance the expression, despite its psychological probability, 'strikes against' the critic's feelings 'as a note out of time and as not coalescing with that *pastoral* tint which gives such a charm to this fourth act'.[2] It is apparently too Macbeth-like for the emotional level of the play. Of course, we may disagree with such fastidiousness; but the criticism itself is significant. There are other considerations to be taken into account in a work of art besides character consistency and psychological truth, and without them psychological truth itself has no merit.

These considerations are what Coleridge sometimes calls poetic or 'aesthetic logic'. What offends the aesthetic logic is for Coleridge of graver consequence than what offends realism. For instance, to observe poetic logic the storm in *The Tempest* has to be represented as 'not in strictness natural'. To harmonize with the 'meaning' of the play it has to be represented in such a way that we are given only 'the bustle of a tempest, from which the real horrors are abstracted'.[3] Coleridge is abundantly aware that the plays are primarily poetic drama and not psychological documents. In the comparison he draws between Massinger and Shakespeare the former is praised for his realism: in his 'delineations objects appear as they do in nature, have the same force and truth and produce the same effect upon the spectator'. But Massinger, he goes on, 'is not a poet of high

[1] *SC*, I, 100. Of course, it may be objected that what Coleridge really wanted Shakespeare to do was to give the romantic idealized picture of womanhood he himself often entertained. It may be so. But this still shows that he did not consider the object of a poetic dramatist to represent men strictly as they are.

[2] *Raleigh*, p. 91; *SC*, I, 120.   [3] *SC*, I, 132.

imagination', and it is not enough for poetic drama to be simply truthful. Shakespeare, on the other hand:

is beyond this; he always by metaphors and figures involves in the thing considered a universe of past and possible experiences; he mingles earth, sea, and air, gives a soul to everything, and at the same time that he inspires human feelings, adds a dignity in his images to human nature itself.[1]

That Coleridge was not really satisfied with the psychological analysis of Shakespeare's characters as an end in itself is seen in his insistence that in Shakespeare we neither find what he calls 'ventriloquism' nor are we faced with characters composed of flesh and blood and completely independent of their creator. Ventriloquism is the term Coleridge uses to describe the lack of sufficient detachment in the dramatic poet from his creations, to denote the absence of what T. S. Eliot once called the 'third voice' of poetry. If a dramatist presents to us characters all speaking the same voice, which is directly the poet's own voice, then he is a ventriloquist.[2] Shakespeare, Coleridge tells us, is no ventriloquist; his characters are more than sufficiently independent of him and remarkably distinguished from one another. Each has a life of its own and each speaks its own voice. That is why Shakespeare seems to be 'characterless'.[3] But this does not mean that his characters are not basically poetic creations:

In the meanest characters, it was still Shakespeare; it was not the mere Nurse in *Romeo and Juliet*, or the Dogberry in *Much Ado About Nothing*, or the blundering Constable in *Measure for Measure* . . . We know that no Nurse talked exactly in that way, tho' particular sentences might be to that purpose.

The Shakespearean universe is therefore peopled not by historic beings, but by the creatures of the poet's imagination, which, however independent they may be, still have their relation to the poet. For the characters, we remember, are essentially products of 'meditation'. Just as Shakespeare is no ventriloquist he is not lost in his creations either. Coleridge expresses this cryptically: 'The poet lost in his portraits contrasted with the poet as a mere

---

[1] *MC*, p. 96.
[2] T. S. Eliot, *The Three Voices of Poetry* (1953); Snyder, *Coleridge on Logic and Learning*, p. 60.   [3] *SC*, I, 82; cf. *TT*, 12 May 1830.

ventriloquist; wonderful union of both in Shakespeare.' The poet indeed speaks in every play, but his voice, in the mature plays at least, is not the voice of any one particular character. We hear it rather, as Coleridge puts it, 'by way of continuous undersong',[1] and its message lies in the total meaning of every play.

Indeed in the immature Shakespeare, and in a very few parts of his mature works (e.g. the Captain's speech in the second scene of *Macbeth*, in which Shakespeare drops the dramatic style and in its stead uses a 'mere style of narration') the author's voice is heard, to use Coleridge's word, 'palpably'.[1] In such parts we find 'thoughts and descriptions, suited neither to the passion of the speaker, nor the purpose of the person to whom the information is to be given', but for a moment the author himself addresses directly the audience or the reader. For a moment Shakespeare's 'negative capability' disappears and his poetry has a 'palpable design upon us', as Keats would say. Of course we can reply by saying that in some cases the dramatic style proper is suspended for higher purposes, perhaps for the sake of the introduction of some significant phrase that is meant to orientate our response to a particular situation or of an image that will set the appropriate atmosphere. But from the point of view of dramatic technique Coleridge would consider this a lapse, and in his mature works Shakespeare very often achieves these effects while simulataneously maintaining the dramatic style, and ventriloquism is the last charge that can be levelled at him.

Importance of psychological truth

Although he did not regard psychological truth as the objective of the dramatic poet, Coleridge did not underrate its importance. He knew that in order to convey its meaning a play, at least a serious play, ought to have a certain degree of probability. Indeed there are one or two of Shakespeare's serious plays of which 'the interest and situations...are derived from the assumption of a gross improbability'. Both *Lear* and *The Merchant*

---

[1] *SC*, I, 96; cf. I, 207: 'The consciousness of the poet's mind must be diffused over that of the reader or spectator; but he himself, according to his genius, elevates us, and by being *always in keeping* prevents us from perceiving any strangeness, tho' we feel great exaltation.'

of Venice start with a postulate which we have to accept unquestioningly. But Coleridge points out that in such cases we are dealing with an old tale. Not only were the stories known either in histories or in ballad form or in both in Elizabethan times but they had sometimes been already dramatized. This fact would lessen then, if it did not remove altogether, the sense of improbability and the unfamiliarity of the poet's world which a modern recipient, unacquainted with these, might feel. The conduct of Lear in the first scene, Coleridge observes – and the same thing applies to that of Shylock – follows 'an old story, rooted in popular faith – a thing taken for granted already, and consequently without any of the *effects* of improbability'. Besides, Shakespeare, Coleridge explains, counteracts the possible effect of improbability in different ways. For instance, the glaring absurdity of Lear in the first scene is lessened by 'the little admixture of pride and sullenness' which he finds in Cordelia's answer 'Nothing'. Further, the interest in the improbable postulate is dropped the moment it has served its purpose, and by introducing the Kent episode the attention is 'forced away from the nursery-tale'.[1]

But the important thing is that it is only the initial postulate which we have to accept. In the development of the drama there is nothing purely arbitrary and accidental. The characters reveal enough psychological realism to make the dramatic experiences possible. Or, to quote Coleridge, the tale in both plays is 'merely the canvas to the characters and passions, a mere *occasion* – not [as in Beaumont and Fletcher] perpetually recurring, as the cause and *sine qua non* of the incidents and emotions'.[1] The incidents and emotions form the body of the dramatic experience, and because genuine dramatic experience is first and foremost a kind of apprehension of reality, a great dramatist, in spite of all the conventions in the world, cannot afford to give us such a distorted representation of reality as to preclude all psychological probability. Of drama, perhaps more than of anything else, Coleridge's words remain true:

Like the moisture or the polish on a pebble, genius neither distorts nor false-colours its objects; but on the contrary brings out many a vein

[1] *SC*, I, 59–61.

and many a tint, which escapes the eye of common observation, thus raising to the ranks of gems what had been often kicked away by the hurrying foot of the traveller on the dusty high road of custom.[1]

The reason why Coleridge finds the tragedies of Beaumont and Fletcher deficient is that they 'proceed upon something forced and unnatural; the reader never can reconcile the plot with probability, and sometimes not with possibility'.[2]

Much was written in the first half of this century to deny psychological realism to Shakespeare's major characters, and to propagate the strange notion that because a dramatist works primarily for the stage his sole object is the momentary excitation of emotions by tricks and illusions. It is difficult to see how the Schückings and the Stolls who asserted that Shakespeare's major characters are not psychologically convincing (without showing us how they could be otherwise convincing) could find in the plays any permanent relevance to human reality. This so-called 'historical' or 'realistic' movement has virtually run its course. There is now a noticeable swing back to a more orthodox position which recognizes that the relation between drama and truth to human feeling is of the greatest importance. It no longer seems necessary to emphasize how right Coleridge is in stressing this importance or to defend him against the attacks of the 'realists'.

Coleridge knew very well that a Shakespeare play is not meant to create the illusion of absolute reality. That is why methods that assume naturalistic criteria, whether they are used by Morgann, Ernest Jones or F. L. Lucas, are wrong because they start from the wrong assumption. But this does not mean that we are dealing with a world completely alien from ours, which is nothing but a set of gorgeously attired walking abstractions declaiming a good deal of fine verse. It is a world of human relevance. A poet can never convey his serious dramatic vision of life unless his medium, the world we are witnessing, is convincing enough. In *Biographia Literaria* (ii, 5) Coleridge explains that the object of 'adherence to the truth of nature' is 'to excite the sympathy of the reader', to arouse in him the necessary degree of concern and interest. This is precisely

[1] *BL*, ii, 121.   [2] *SC*, ii, 34.

Shakespeare's greatness, and the secret of his superiority over his contemporaries. Whereas most of them presented only those 'abstractions', or the wooden conventional characters based upon them, coming to life now and then, Shakespeare, by transcending these conventions and the 'primitive technique', managed to make his world convincing to us. The conventions can perhaps be seen through his characters, but certainly in the mature works, they are not the characters themselves. Although Coleridge did not prove his case in a detailed, scholarly fashion, he was right when he said:

No one can understand Shakespeare's superiority fully until he has ascertained, by comparison, all that which he possessed in common with several other great dramatists of his age, and has then calculated the surplus which is entirely Shakespeare's own.[1]

Shakespeare's power of realizing his 'values' in concrete human situations is entirely his own, and cannot be explained away by reference to contemporary dramatic conventions.

Character therefore has to be consistent; it has to conform to the general psychology of man. The 'accidental' in the initial assumption of a play is not as serious a fault as in the character; and yet we are shown by Coleridge how the effects of the former in Shakespeare are counteracted by the fact that the accidental there was part and parcel of the common tradition of the time. As for the characters Shakespeare is too great a dramatist to present us with the purely arbitrary in them. In *Lear*, Coleridge writes:

The *accidental* is nowhere the groundwork of the passions, but the καθόλον, that which in all ages has been and ever will be close and native to the heart of man – parental anguish from filial ingratitude, the genuineness of worth, tho' coffered in bluntness, the vileness of smooth iniquity.[2]

These are some of the values the play expresses. They are primarily moral rather than psychological. But they have to be placed in a universe not unlike ours so that they may have relevance to our experience. As early as 1796 Coleridge realized that necessity. The reason for his strictures on the type of

[1] *TT*, 12 May 1830.   [2] *SC*, i, 59.

111

'romances' in which 'the order of nature may be changed whenever the author's purposes demand it' is that it is 'incapable of
exemplifying a moral truth'. If the author only works '*physical
wonders*' no serious criticism can be levelled against him, but
'the first *moral* miracle which he attempts' will disgust our
judgement. We cannot avoid judging by our own experience as
human beings. Once the situation in which the characters are
placed, however improbable that may be, is accepted, then 'how
beings like ourselves would feel and act in it, our own feelings
sufficiently instruct us'.[1] Consequently Coleridge would not
have a dramatic character that is purely vicious. For a character
completely devoid of the common feelings of humanity is not an
adequate representation of it. It is monstrous and therefore unnatural. That is perhaps what caused Coleridge to make the
rash generalization that Shakespeare 'became...all beings but
the vicious'.[2]

Motivation

Consistency of character, however, in Coleridge's view, does not
mean perfectly adequate motivation, and it certainly does not
imply that a character's behaviour is absolutely determined
beforehand, the thing which obtains in complete types. The
rationalist approach to character reduced it to a neat chain of
cause and effect. *L'ésprit simpliste* behind it could only lead to an
inadequate and rather naïve conception of personality. To hold
that man is a completely rational animal is to believe that his
actions proceed from completely rational motives. If the behaviour of a dramatic character does not tally perfectly with its
conscious motives, the character is dismissed as inconsistent and
not true to human nature. It is significant that the critic who
wrote the best essay on Shakespeare in the eighteenth century
was the one who raised his voice against the concept of rationality. 'We might indeed, if we chose it, candidly confess to one
another that...we are by no means so rational in all points as

[1] *MC*, pp. 371–3. Note the similarity between Coleridge's view and that of Lessing.
See *Hamburgische Dramaturgie*, No. 45. There is no question of influence here.
[2] *SC*, ii, 204. In *TT*, 5 April 1833, Coleridge admits that 'Regan and Goneril are
the only pictures of the unnatural in Shakespeare – the pure unnatural; and you
will observe that Shakespeare has left their hideousness unsoftened or diversified
by a single line of goodness or common human frailty.'

we could wish,' said Maurice Morgann.[1] But his voice was not hearkened to, and he himself did not always distinguish between nature and art, so that he sometimes lost himself in a wilderness of irrelevancies.

Like Morgann, Coleridge realized the inadequacy of the rationalist concept of personality. Complete consistency and intelligibility, Coleridge believed, is not human:

> It is not the *wickedness* of *Don Juan*, therefore, which constitutes the character an *abstraction*, and removes it from the rules of probability; but the rapid succession of the correspondent acts and incidents . . . *Don Juan*, is from beginning to end, an *intelligible* character: as much so as the *Satan* of Milton.[2]

Hence the residue of mystery in nearly all the major characters of Shakespeare, the mystery which, in their attempts to make the characters completely intelligible by an appeal to such things as the history and the conventions of the Elizabethan stage, the modern rationalist critics explain away at the expense of impoverishing the immensely rich content of the characters. To claim with the modern realists that Shakespeare's characters are psychologically impossible creations and must therefore be mere illusions, because their conscious motives do not always explain adequately their actions, is to suppose that man is a completely rational animal. This is to hark back to the rationalist approach, the approach of Rymer and the late eighteenth-century critics. Only a superficial view of psychology, which holds that man lives only on the conscious level and that his actions are commensurate with his conscious motives, can regard, for instance, the characters of Brutus and Iago as 'unnatural' because Brutus's avowed motives are not adequate, and Iago's cannot be reconciled with his actions. Because of his habit of introspection, and his fascination with dreams and cognate experiences, Coleridge was aware of the unconscious forces underlying human personality, of the inadequacy of motives to account completely for its behaviour.

Coleridge's own view of motives is interesting, and may explain his approach to the Shakespearean character more fully.

---

[1] Morgann, *Falstaff*, p. 8.   [2] *BL*, II, 186.

For what is a Motive? Not a thing, but the thought of a thing. But as all thoughts are not motives, in order to specify the class of thoughts we must add the predicate, 'determining' and a motive must be defined a determining thought. But again, what is Thought? – Is this a thing or an individual? What are its circumscriptions, what the interspaces between it and another? Where does it begin? Where does it end? – Far more readily could we apply these quotations to an ocean billow, or the drops of water which we may imagine as the component integers of the ocean. As by a billow we mean no more than a particular movement of the sea, so neither by a thought can we mean more than the mind thinking in some one direction. Consequently a motive is neither more nor less than the act of an intelligent being determining itself . . . It is not the motives govern the man, but it is the man that makes the motives: and these indeed are so various, mutable and chameleon-like that it is often as difficult as fortunately it is a matter of comparative indifference, to determine what a man's motive is for this or that particular action. A wise man will rather enquire what the person's general objects are – what does he habitually wish? – thence deducing the state of the will and the impulses, in which that state reveals itself and which are commonly the true efficient causes of human actions: inasmuch as without these the motive itself could not have become a *motive*.[1]

Thus an analysis of motives resolves itself into an analysis of the whole personality. The motive, in the sense of a single conscious determining thought, becomes not only very difficult to detect, but meaningless. For the motive in reality is the *whole* being moving in a certain direction at a particular moment. What matters is the whole man, his principle of individuation, so to speak: what matters is not 'motive-mongering', but 'the individual self'.[2] The motives in the common sense of the word behind Iago's action are not adequate, and Coleridge is fully aware of it. But he does not dismiss the character as a psychological impossibility:

Without the perception of this truth it is impossible to understand the character of Iago, who is represented as now assigning one, and then another, and again a third, motive for his conduct, all alike the mere fictions of his own restless nature, distempered by a keen sense of his intellectual superiority, and haunted by the love of exerting power, on those especially who are his superior in practical and moral excellence.

[1] Snyder, *Coleridge on Logic and Learning*, pp. 132–3.   [2] *SC*, i, 33.

Yet how many among our modern critics have attributed to the profound author this the appropriate inconsistency of the character itself.[1]

The living principle beneath Iago's character renders his actions sufficiently explicable. To go much further is to presuppose that a living person is perfectly intelligible. And after all, as Coleridge was fond of saying, *omnia exeunt in mysterium*.[2] Eliot was right when he said that 'one of the gifts of the Romantic Movement to Shakespeare criticism' was the recognition of 'an element of mystery' in Shakespeare's characters.[3] More than any other critic Coleridge was sensitive to this element, especially because of his views on the nature of motives. Of all his predecessors only one, Morgann, had somewhat similar views on 'motives':

The Understanding seems for the most part to take cognizance of *actions* only, and from these to infer *motives* and *character*; but the sense we have been speaking of proceeds in a contrary course, and determines of *actions* from certain *first principles of character*, which seem wholly out of the reach of the Understanding.[4]

It is this element of mystery that modern rationalist critics, like those of the eighteenth century, endeavour to exorcise from the plays. The realist critics fought shy of mystery with the same zeal and embarrassment as the logical positivists shunned metaphysics; and perhaps there is more than a surface connection between the two movements. But T. S. Eliot in the thirties admitted that this gift of the Romantic Movement is 'one for which, with all its excesses, we have reason to be grateful'. We should remember that if the characters of Shakespeare act not on a rational principle, but 'on the immediate impulse of feeling', if they do not give us a cogent rational explanation of their action, it is not because of their unreality, but because of their essential psychological realism. And as the author was not a psychological

1 *Omniana*, I, 29–30.
2 *AR*, p. 91. For a somewhat laboured attempt to relate Coleridge's view of Iago (and of the whole play) to his 'metaphysical conception' see Elinor Shaffer, 'Iago's Malignity Motivated: Coleridge's Unpublished "Opus Magnum"', *Shakespeare Quarterly*, XIX, no. 3 (Summer, 1968), pp. 195–203.
3 H. Granville-Barker and G. B. Harrison (eds.), *A Companion to Shakespeare Studies* (1949), p. 298.
4 Morgann, *Falstaff*, p. 6.

115

novelist he could not intrude in his own person and analyse in detail the motives of his characters.

Varying degrees of psychological realism

The degree of probability and psychological realism, however, seems to be determined by the seriousness of the vision expressed.[1] When we are no longer immediately involved, we remain outside the threshold of the dramatic proper. In *The Comedy of Errors* Shakespeare provides an example of this. It is a farce in the strict sense of the term. In a farce it does not matter if we cannot identify to the requisite degree the world that is being unfolded to us with our own. It is perhaps necessary that we should abstain from such an identification, for as a rule the effect of farce, as farce, diminishes in proportion to the decrease in detachment with which we view it. To secure that detachment there is no attempt in farce to make its world probable or convincing. As distinguished from comedy, and naturally from tragedy, farce is not only 'allowed', but it 'requires' extraordinary licence in its fable. 'The story need not be probable, it is enough that it is possible.' The accidental, which, if it is allowed to remain accidental, mars serious drama, is the domain of farce: 'A comedy would scarcely allow even the two Antipholuses...But farce dares add the two Dromios, and is justified in so doing by the laws of its end and constitution.' But it is significant that in farce we are not concerned with the question of values. If there is any dramatic form which aims at producing a mere emotion, it is farce, which is on the same level as melodrama. Every liberty is taken by the dramatist to achieve his end, which is the production of 'laughable situations'. Farce is the lowest form of drama, for who would think of comparing *The Comedy of Errors* with *Othello* or *The Tempest*? If a farce produces 'strange and laughable situations' it has achieved its end.[2] But great drama cannot be satisfied with skimming the surface of the human spirit. It has to touch its depths and uncharted seas, enlarging our awareness of the human situation itself.

Dramatic probability, again, depends on the emotional level of a situation and the degree of excitement in which the mind is supposed to be:

[1] *SC*, I, 130. [2] *Ibid.* I, 99.

Many obvious improbabilities will be endured as belonging to the groundwork of the story rather than to the drama, in the first scenes, which would disturb or disentrance us from all illusion in the acme of our excitement, as, for instance, Lear's division of his realm and banishment of Cordelia.[1]

Consequently the degree of psychological realism varies from one character to another, in proportion to the importance of the role a character plays in the particular drama, together with the emotional level of the dramatic world it inhabits. Generally speaking it is not necessary that characters in comedy should possess the same degree of psychological reality as those in tragedy. For instance, Coleridge finds that Prospero's behaviour in interrupting the courtship between Ferdinand and Miranda (i. ii. 451ff.) is not sufficiently motivated. Now a critic who regards psychological realism as the end of drama would either condemn this behaviour as psychologically unconvincing, or else try to reconcile it with Prospero's character. Hazlitt, for example, follows the second course, maintaining that it is 'in character with the magician, whose sense of preternatural power makes him arbitrary, tetchy, and impatient of opposition', which is rather straining the character for the sake of preserving the psychology. Likewise Schücking finds in his behaviour something of a humourless schoolmaster, and Dover Wilson regards him as 'a terrible old man almost as tyrannical and irascible as Lear at the opening of his play'. But such interpretations cannot be convincingly corroborated by the text. Coleridge admits the absence of complete psychological probability, but still considers Prospero's alleged reason 'lest too light winning Make the prize light' to be a sufficient motive 'for the ethereal connexions of the romantic imagination, although it would not be so for the historical'. In other words, a romance does not require the same degree of psychological probability as a play at a higher emotional level. It is therefore irrelevant to ask for the same degree of psychological probability in *The Tempest* as in *Macbeth*, since the former is deliberately 'pitched in a lower key throughout'.[2]

[1] *Ibid.* I, 130.
[2] *Hazlitt*, IV, 242; L. L. Schücking, *Character Problems in Shakespeare's Plays* (1922), pp. 243ff.; J. Dover Wilson, *The Meaning of the Tempest* (1936) quoted by E. M. W. Tillyard; *Shakespeare's Last Plays* (1951), p. 54; *SC*, I, 135–6.

Similarly when Coleridge discusses *The Winter's Tale*, he writes that 'it seems a mere indolence of the great bard not to have in the oracle provided some ground for Hermione's seeming death and fifteen years concealment, voluntary concealment'. By suggesting that Shakespeare could have remedied the fault by the mere addition of some such 'obscure sentence' to the words of the oracle as 'Nor shall he [i.e. Leontes] ever recover an heir if he have a wife before that recovery', Coleridge's intention is not to make the behaviour of Hermione rational in the strict sense, or, as Miss Bradbrook thinks, to 'relieve her from a possible charge of hard-heartedness', but rather to create that quantum of probability necessary for drama. But he realizes that in a romance like *The Winter's Tale* no great degree of probability is aimed at. It is, he remarks, 'on the whole exquisitely respondent to its title'.[1]

It is not only in romances that psychological probability can *to some extent* be sacrificed; even in a serious tragedy a minor character may be deliberately unrealized and made quasi-symbolical. For instance, the Fool in *Lear* is not altogether a realistic clown. He is 'no comic buffoon to make the groundlings laugh, no forced condescension of Shakespeare's genius to the taste of his audiences'. The eighteenth century had generally thought he was, and consequently he was cut out in the stage productions of the time (he was not restored to the stage until 1838). Of course, there were individual critics in the eighteenth century, like Tom Davies, who objected to the tampering with Shakespeare's text, particularly as the century drew to its close. But it was Coleridge who pointed out the exact nature of the Fool in *King Lear*. The Fool, he wrote, is 'brought into living connection with the pathos of the play, with the sufferings'; since Cordelia's departure, Shakespeare tells us, the Fool 'hath much pined away'. He has an important symbolical function to fulfil: he acts as an impersonal commentator on, and a pointer to, what goes on in the mind of Lear. For instance, the Fool's 'grotesque prattling' at the end of the first act 'seems to indicate the dislocation of the feeling that has begun and is to be continued' in the mind of Lear himself.[2]

In the serious plays, however, the degree of roundness and

---

[1] *SC*, I, 119; Bradbrook, *Elizabethan Stage Conditions*, p. 84.   [2] *SC*, I, 63–4.

psychological truth of the main characters naturally increases with the maturing of Shakespeare's genius. Coleridge detected the formal nature of the characters where it is obvious in the early plays. For instance, in *Richard II* he noticed that characters are formal in the sense that they have no more reality than the poet assigns to them in certain situations, that they have no third dimension, so to speak. The result is that a character may say something in a particular situation which is patently out of character. For a moment it ceases altogether to be an individual character and acts as a chorus utering general truths that bear no relation to its own nature. This inorganic quality in character, Coleridge remarks, belongs only to Shakespeare's early work. In the case of *Richard II*, he tries to account for this feature, saying that Shakespeare takes the historical reality of his characters for granted, and assumes that it is equally known to his public, with the result that he is not so much concerned with impressing his audience with their reality (as he does with his non-historical characters) as with pointing out certain truths. Hence a character may act as itself and as a Greek chorus, not indeed at one and the same time as is the case sometimes in the mature works, but at different moments. But this explanation is very shaky, as Coleridge himself realizes. His idolatry here drives him to find excuses for Shakespeare's artistic lapses, where there can be none. For in the same breath he declares that it does not exactly '*justify* the practice', and remarks that this fault in dramatic conception and technique is 'infrequent in proportion to the excellence of Shakespeare's plays'.[1]

Coleridge was also aware how a number of Shakespeare's characters fall into certain types, and he traced the development of these types in Shakespeare's hands. Just as he found that an early work like *Love's Labour's Lost* mirrors, in a minor form, some of the qualities of the later productions, so he saw that Berowne and Rosaline are the prototypes of Benedick and Beatrice. Berowne is also the prototype of Mercutio as well. Costard is the 'groundwork' of Tapster in *Measure for Measure*, and Dull of Dogberry. The pedant in Holofernes is the germ of his equivalent in Polonius. Launce in *Two Gentlemen* fore-shadows Launcelot in *The Merchant of Venice*. 'True genius,'

---

[1] *Ibid.* i, 146.

says Coleridge, 'begins by generalizing and condensing; it ends in realizing and expanding. It first collects the seeds.' Thus by comparing the earlier with the later works we can watch the development of the dramatic artist in Shakespeare. In *Love's Labour's Lost* there are 'many of Shakespeare's characteristic features' in which we find all the potentialities of his maturity. In them, as it were, we see 'a portrait taken of him in his boyhood'.[1] The earlier sketches seem to be studies for the later finished works. But they are not studies made with the object of furnishing material to be exhibited in a portrait gallery. Each of these characters, although broadly it conforms to a type, serves a particular purpose in the play from which it derives its existence. And it is always a dramatic purpose. Berowne, Mercutio, and Benedick belong to the same family, but they fulfil different functions. There would have been no tragedy in *Romeo and Juliet* if Mercutio, with his nobility, charm and generosity, which endear him to Romeo, had not been there to be sacrificed. Conversely without Benedick *Much Ado* would have been no comedy. The education of Berowne is essential to the meaning of the play of which he is a part.[2]

The main characters in the mature works obviously grow beyond the limits of types and conventions. Coleridge realizes that the ground work of Hamlet, for instance, is the melancholy type. He sees his affinity to the melancholy Jacques. But he is sensitive, as who cannot be, to the complexity of Hamlet's character, to his growing beyond the conventional framework of the type. The speech 'To be or not to be...', he remarks, is appropriately given to Hamlet, but 'it would have been too deep' for Jacques. He also intimates that Hamlet's doubts concerning the Ghost's message are not the unjustified doubts of a diseased character in the face of contrary evidence. Rather he places the conflict in Hamlet's mind in the larger context of contemporary opinion. Coleridge goes to the writings of Sir Thomas Browne, to support his view that until the staging of the play within a play Hamlet's misgivings about the possibility of the Ghost being the incarnation of the devil, and his consequent fears of damnation, are both genuine and sincere.[3] Hamlet's

[1] *SC*, I, 92–3. cf. 99; II, 108.   [2] *Ibid*. II, 132; I, 226.
[3] *Ibid*. I, 28–9. For the following discussion of Hamlet's character see *ibid*. I, 23–40.

predicament is therefore a real one; his sorrows are not artificial sorrows spun round a mere melancholic humour.

Analysis of major characters

In the analysis of the major characters, the type of analysis which began in the form of observations from without in the early eighteenth century and took a more inward turn later in the century, Coleridge may be said to have carried on the achievement of his predecessors. But he was better qualified than many of them. He had an exceedingly sharp eye for the subtle distinctions between one character and another, and noted the minutest change from one moment to another in the emotional life of each character. Unlike Richardson, he did not often force the text to agree with a preconceived simple moral or psychological theory. Rather he had an open, sensitive and perceptive mind, with the result that nearly all the outstanding traits in the characters he dealt with are all there in his accounts. For instance, his analysis of the character of Hamlet, however much one may disagree with his final interpretation, is masterly. His account of the salient points in the character is just and almost exhaustive. He noted his meditativeness, his habit of introspection, his morbid preoccupation with death, his melancholy, his *tedium vitae*, his fits of passion, his 'half-false' madness, his wild jesting immediately after his fateful interview with the Ghost (the ludicrous is 'a common mode by which the mind tries to emancipate itself from terror'), his exuberancy of mind, his fondness for puns and ambiguities (and all that it means), his tendency to generalize his situation, his gentlemanly manners, his nobility of soul, etc.

It is worth saying that the charge that Coleridge identifies himself with the character under consideration is largely ill-grounded and certainly exaggerated. It is only true of his criticism of Hamlet, where he interprets his delay in the light of his own personal tragic experience. But we must remember that he was aware of that: 'I have a smack of Hamlet myself,' he once said.[1] On the other hand, it was his constant belief that 'the

---

[1] Cf. *CL*, IV, 611 (letter to John Morgan, November 1815) : 'To-morrow morning, I doubt not, I shall be of clear and collected Spirits; but tonight I feel that I should do nothing to any purpose, but and excepting Thinking, Planning, and

essence of poetry [is] *universality'*. Great poetry, he maintained, does not address itself to 'personal feeling' and 'the sympathy arising from a reference to individual sensibility' is only 'a spurious sympathy'. It is not a proper response to the work. That is precisely why a character like Hamlet 'affects all men'.[1] And he always maintained that a Shakespearean character is both an individual and a species. Besides it is only right to observe that in his remarks on the other characters of the play he never commits the mistake of seeing them through Hamlet's eyes. In fact he seems to be sure (and he substantiates his view from the text) that 'Shakespeare never intended us to see the King with Hamlet's eyes'.[2] Similarly he tells us that we are not supposed to regard Polonius as the prejudiced Hamlet sees him:

> It was natural that Hamlet, a young man of genius and fire, detesting formality, and disliking Polonius for political reasons, as imagining that he had assisted his uncle in his usurpation, should express himself satirically; but Hamlet's words should not be taken as Shakespeare's conception of him.[3]

Coleridge also points out another reason for Hamlet's dislike of Polonius, namely his thwarting the love affair between him and Ophelia.[4] But if his self-identification with the character of Hamlet were as complete as it is often made out to be, he would certainly have seen the other characters through Hamlet's eyes, as indeed some critics have done. It is therefore not just to imply that Coleridge's *Hamlet* is merely 'an attempt to present Coleridge in an attractive costume'.[5]

Or take his searching analysis of Lear's character – an analysis which is both psychological and dramatic. From the psychological point of view he finds that Lear at the opening of the play suffers from 'a mixture of selfishness and sensibility'. He is selfish in the sense that he has an 'intense desire to be intensely beloved', but his selfishness is of a feeble kind: Lear is not self-sufficient, since he craves for the absolute love of his daughters. His sensibility is enforced by his rank and the long habit of obtaining

Resolving to resolve – and praying to be able to execute', and his summing up of the character of Hamlet (in *SC*, II, 198) and *TT*, 24 June 1827.

[1] *SC*, II, 9.   [2] *Ibid*. I, 34.   [3] *Ibid*. II, 266–7.   [4] *Ibid*. I, 30.
[5] T. S. Eliot, *Selected Essays* (1948), p. 33.

complete obedience. This last converts his selfish 'wish into claim and positive right, and the incompliance with it into crime and treason'. Hence his tyranny and his moral inability to resign his sovereignty even at the very moment he has divided his kingdom, which shows itself in his punishment of Kent.

The psychological method, however, is not pursued beyond proper limits. There is just enough psychological realism in the character: 'the mixture of selfishness and sensibility', we are told, is 'strange but by no means unnatural'. Lear is not a complete flesh and blood individual, and 'any addition of individuality' (to his old age and lifelong habits of being promptly obeyed), Coleridge writes, would be 'unnecessary'. But Shakespeare resorts to a subtle dramatic method in his delineation of Lear. Lear's character becomes distinguished sufficiently for dramatic purposes, as the play unfolds itself, by the relations of others to him. Thus the 'passionate affection and fidelity' of Kent – who is 'the nearest to perfect goodness of all Shakespeare's characters' – 'acts on our feelings in Lear's own favour'. We feel that 'virtue itself seems to be in company with him', just as vice and evil in the person of his daughters and Edmund seem to be against him. This too mitigates whatever bad effect his extreme folly, pride and irascibility may have on us. In fact Shakespeare manages most cunningly to make all his faults 'increase our pity. We refuse to know them otherwise than as means and aggravations of his sufferings and his daughters' ingratitude.' And from the beginning Shakespeare has seen to it that Lear's selfishness is not that of a vicious character, but of 'a loving and kindly nature'.[1]

Shakespeare's methods of characterization

Shakespeare pursues more than one method of characterization. In his discussion of these methods Coleridge is enlightening. For instance, he points out, by implication, what we may call the method of single characterization. This is the usual method, which seems to consist in the dramatist's concentration on individualizing a character mainly through soliloquy and self-exploration as well as impersonal commentary by other characters. Of this method Hamlet would be a good example. But there

[1] *SC*, I, 55–65.

is also the method of double characterization. We find that the speeches in which one character describes another quite often reveal to us both characters at once. This method of double characterization Coleridge detects in *Macbeth*, where Lady Macbeth in her famous soliloquy describes her husband: 'Macbeth [is] described by Lady Macbeth so as at the same time to describe her own character.'[1] This method is too subtle to be reduced to a single formula: at one time a speech works one way, at another time it works another way. But there are times when it works both ways at once. It is futile to attempt to find any single law which, we may suppose, Shakespeare consciously or unconsciously follows scientifically, since we shall have to allow for numberless exceptions to any law that our ingenuity may cause us to discover. Such laws as Schücking's 'Principle of the Objective Appropriateness of Dramatic Testimony' and so forth are the result of a naïve application of scientific method to such a subtle thing as poetic drama. Coleridge indeed has said that poetry has a logic of its own as severe as that of science, but the logic of poetry is not the same as that of science. When Iago tells us that there is a daily beauty in Cassio's life that makes him ugly we believe him. But when he tells us of Othello that he is 'horribly stuff'd with epithets of war' we do not. The reason is that we cannot take at any point one character's description of another for gospel truth without taking into consideration the nature of the character as well as the dramatic situation. As Coleridge writes, 'It is a common error to mistake the epithets by the *dramatis personae* to each other, as truly descriptive of what the audience ought to see or know'.[2] What is always needed is critical tact, the kind of tact a great critic like Coleridge reveals. Otherwise our criticism will become mechanical, we shall misread the text and find ourselves beset by all kinds of spurious problems.

Coleridge notes another method of characterization in Shakespearean drama. He often draws attention to what may be called the relational method, which, by its economy and indirectness, seems to be more germane than the other two to poetic drama proper. By this method a character is further defined, not by additional psychological delineation so much as by the rela-

---

[1] *SC*, I, 71. [2] *Ibid.* I, 47.

tion which other characters bear to it. Thus Ophelia's attitude to Polonius, her 'reverence of his memory', acts in his favour and shows that 'Shakespeare never intended to represent him as a mere buffoon'. Similarly, but more powerfully, Kent's relation to Lear, his absolute faithfulness and devoted service to him, help to define Lear's character and our response to him.[1] Our interest in Helena in *All's Well that Ends Well* is determined 'chiefly by the operation of the other characters, – the Countess, Lafeu, etc. We get to like Helena from their praising and commending her so much.'[2] But there is really no sharp separation between these three methods, for often the three can be seen at work together in the delineation of the same character, although usually either the one or the other is more dominant at a time.

Psychological realism and the exigencies of poetic drama

From Coleridge's treatment of Shakespeare's characters it is obvious that he does not regard the main characters in the great plays as purely conventional or as mere theatrical types. On the contrary, he sees in them a proof of Shakespere's firm grasp of concrete human situations. Not only does he note the different and subtle methods of characterization employed by Shakespeare, as well as the fine shades of distinction between one character and another, but he also points out how the characters develop. And he is sometimes aware of the dramatic technique Shakespeare occasionally uses to reconcile the audience to that development. For instance, he shows how Shakespeare withdraws Lear after the storm scene, where we find the 'first symptoms of positive derangement', for a whole scene 'in order to allow an interval for Lear in full madness to appear'.[3] In fact, in his treatment of the mature plays, there is a firm assumption that there is nothing primitive about Shakespeare's characterization. In order to arrive at a sound view of a character, Coleridge often considers the very expression it uses, the imagery and even at times the rhythm of its speech. He points to the 'set, pedantically antithetic form' of the King's speech at the beginning of the second scene of the first act of *Hamlet*, and 'the laboured rhythm and hypocritical overmuch' of Lady Macbeth's welcome to Duncan.[4] The result is a

---

[1] *SC*, II, 266–7; I, 61.   [2] *TT*, 1 July 1833.   [3] *SC*, I, 66.
[4] *Ibid.* I, 22, 73. For a detailed treatment of this point see ch. 6.

more sensitive and broadly-based criticism than the so-called objective interpretation. Ironically enough, 'scientific' criticism often ends by being downright dogmatic. For instance, having stated his principle of the sufficiency of 'expressly stated reasons' for action for the understanding of a character (in this case the reasons stated by the King in *Hamlet*, IV. v. 76), Schücking goes on to 'conclude with certainty' that Shakespeare wanted us to know that Ophelia's madness is caused solely by her father's death, and that Hamlet's desertion has nothing to do with it. On the other hand, a detailed analysis of Ophelia's speeches like the one attempted by Coleridge shows us how the two thoughts – her father's death and her lover's desertion – remain inseparable in her mind.[1]

Yet, it would be wrong to think that Coleridge was blind to the exigencies of poetic drama and to the basic conventions which its nature imposes.[2] Let it be admitted that Coleridge at times forgot his own precepts and hunted for psychological truths for their own sake. For in his writings on Shakespeare there are in fact two Coleridges, or, to use Stephen Potter's words, a Coleridge and an S.T.C. We have seen how his theory of poetry consists of two incompatible theories, each having its different assumptions as well as its different consequences in his practical criticism. Whereas his theory of imagination led him to the conception of a work of art as one in which psychological truth is only a means, his pleasure theory led to different conclusions altogether. Consequently because Coleridge found that in Shakespeare's major characters 'the reader never has a mere abstract of a passion, as of wrath or ambition, but the whole man is presented to him', he sometimes dwelt on the psychological insight and subtlety with which Shakespeare presents the whole man, as if these were the ultimate end of dramatic excellence:

Shakespeare has this advantage over all dramatists – that he has availed himself of his psychological genius to develop all the minutiae of the human heart: showing us the thing that, to common observers, he seems solely intent upon, he makes visible what we should not otherwise have seen: just as, after looking at distant objects through a telescope, when we behold them subsequently with the naked eye, we

[1] *SC*, I, 33; *Schücking, Character Problems*, p. 225.
[2] J. I. M. Stewart, *Character and Motive in Shakespeare* (1949), p. 6.

see them with greater distinctness, and in more detail, than we should otherwise have done.[1]

When he declared that 'one main object' of his lectures is 'to point out the superiority of Shakespeare to other dramatists' and that 'no superiority can be more striking, than that this wonderful poet could take two characters, which at first sight seem so much alike, and yet, when carefully and minutely examined, are so totally distinct'[2] – like Hazlitt, he was simply writing in the eighteenth-century tradition of Thomas Whately. Numberless parallel passages, particularly from late-eighteenth-century criticism, can easily be produced. And by stating that 'every one wished a Desdemona or Ophelia for a wife'[3] he was already paving the way for such irrelevant and sentimental works as Mrs Jameson's *Shakespeare's Heroines*.

In fact it is abundantly clear that by calling Shakespeare a philosopher Coleridge sometimes meant simply that in his creations he reveals profound insight into the psychology of man. For example, when he compared Fletcher's Rollo with Shakespeare's Richard III he wrote:

as in all his other imitations of Shakespeare, he was not philosopher enough to *bottom* his original. Thus, in Rollo, he has produced a mere personification of outrageous wickedness, with no fundamental characteristic impulses to make either the tyrant's words or actions philosophically intelligible.[4]

In the 'Essay on Method' Coleridge, exactly in the manner of Kames and Richardson, illustrates a psychological truth by examples drawn from Shakespeare's characters. But it would be unfair to overlook the two different views of character expressed in the 'Essay on Method' itself. While looking upon the characters as concrete illustrations of psychological truths, unlike his predecessors, Coleridge shows that he is sufficiently aware of the difference between art and reality. The Hostess and the Tapster, it is true, illustrate the want of method in the 'ignorant and unthinking'; but they differ from their counterpart in real life 'by their superior humour, the poet's own gift and infusion'.[5]

Generally, however, Coleridge's conception of Shakespearean

---

[1] *SC*, ii, 131–2.   [2] *Ibid.* ii, 182.   [3] *TT*, 27 September 1830; cf. *SC*, ii, 127–8.
[4] *MC*, p. 84.   [5] *SC*, ii, 339.

drama is not naturalistic. Referring to contemporary naturalistic drama he writes that it is:

utterly heterogeneous from the drama of the Shakespearean age, with a diverse object and a contrary principle. The one was to present a model by *imitation* of real life, to take from real life all that is what it ought to be, and to supply the rest – the other to *copy* what *is*, and as it *is* . . . In the former the difference was an essential element; in the latter an involuntary defect.[1]

We should not now put the difference between the two types so strongly, or in these terms; but from our earlier discussion of what Coleridge meant by the antithesis he drew between 'copy' and 'imitation', we may perceive the force of his distinction here. Of course, Coleridge was aware of the conventions inherent in the dramatic form itself, from 'dark scenes' to 'asides' and dialogue.[2] He finds no contradiction in the behaviour of Portia, who speaks excellent English, when she rejects her English suitor on the grounds that she cannot speak his language. On the contrary he regards it as an example illustrating the essentially conventional nature of drama.[3]

Poetic drama has still further specific exigencies. According to Coleridge, its proper domain lies in that middle state between pure conventionalism on the one hand, and pure naturalism on the other. A purely conventional poetic play will be more akin to poetry than to drama, for drama is after all a living action; just as a purely naturalistic play may be drama, but not poetry. Making allowance for Coleridge's prejudiced view of Greek drama, which he seems to have derived from Schlegel, but which he later repudiated,[4] this is what he meant when he said that 'on the Grecian [plan] a man could be a poet, but rarely a dramatist; on the present a dramatist, not a poet'. This is also the assumption behind his discussion of the way a dramatic poet should use language:

It cannot be supposed that the poet should make his characters say *all* that they would, or taking in his whole drama, that *each* scene, or *paragraph* should be such as on cool examination we can conceive it likely that men in such situations would say, in that order and in that *perfection*.

[1] *MC*, p. 49. [2] *SC*, I, 51. [3] *Ibid*. I, 128; cf. *MC*, p. 452.
[4] *SC*, II, 161, n.1; *MC*, p. 395.

Yet, on the other hand, Coleridge deems a certain amount of realism necessary for good poetic drama. 'According to my feelings, it is a very inferior kind of poetry in which, as in the French tragedies, men are made to talk what few indeed, even of the wittiest men can be supposed to converse in' and which is the 'actual produce of an author's closet'.[1] It is again the happy union of 'the poet lost in his portraits' and 'the poet as a mere ventriloquist' that is needed.

It is wrong then to assume that Coleridge conceived of a Shakespearean play as a kind of naturalistic drama (or a novel), only written in verse. This is largely the eighteenth-century view, but not that of Coleridge. Novelists, he says, 'describe with more minuteness, accuracy, and truth, than is consistent with poetry'.[2] In *Biographia Literaria* we are told that 'if metre be superadded' to a work, 'all other parts must be made consonant with it'.[3] And he always considered Shakespearean drama primarily as a kind of poetry. This could be seen even in his views on acting. 'A great Actor, comic or tragic,' he wrote, 'is not to be a mere *Copy*, a *fac simile*, but an *imitation* of Nature.' He is in fact 'Pygmalion's Statue, a work of exquisite *art*, *animated* and gifted with *motion*, but still *art*, still a species of Poetry'.[4] And he attacked the contemporary stage representations of Shakespeare because in their drive for naturalism they sacrificed the poetry of the plays.[5] In fact, one can go further and claim that he was even aware of some of the conventions of speech in Elizabethan drama itself – though not as conventions – the kind of thing that has been pointed out by M. C. Bradbrook, Madeleine Doran and other scholars. He noted the patterned sententious speeches which were usually formalized by rhymes,[6] as well as the insertion of little poems in the dialogue, to which Shakespeare drew attention by the use of incomplete metre. But it does not require any deep study to be convinced that Coleridge's interest in Shakespeare's poetry is as great as, if not greater than, his interest in character.

The use of poetry therefore entails a specific treatment of character. In Shakespearean drama characters are essentially the product of 'meditation'; 'they are the embodiments of 'ideas' or

[1] *SC*, I, 203–4, 206.   [2] *Ibid.* II, 67.   [3] *BL*, II, 9; cf. 33n.   [4] *CL*, III, 501.
[5] See Appendix A.   [6] *SC*, I, 146, 157.

'values', for 'Meditation looks at every character with interest, only as it contains something generally true, and such as might be expressed in a philosophical problem'.[1] Coleridge often talks about 'the germ of a character' which it is 'of such importance to understand',[2] meaning the idea round which the character is built and the value which it is meant to convey. Once the mind seizes hold of the 'Idea' of a character 'all the speeches receive the light and attest by reflecting it'. The idea of a character is, of course, something different from mere psychological truth and from the 'ruling passion' which was so popular with the eighteenth-century character-critics. Shakespeare does not give us 'psychologic portraiture', as naturalist dramatists do, but rather a 'living balance' between psychologic portraiture and general truths: 'It is not the poet's business to analyse and criticize the affections and faiths of men, but to assure himself that such and such are affections and faiths grounded in human nature, not in mere accident of ignorance or disease.'[3]

We may not accept the values Coleridge finds in this Shakespearean character or that. We may find his interpretation of Hamlet's character too personal or his view of the values behind Falstaff's too solemn. But the search for a pattern underlying the character, and indeed the whole play, a pattern of moral and philosophical implications is significant. And one of the results of the search is the realization of the profundity, the rich and closely knit texture, the organic unity of the plays. Unlike characters in naturalistic drama, Shakespeare's characters 'from Othello and Macbeth down to Dogberry and the Gravedigger, may be termed ideal realities. They are not the things themselves, so much as abstracts of the things, which a great mind takes into itself, and there naturalizes them to its own conception.'[4] Yet they are not abstractions, for they have sufficient psychological realism and individuality. Unlike Ben Jonson's characters, which are 'almost as fixed as the masks of the ancient actors; you know from the first scene – sometimes from the list of names – exactly what every one of them is to be', Shakespeare's grow and develop.[5] They are alive, but their life is not that of pure naturalism. And Coleridge knew how an author deliberately 'unrealizes

[1] *SC*, ii, 117.   [2] *Ibid.* i, 33.   [3] *Ibid.* i, 227–8.   [4] *Ibid.* ii, 162.
[5] *MC*, p. 46.

his story, in order to give a deeper reality to the truths intended'.[1]

Characters in Shakespearean drama are therefore both individuals and species at one and the same time, and that is what characters in poetry should be. Coleridge declares his full faith in 'the principle of Aristotle that poetry as poetry is essentially *ideal*...that its apparent individualities of rank, character or occupation must be *representative* of a class'.[2] That is why he attacked the '*matter-of-factness*' in some of Wordsworth's poems – a phrase which he coined to mean 'a laborious minuteness and fidelity in the representation of objects, and their positions' and 'the insertion of accidental circumstances in order to the full explanation of his living characters, their dispositions and actions'. These circumstances, he continues, 'might be necessary to establish the probability of a statement in real life, where nothing is taken for granted by the hearer; but appear super-fluous in poetry, where the reader is willing to believe for his own sake'.[3] The difference between Coleridge's position and that of Priestley and other eighteenth-century sensationalist critics cannot be more obvious. In a footnote Coleridge explains his position further:

Say not I am recommending abstractions; for these class-characteristics which constitute the instructiveness of a character are so modified and particularized in each person of the Shakespearean Drama, that life itself does not excite more distinctly that sense of individuality which belongs to real existence. Paradoxical as it may sound, one of the essential properties of Geometry is not less essential to dramatic excellence; and Aristotle has accordingly required of the poet an involution of the universal in the individual. The chief differences are, that in Geometry it is universal truth, which is uppermost in the con-sciousness; in poetry the individual form in which the truth is clothed.[4]

Because characters in Shakespearean drama are general no less than individual they are 'clothed...not with such as one gifted individual might *possibly* possess, but such as from his situation it is most probable beforehand that he would possess'.[5] Hence the importance of the dramatic situation. For the truth of a character is the truth of the experience that it undergoes in a given situation and in none other. A character is only a con-

[1] *Ibid.* p. 306. [2] *BL*, II, 33–4. [3] *Ibid.* II, 101. [4] *Ibid.* II, 33n.
[5] *BL*, II, 33–4.

stituent of a whole and, disengaged from it, would have no meaning, or at least would not mean the same thing. For it is only alive in the particular situation conceived by the poet. The pattern of the whole work is of great importance, not only in poetry, but in the other arts as well: 'The *Helen* of Zeuxis is said to have been composed from different features of the most beautiful women of Greece but yet it would be strange to say that the Helen of Zeuxis had existed anywhere but in the picture.'[1] In *Biographia Literaria* he writes that 'the fairest part of the most beautiful body will appear deformed and monstrous if dissevered from its place in the organic Whole'.[2] Hamlet's madness, feigned or real, is not a study in madness as such, and is not meant to reveal the character of Hamlet abstracted from the situation. It rather consists in 'the full utterance of all the thoughts that had past thro' his mind before – in telling home truths'. It is born of, and reflects upon, the wider issues of the play. Similarly Ophelia's madness brings out most clearly some of these issues. In her singing we find the 'conjunction of these two thoughts that had never subsisted in disjunction, the love for Hamlet and her filial love'. Her madness has its roots in the dramatic situation, and the thoughts that come rushing into her disordered mind in rapid succession are formed of the 'cautions so lately expressed and the fears not too delicately avowed by her father and brother concerning the danger to which her honour lay exposed'.[3] Far from being a 'mere piece of Dutch painting', the character of the Nurse in *Romeo and Juliet* is not only 'exquisitely generalized', but it is also made 'subservient to the display of fine moral contrasts'. It derives its full significance from the whole dramatic situation of which it forms a part.[4]

Each play is then an individual work of art. The poet is interested in creating, not a portrait gallery, but an organic whole. The characters have to be convincing, to be sure; but because they inhabit a particular world they bear a necessary relation to one another. While 'his eye rested upon an individual character, Shakespeare always embraced a wide circumference of others, without diminishing the separate interest he intended to attach to the being he portrayed'.[5] Coleridge often admired what

[1] *Ph L*, p. 234.   [2] *BL*, I, 162.   [3] *SC*, I, 33–4.   [4] *Ibid.* II, 204.
[5] *Ibid.* II, 33–4.

he called 'the keeping of the character' of the individual play. For instance, in *Richard II*, not only are the principal characters, Richard II, Bolingbroke, and York, easily distinguished from one another, but 'the keeping of all is most admirable'.[1]

The beautiful *keeping of the character* of the play is conspicuous in the Duke of York. He, like Gaunt, is old, and, full of religious loyalty struggling with indignation at the king's vices and follies, is an evidence of a man giving up all energy under a feeling of despair.[2]

– which, in turn, is what happens to Richard himself. This is what Coleridge means when he describes a Shakespearean play as a *syngenesia*: in a Shakespearean play, he writes, the *dramatis personae* were not 'planned *each by itself*', but 'the play is a *syngenesia* – each has indeed a life of its own and is an *individuum* of itself, but yet an organ to the whole – as the heart, etc...of *that* particular whole'.[3]

[1] *Ibid.* ii, 183–4.   [2] *Ibid.* ii, 280.   [3] *MC*, p. 95.

5

Character and morality

Coleridge a moral rather than a psychological critic

We have seen that, although Coleridge thought psychological probability essential to a major character in a serious play, he generally did not regard psychological truth as the ultimate end of a Shakespearean play or the main occupation of the Shakespearean critic. A Shakespearean play is primarily a work of art, or, as he put it, a 'syngenesia'. As poetry it has for him a serious 'meaning', which lies not in the psychological truths it reveals in its characters, but in the moral values of which it is the concrete expression. In this respect Coleridge can be called a moral, rather than a psychological, critic – although we shall have to modify the sense of the word 'moral' here so as to distinguish between his standpoint and that of eighteenth-century critics like Gentleman, Richardson or Mrs Griffith who hunted mainly for the explicit moral in the plays. Coleridge, we hardly need to say, is too subtle a mind to offer us crudities of the type that *Hamlet* teaches that 'murder cannot lie hid', *Romeo and Juliet* the 'danger of disobedience in children', or that *Othello* provides an admonition against 'disproportionate marriages'.

Poetry, in Coleridge's view, belongs essentially to the world of the spirit; it is the product of an act of 'meditation' on the human condition, and that is why it embodies spiritual values. Dramatic poetry, especially, because it deals directly with the moral or spiritual world, cannot be divorced from morality in the broad sense of the term. Consequently in his criticism of Shakespeare's plays Coleridge always points to the intimate connection between characters and moral issues. He would never accept, for instance, Blake's view that 'Goodness or Badness has nothing to do with Character'. He would agree with him that 'a Good Apple tree or a Bad is an Apple tree still',[1] but he would

---

[1] William Blake, *Poetry and Prose*, ed. Geoffrey Keynes (1948), p. 582.

point out that the case of man is different. Man is such because of his self-consciousness: this is the starting-point of Coleridge's dynamic philosophy. But self-consciousness also means to him reason and the moral sense. Goodness or badness, therefore, is not 'another consideration', as Blake believes: on the contrary, in Coleridge's opinion, the moral sense is part of the very concept of man. That is why moral considerations carry such a heavy weight in Coleridge's criticism of Shakespeare.

It is his moral approach to the plays which determines his interpretation of this character or that, of this play or the other. This is apparent in much of his criticism of the plays. But it is his treatment of *Othello* which seems to me to reveal this moral approach in a peculiar and significant way. It may therefore be illuminating on this point to examine his treatment of this particular play first and in some detail. Before we can discuss his general interpretation of it, however, it is necessary at the outset to clarify certain points regarding a statement he once made to describe Iago's commentary on his own vicious machinations. I mean the celebrated phrase 'the motive-hunting of motiveless malignity',[1] which has led him into some trouble with certain modern critics, and indeed passed current as the summing up of his judgement on Iago's character. Besides, as will be seen later, his interpretation of the character of Iago is an integral and important part of his interpretation of the whole play.

Coleridge's criticism of 'Othello'

That the phrase means, as it is often understood to mean,[2] the complete absence of all motives behind Iago's actions is far from the truth. Coleridge points out the two passions that rankle in Iago's breast: disappointment and envy. Further he even concedes that Shakespeare has compromised on the dubious question of Othello's alleged adultery with Emilia. But he also realizes that when we have exhausted all that could be said about Iago's alleged motives, there will still remain something inexplicable and inscrutable about his villainy, something which cannot be accounted for by the application of a rational chain of cause and effect. And, taking into account Coleridge's own views on

---

[1] *SC*, I, 49. For the following discussion see *ibid*. I, 46–54.
[2] See, e.g., A. C. Bradley, *Shakespearean Tragedy* (1950), p. 209.

motives which we have already discussed, this is not because of Iago's unnaturalness, but because he is too alive a character to be reduced to any one wholly intelligible formula.

It is here that Coleridge's dissatisfaction with the purely rational approach betrays itself. In Iago Shakespeare has given us a character who is alive and convincing, and yet whose behaviour cannot be elucidated rationally – a problem which caused some previous critics (like Francis Gentleman, Richard Hole, and Lord Chedworth) either to make capital out of inadequate motives or else to supply him with motives of their own.[1] It is significant that William Richardson, who attempted an analysis of Shakespeare's major characters such as Hamlet, Lear, and Macbeth, did not venture to tackle Iago, although he dealt with minor characters like Jacques and Imogen. For what 'leading passion' in the eighteenth-century sense could be found in him? Unlike some of the eighteenth-century critics (for instance, Richard Hole), Coleridge does not lose himself in a morass of speculation as to whether and how Othello commited adultery with Iago's wife, whether Iago was a good man before this happened, and like questions. Instead he sees that in Iago we are faced with the inscrutable element of evil in human existence. But evil is not an abstract quality thrust upon him inorganically, from without, so to speak. It comes from within him, and is his whole 'individual self'. The scientific Shakespearean criticism of Schücking is committed to accepting Iago's avowed motives for gospel truth, and the historical method of Miss Bradbrook leads her to think that 'his explanation must plainly be accepted'. But it is amusing to watch Schücking attacking Coleridge's view of Iago, and yet, after a long-winded analysis, ending by declaring that 'the reasons alleged by Iago for his actions do not strike as the real impelling forces' – which is the very position of Coleridge. But Schücking considers the inconsistency between Iago's avowed motives and his actual behaviour an artistic 'mistake' by Shakespeare. Yet if 'we see him [i.e. Iago] actuated by hellish malignity'[2] we must not think he is the less

1 E. H. Seymour, *Remarks Critical, Conjectural and Explanatory upon the Plays of Shakespeare* (1805), II, 320; *Bell's Edition of Shakespeare's Plays* (1774), I, 178; Babcock, *Genesis of Idolatry*, p. 141.
2 L. L. Schücking, *Character Problems*, pp. 207–13; M. C. Bradbrook, *Themes and Conventions of Elizabethan Tragedy* (1935), p. 65.

human or alive for it. It is indeed better to be true to our response and admit the embarrassing truth that he is a fearfully alive character, inscrutable as we may find him.

Such an interpretation as Coleridge's, which endows Iago with exceptional 'will in intellect', and regards him as the incarnation of evil, naturally makes him a major figure in the tragedy, and not just a type as Stoll thought or a mere necessary piece of dramatic mechanism as Leavis argued. Coleridge objects to the representation of Iago on the stage as 'a fellow with a countenance predestined for the gallows', and not as 'an accomplished and artful villain, who was indefatigable in his exertions to poison the mind of the brave and swarthy Moor'.[1] Coleridge may not have been fully conscious that the character of Iago is based upon the Machiavellian type. But his analysis of some of the salient points in his character accords with the Elizabethan notion of the Machiavellian villain. In Iago, Coleridge writes, Shakespeare gives us a human quality magnified to the exclusion of other human attributes: his character consists in his being 'all will in intellect'. He is the type that sets himself on a higher level than the rest of humanity; he does not share 'the frail nature of man', or his passions. No moral considerations can stand in his way. On the contrary, he coldly and unflinchingly uses the rest of humanity purely for his convenience, and as tools with which to achieve his ends. His end is always to assert his superiority, and if he suffers from any passion at all, it is pride in doing so. In his relationship with Roderigo, Coleridge remarks, pride is by far stronger than 'the love of lucre'. All these are roughly the qualities of the conventional Machiavellian villain, but only roughly. For he is not a cold compound of conventions; in him all these qualities spring to life. He is 'a being next to devil, only *not* quite devil' and yet he is made perfectly convincing. And that is the mystery of Shakespeare's genius. But alive as he is, he is clearly meant to be a medium for certain 'values', what Coleridge calls 'Iagoism'. Iago's 'passionless character', which is 'all will in intellect' is 'a bold partisan here of a truth, but yet of a truth converted into falsehood by the absence of all the modifications by the frail nature of man'.

The question of the importance of Iago's character is crucial to

[1] *SC*, ii, 277.

Coleridge's interpretation of the whole play. Coleridge, we remember, does not consider *Othello* a tragedy of jealousy. He
notes how Shakespeare idealizes Othello's character as well as
the relationship between him and Desdemona,[1] how he empha-
sizes his nobility, his 'self-government'. In support of his
interpretation Coleridge finds abundant evidence. For instance,
he draws attention to Othello's calm reply: 'It is better as it is'
to Iago when the latter tells him how he has thought of attacking
Brabantio. Shakespeare, he says, seems to have made Othello
'above low passions'. Othello would not let Desdemona accom-
pany him to Cyprus until he has obtained the consent of the
senate. His agreeing to taking her with him is motivated mainly
by the wish to grant her her desire. His trusting nature appears
most clearly in his speech to the Duke at the Senate House,
where he asks that Iago, 'a man of honesty and trust' should be
given the charge of bringing her to Cyprus. Coleridge asks us to
consider Othello's description of himself as one 'not easily
wrought'. Jealousy is not the quality emphasized in the important murder scene, in the dialogue between Othello and Desdemona before he murders her. Othello is not jealous in the sense
that in him 'there is no predisposition to suspicion':

Iago's suggestions are quite new to him; they do not correspond with
anything of a like nature previously in his mind. If Desdemona had, in
fact, been guilty, no one would have thought of calling Othello's conduct that of a jealous man. He could not act otherwise than he did with
the lights he had; whereas jealousy can never be strictly right.[2]

Because Coleridge was only too aware of the idealized nature
of Othello's character he did not see his tragedy or, indeed, the
whole drama as a tragedy of jealousy. But why was Coleridge so
anxious, as indeed he often was, to draw our attention to this?
The point which Coleridge was intent on demonstrating seems
to me to be that the tragedy of *Othello* is not centred on a psychological problem. Indeed for him the tragedy would have lost its
meaning, or, at least, a great deal of its meaning, if the hero had
been portrayed by Shakespeare as a psychologically unstable
character from the start. It is doubtful if an 'abnormal' personality could be tragic in Coleridge's sense, since such a personality

[1] *SC*, I, 124, 48.   [2] *TT*, 24 June 1827.

would fail to be sufficiently representative. And character in tragedy, we are told by Coleridge, must be no less a species than an individual.

Coleridge was careful to point out that, given the *Othello* world, Othello's feelings are what 'any man would and must feel who had believed of Iago as Othello'.[1] With his vigilant reading of Shakespeare's poetry he could not pass unheedingly the repetition of the epithet 'honest'. Not only Othello, but the other characters as well apply the word to Iago. Coleridge knew that Shakespeare could not repeat the words 'honest, honest Iago' accidentally, and he therefore set about viewing the whole tragedy from the point of view which seemed to him to have been stressed by Shakespeare. Othello could not but believe Iago, because of his subtlety of deception, as, indeed, the rest of the characters did (including Roderigo himself, who had no illusions as regards Iago's dishonest behaviour to others), and because Shakespeare has intentionally endowed him with a firm faith in his honesty and love.

Because Othello's character is deliberately ennobled by Shakespeare, and his attachment to Desdemona highly spiritualized, his tragedy becomes not the tragedy of a jealous man as much as that of a noble man who has been deceived into seeing his ideal (where he has garnered up his heart, and the loss of which would bring chaos in his universe) thrown in the mire:

Jealousy does not strike me as the point in his passion; I take it to be rather an agony that the creature, whom he had believed angelic, with whom he had garnered up his heart, and whom he could not help still loving, should be proved impure and worthless . . . It was a moral indignation and regret that virtue should so fall: 'But yet the *pity* of it, Iago! O Iago! the *pity* of it, Iago!' In addition to this, his honour was concerned: Iago would not have succeeded but by hinting that his honour was compromised.[2]

Othello's experience is therefore nearer to that of Troilus than to that of Leontes in *The Winter's Tale*, or Leonatus in *Cymbeline*. But this is not all, for the truth Othello has to face is much harsher and more bitter than Troilus has ever known. The humiliation of such a noble mind as Othello's is brought about

[1] *SC*, i, 125.　　[2] *TT*, 29 December 1822.

by the villainy of one who is both man and the incarnation of evil, for, apart from its ultimately mysterious nature, Iago's evil acquires superhuman dimensions by being aided by chance or fate. Tempted by the devil Othello mistakes appearance for reality, and having lived appearance through, he discovers, when it is too late, that it is only an appearance and that reality is what he has irretrievably discarded. The tragedy of *Othello* then is the tragedy of the enormity of human deception and the fearful blunders of the spirit. This, as I understand it, is Coleridge's interpretation of the play. It is true that he did not put it precisely in these terms, but what I have attempted here is only a recon-struction, based upon his various abrupt and fragmentary com-ments and suggestions.[1]

Coleridge no doubt goes to extremes when he denies Othello jealousy altogether. When he attempts to prove his case he seems on the whole to be thinking of him before the temptation, rather than after. At least he seems to select deliberately only those examples which support his view and omit others equally significant. But if he concentrates on Othello's mind before the temptation it is because his object seems to be to deny Othello a jealous disposition. Coleridge's arguments are directed to the one end of proving that Othello's jealousy is not 'a *vice* of mind, a culpable despicable tendency'. In other words, the behaviour of Othello until Iago's devilish temptation is not that of a jealous man. His jealousy is not the child of his own soul; it does not arise within him as a result of previous suspicions and a poisoned imagination. Unlike Leontes he does not get excited by the most inadequate causes'.[2] It needed the wiles, tricks and insinuations, the masterly suggestion, the hypnotizing and the blinding of none less than an Iago, whom every character in the *Othello* world trusts, to set it in motion. But, one may ask, since nearly all the qualities which he tabulates as the 'natural effects and concomitants' of jealousy can be, and have already been, found in Othello's behaviour once Iago's medicine starts working, is it just perversity that makes Coleridge blind to Othello's jeal-

---

[1] Tact is needed in any attempt to reconstruct Coleridge's position; otherwise one may get very strange results as in, e.g., Lois Josephs, 'Shakespeare and a Coleridgean Synthesis: Cleopatra, Leontes and Falstaff', *Shakespeare Quarterly*, xviii, no. 1 (Winter, 1967), pp. 17–21. [2] *SC*, i, 122–3.

ousy after the temptation? In denying Othello a jealous temperament we have seen that his object is really to make the problem
of the play moral rather than psychological. But why does he
omit to note his jealousy after the temptation? Coleridge seems
to go astray here, because he has seen the other sides of Othello's
character, which if we missed or overlooked the play would be
the poorer. Coleridge is the first critic to point out the ambival-
ence in Othello's feelings towards Desdemona,[1] and by insisting
on the other side of Othello's character he has helped us, who
are not blind to his jealousy, to have a clear view of this ambival-
ence. By emphasizing such qualities as Othello's love for Desdemona (which can be seen, though intermittently, in the whole of
the play) and its idealized nature, the sense of overwhelming
pity he feels at the downfall of his ideal, his conception of ven-
geance as an honourable act of justice and duty, Coleridge has
made us aware of the complexity of Othello's feelings in a way
which no interpretation of Othello as a merely jealous man can
do. This complexity Coleridge traces even in the very imagery
in which Othello expresses himself.[2]

'Hamlet' and 'Macbeth'

As in *Othello* the issues raised in the other plays are moral. In
fact, the meaning Coleridge finds behind Shakespeare's plays is
always a moral rather than a psychological meaning. With the
possible exception of *Hamlet*, the great tragedies present to him
moral issues. But even in *Hamlet*, although he is clearly fascin-
ated by the particular complexity of the hero's character, ultimately the question he stresses is really one of conduct. 'Action
is the chief end of existence',[3] which is the summing up of his
interpretation of *Hamlet*, is, after all, not a psychological but a
moral assertion. One and the same problem, I suppose, can be
put both in psychological and in moral terms; and we can to
some extent translate from the one set of terms to the other.
But it is a question of emphasis. And the emphasis Coleridge
lays, as far as his recorded criticism shows, is on the moral
rather than the psychological side. He is not contented with
saying that Iago, for instance, behaves as he does because the
make-up of his personality is such and such. He is always

[1] *Ibid.* II, 276; *TT*, 29 December 1822. [2] *SC*, I, 54. [3] *Ibid.* II, 197.

introducing value judgements, which are extraneous to psychology: in Iago, he says, intellect is developed at the expense of the moral reason. In other words, he does not merely attempt to explain why characters behave as they do, but he always asks whether or not they behave as they ought to behave, and from thence tries to find the moral values which the author intends that they should represent. 'Iagoism' therefore is not a psychological, but a moral term. Recently Paul Deschamps has attempted to describe Coleridge's approach (which he clearly finds to be a compromise between the psychological and the moral) by calling it 'une sorte de psychanalyse idéaliste'. Coleridge's method, he says:

a la rigueur de la psychanalyse; comme elle, elle essaie d'atteindre au-delà de la zone claire de la conscience les regions profondes où se cachent les mobiles véritables des actions de l'homme. Mais ce que découvre Coleridge, lorsqu'il pénètre ainsi dans le domaine du subconscient, ce sont des besoins profonds de l'âme, et non pas seulement des instincts élémentaires liés aux grandes lois physiologiques, comme le fait la psychanalyse moderne.[1]

The problem of Macbeth, to take another example, is chiefly moral. Coleridge's interpretation of his character is that he is a man deceived in himself. Before the murder he is continually mistaking the voice of his conscience for mere prudence, and after it for 'fear from external danger'. Coleridge realizes that Macbeth's words are not to be taken at their face value, and he is fully aware of the profundity of Shakespeare's conception. Macbeth is not the incarnation of evil: if he were his conflict would have been predominantly external, which clearly is not the case. To show that the trouble is really spiritual, Coleridge contrasts 'the ingenuity' with which he 'evades the promptings of conscience before the commission of a crime' with 'his total imbecility and helplessness when the crime had been committed, and when conscience can be no longer dallied with or eluded'. Macbeth, he says:

in the first instance enumerates the different worldly impediments to his scheme of murder: could he put them by, he would 'jump the life

---

[1] Paul Deschamps, *La Formation de la pensée de Coleridge* (1772–1804) (Didier, 1964), p. 263.

to come'. Yet no sooner is the murder perpetrated, than all the concerns of this mortal life are absorbed and swallowed up in the avenging feeling within him: he hears a voice cry: 'Macbeth has murder'd sleep: and therefore, Glamis shall sleep no more.'

Like Lady Macbeth, Macbeth then is 'never meant for a real monster'.[1]

Yet it cannot be said that, because he is deceived in himself and because he mistakes the voice of his own conscience for mere prudence, he does not undergo a moral conflict. Nor can his partial ignorance of his own soul relieve him of the responsibility in Coleridge's eyes. 'In the tragic,' Coleridge believed, 'the free-will of man is the first cause.'[2] The deepest tragic effect is produced when a play presents an opposition between an individual ('springing from a defect in him') and 'a higher and intelligent will'. To deny Macbeth his part in bringing about his downfall and the downfall of others by minimizing or ignoring the importance of his choice is, according to Coleridge, to misrepresent Shakespeare's play. Wilson Knight, to take, by way of contrast, an example of the type of critic who overlooks the significant role of Macbeth's choice, asserts that the concept of willpower has no place in *Macbeth*. Macbeth, he writes:

is helpless as a man in a nightmare: and this helplessness is integral to the conception – the will-concept is absent. Macbeth may struggle, but he cannot fight: he can no more resist than a rabbit resists a weasel's teeth fastened in its neck, or a bird in the serpent's transfixing eye. Now this Evil in Macbeth propels him to an act absolutely evil.[3]

And he entitles his essay on *Macbeth* 'The Metaphysic of Evil'. No doubt the supernatural in this play plays a powerful role and Knight is acutely sensitive when he points out how Macbeth seems to be literally possessed by evil. But to make this a final verdict on his character, to rob him of his responsibility of choice would be strongly opposed by Coleridge. Without detracting from the importance of the supernatural in the tragedy or denying the metaphysical quality of its evil, Coleridge insists that the human also has its place. As he sees it, evil in Macbeth is

[1] *SC*, I, 80; II, 270; *MC*, p. 449.   [2] *SC*, II, 278; cf. I, 138.
[3] G. Wilson Knight, *The Wheel of Fire* (1937), pp. 167–9.

not exclusively imposed from above. In fact, he tries to account for the nightmare-like experience Macbeth seems to be undergoing before the murder of Duncan by the fascination evil holds for the sinful soul in spite of the soul's full realization of its nature:

When once the mind, in despite of the remonstrating conscience, has abandoned its free power to a haunting impulse or idea, then whatever tends to give depth and vividness to this idea or indefinite imagination increases *its* despotism, and in the same proportion renders the reason and free will ineffectual. Now fearful calamities, sufferings, horrors, and hair-breadth escapes will have this effect far more than even sensual pleasure and prosperous incidents. Hence the evil consequences of sin in such cases, instead of retracting and deterring the sinner, goad him on to his destruction. This is the moral of Shakespeare's *Macbeth*.[1]

And he therefore praises 'the consummate art' with which Shakespeare makes Lady Macbeth first use 'herself as incentives what his [i.e. Macbeth's] conscience would perhaps have used as motives of abhorrence', referring to her use of Duncan's presence in their castle as an argument in favour of his 'taking off' (i. v. 60ff.). Lady Macbeth, we are told, does the same thing to herself in her soliloquy immediately after hearing the news of Duncan's intended visit.[2]

Unlike the eighteenth-century rationalist critics, Coleridge realizes fully the function of the supernatural in Shakespearean tragedy. We have seen how in spite of the excessive praise lavished on Shakespeare's masterly treatment of the supernatural, the full dramatic significance of the supernatural in the plays was not realized in an age that regarded itself as enlightened. Critics like Gentleman doubted if such 'false creations of the brain' as ghosts should ever be represented on the stage since they 'play upon our passions in flat and absurd contradiction to our reason' and he condemned the supernatural in *Macbeth* as well as in other plays. Tom Davies, who generally respected Shakespeare's text, suggested that *Macbeth* should be produced 'without the help of such ghostly aid', and both he and Morgann remarked that the Witches on the stage produced a comical effect upon the audience.

[1] *MC*, p. 293.   [2] *Macbeth*, i, v. 39ff. See *SC*, i, 73.

144

Richardson gives a self-contained rational account of Macbeth's development:

The growth of Macbeth's ambition was so imperceptible, and his treason so unexpected that the historians of an ignorant age, little accustomed to explain uncommon events by simple causes, and strongly addicted to a superstitious belief in sorcery, ascribed them to praeternatural agency.[1]

Different indeed is Coleridge's attitude. In *Macbeth*, he says, not only are the Weird Sisters embodiments of the Fates and Furies at once, but they also provide the keynote to the play. But their supernatural power of knowledge does not relieve Macbeth of the heavy burden of choice laid on his shoulders. Indeed part of their prophecy was fulfilled, but the major and crucial part 'king hereafter' was 'still contingent, still in Macbeth's moral will'. And the preservation of the freedom of will is regarded by Coleridge as essential for Shakespearean tragedy: it is the hero's particular choice which brings about the tragedy. The fact that the hero, once he has made the fatal decision, is no longer the free agent he was before making it, does not make of him a determined being from the start. It is Macbeth's diseased will, his succumbing to temptation that brings about his downfall, in spite of the fact that the Weird Sisters are endowed with foreknowledge, and they predict the future events pertaining to his life.

The problem as Coleridge poses it resembles its equivalent in theology, but, as this is poetry and not metaphysics or theology, what matters is the general idea: 'the *general* idea is all that can be required from the poet, not a scholastic logical consistency in all the parts so as to meet metaphysical objections'. To curtail the power of the supernatural without nullifying it altogether, Macbeth is shown as 'rendered *temptable* by previous dalliance of the fancy with ambitious thoughts'. Coleridge points out how, at the prophecies of the Weird Sisters, Macbeth's violent reactions are sharply distinguished from 'the *unpossessedness* of Banquo's mind'.[2] He contrasts (in the words of his reporter):

the talkative curiosity of the innocent-minded and open-dispositioned Banquo, in the scene with the Witches, with the silent, absent, and

[1] *Richardson*, p. 38.   [2] *SC*, i, 67–9.

brooding melancholy of his partner. A striking instance of this self-temptation was pointed out in the disturbance of Macbeth at the election of the Prince of Cumberland.[1]

Nevertheless, Coleridge does not underrate the importance of the supernatural, for 'before Macbeth can cool' from the effect of the Weird Sister's prophecies, he writes, 'the *confirmation* of the tempting half of the prophecy [arrives] and the *catenating* tendency [of the mind is] fostered by the sudden coincidence'.[2] Thus the world of tragedy is the moral world, although in it there is sufficient room for the unknown forces in human existence.

Evil and the balance of moral forces in tragedy

In the moral world evil exists in its own right as much as good. It is metaphysical, in the sense that it is necessary and universal and cannot be explained away. Its existence is 'essentially such, not by accident of outward circumstances, not derived from its physical consequences, nor from any cause, out of itself . . . *Omnia exeunt in mysterium*'.[3] Alfred Harbage was therefore obviously wrong in saying that Coleridge did not really believe in evil. Coleridge is no believer in a pre-established harmony after Shaftesbury's fashion, and that, at least, is one reason why he does not demand poetic justice, as most of the eighteenth-century critics have done: in his lectures we find him vindicating 'the melancholy catastrophe' of *Lear*.[4] That he does not in his criticism of Shakespeare flinch from the existence of evil cannot be better illustrated than in his acceptance of Iago's character in spite of his mysterious villainy. But the relation between tragedy and morality is, in Coleridge's opinion, an intimate and important one. No tragedy can be great which neglects moral values altogether. It is essential for drama to present a world with which we can identify our own not only psychologically, but morally as well. The one thing may in fact be a corollary of the other. We refrain from this necessary identification when we are faced with a dramatic world made up exclusively of evil. Consequently no dramatic vision can be great which recognizes only evil in human existence.

[1] *SC*, II, 270.   [2] *Ibid.* I, 69.
[3] *AR*, p. 91. See introduction to Terence Hawkes (ed.), *Coleridge's Writings on Shakespeare* (1959), p. 23.   [4] *SC*, II, 219.

Great drama, Coleridge believes, must observe some kind of balance of moral forces. In a tragedy, he says, there must be at least one or more characters 'in whom you are morally interested', whom 'you follow with affectionate feelings'. It is 'impossible to keep up any pleasurable interest in a tale in which there is no goodness of heart in any of the prominent characters'. That is why in spite of 'the fertility and vigor of invention, character, language and sentiment' in Jonson's *Volpone*, Coleridge finds it to be 'a painful weight on the feelings' after the third act. It is precisely for the same reason that he condemns *Measure for Measure*, for in his opinion there is a complete absence of good characters in the play, and he admits that 'Isabella, of all Shakespeare's female characters, interests me the least'.[1] In this particular instance we may deplore the critic's insensitivity to the peculiar form and meaning of the play, although we cannot but agree that the general principle behind his criticism is just. In *Lear*, in which the dramatic vision is impenetrably dark, and evil in man is presented almost to an excess, or, as Coleridge puts it, 'the tragic has been urged beyond the outermost mark and *ne plus ultra* of the dramatic', Shakespeare sees to it that the moral balance is not completely upset. He introduces a character of almost 'absolute goodness' like Kent, and when the utmost evil appears in the shape of 'utter monsters' like Goneril and Regan, Shakespeare takes care that they are 'kept out of sight as much as possible', and that they should be used largely as a 'means for the excitement and deepening of noblest emotions towards Lear and Cordelia'.[2]

Just as a tragedy as a whole must maintain some kind of moral balance, so must the character of the hero. In Coleridge's opinion no completely villainous character can be a tragic hero. In this connection he seems to distinguish between two kinds of evil. There is what he calls 'positive' evil, the kind of evil which is premeditated in cold blood, with full knowledge and ability to act differently. On the other hand, there is the evil that springs 'entirely from defect of character'. The first can only make the villain, the Iago type, whereas the second kind of evil does not offer much resistance to tragic treatment. By denying some measure of responsibility to the character, the dramatist does not

[1] *MC*, pp. 49, 55.   [2] *SC*, I, 57, 61; *MC*, p. 83.

fear to draw his faults 'openly and broadly', and 'without reserve' – as in the case of Richard II, and one may add Macbeth. Our sympathy for such a character will be secured as long as we perceive his eventual 'disproportionate sufferings'.[1] Yet even the villainous characters, if they happen to be major characters as well, Shakespeare often endows with qualities which to some extent call for the admiration of the recipient. For 'power without reference to any moral end' inevitably compels our admiration 'whether it be displayed in the conquests of a Napoleon or Tamerlane, or in the form and thunder of a cataract'. But the admiration is limited and there is no tampering with moral values in Shakespeare's plays. 'By the counteracting power of profound intellects', Coleridge writes, the characters of Richard III and Iago are rendered 'awful' rather than 'hateful'; but awful they remain. Unlike Beaumont and Fletcher, Shakespeare does not resort to the 'trick of bringing one part of our moral nature to counteract another'.[2]

Closely connected with the problem of evil is the question of motivation. Of course, the question is really psychological, and we have seen elsewhere Coleridge's psychological views on it. But in drama there is also a moral aspect to it. Fairly adequate motivation in the case of villainous characters is one of the means of producing the moral balance which in Coleridge's opinion a tragedy must maintain. By making evil *to some extent* explicable a dramatist relieves its intensity. Compared with the introduction of good characters this is really a negative means. It only lessens evil, but does not remove it altogether. There remains a residue, which, as Coleridge thinks, is part of the mystery of existence. Hence the motives account for the evil, without explaining it away. This is essential particularly in the case of a character possessing qualities which are admirable, though amoral:

For such are the appointed relations of intellectual power to truth, and of truth to goodness, that it becomes both morally and poetically unsafe to present what is admirable – what our nature compels us to admire – in the mind, and what is most detestable in the heart, as co-existing in the same invidibual without any apparent connection, or any modification of the one by the other.

[1] *SC*, i, 149.   [2] *Ibid*. i, 58, 60; *MC*, p. 82.

Perhaps the categorical imperative has too large a share in this; yet, on the whole, it still remains true, I think, that:

in the display of such a character it was of the highest importance to prevent the guilt from passing into utter *monstrosity* – which again depends on the presence or absence of causes and temptations sufficient to *account* for the wickedness, without the necessity of recurring to a thorough fiendishness of nature for its origination.[1]

Even Iago does not possess 'a thorough fiendishness of nature'; although he 'approaches' it, he is still convincing as a character. But convincing as he is, in him evil manifests itself in its most powerful and mysterious shape. In a tragedy like *Othello* he is in his proper place, for there is no other character that can be called really evil in the *Othello* world. Roderigo is more a fool than a villain; he is a mere tool and from the very beginning he is as much sinned against as sinning.

But in a play like *Lear*, the introduction of such mysterious evil would precariously upset the moral balance, and would turn the tragic into the monstrous. It 'was most carefully to be avoided'; for the vision is gloomy enough, and there are already Goneril and Regan in it, who represent 'wickedness in an outrageous form'. Consequently evil in a prominent character like Edmund has to be made more explicable. In his discussion of his motives, Coleridge characteristically takes into account his whole personality. In the first place we have the peculiar circumstances of his birth. Further, his father relates these circumstances in his presence 'with a most degrading levity',[2] and in his presence too he expresses his shame in having to acknowledge him as his own son. Since the whole affair was no fault of Edmund's, he feels that 'the pangs of shame personally undeserved' are wrongs and hence his defence of his 'base' birth in his soliloquy. Secondly, we are told by Shakespeare that since his boyhood he had been away from his father and brother receiving his education abroad, and that he will soon be sent away again. Thirdly, besides his being a bastard, the fact that he is the younger brother makes him, in his own words, 'unpossessing', and leaves all the honours to his elder brother. By giving us all this information Shakespeare apparently makes the evil in the character to some extent

[1] *SC*, I, 58. [2] *Ibid.* I, 56. For the rest of the discussion see *ibid.* I, 56–64.

explicable. It is important to note that all this Coleridge finds in the text. He does not disengage the character of Edmund from the dramatic context and analyse it independently, nor does he, like Hazlitt, read it with too modern eyes. Whereas Hazlitt admires Edmund's 'religious honesty' in his admission of his 'plain villainy', and thinks that his speech about the mistaken influence of the stars 'is worth a million', Coleridge says that a person 'can be free from superstition by being below as well as by rising above it', and thinks that Edmund is certainly below it. This, no doubt, is more in keeping with the meaning of the Elizabethan play.[1]

Coleridge finds that Shakespeare's usual practice is to try to make evil partially explicable. He does so even in a minor character like the Second Murderer in *Macbeth*, who is not made 'a perfect monster', but who gives such a description of his life as renders his evil somewhat accountable:[2]

> I am one, my liege,
> Whom the vile blows and buffets of the world
> Have so incensed that I am reckless what
> I do to spite the world. (III. i. 108–10)

In great tragedies like Shakespeare's we do not find 'perfect monsters', for apart from the psychological improbability that attends such beings, tragedy is not meant to arouse pure horror. It is on these grounds that Coleridge once condemned the blinding scene in *Lear* for being too painful. It is true that the scene also wounded the sensibility of many an eighteenth-century critic, but the paradox is that while their theories of the sublime included the element of terror or horror as one of its constituents (Burke in fact resolved the sublime to what is fraught with danger and terror alone), and while the Gothic novel was being born, the blinding of Gloucester was considered too terrible. But Coleridge's view of sublimity is free from such crudities as the eighteenth-century critics entertained. Early in his career (1796) in a review of *The Monk*, a Gothic novel by M. G. Lewis, he stated his opinions quite clearly:

Situations of torment and images of naked horror, are easily conceived; and a writer in whose works they abound deserves our gratitude almost

---

[1] *Hazlitt*, IV, 259; *SC*, I, 62.   [2] *MC*, p. 450.

equally with him who should drag us by way of sport through a military hospital, or force us to sit at the dissecting-table of a natural philosopher . . . Figures that shock the imagination, and narratives that mangle the feelings, rarely discover *genius*, and always betray a low *taste*.[1]

Later on, when Coleridge realized that the blinding of Gloucester is at least formally functional, and saw that Shakespeare makes it less offensive to the moral sense and 'somewhat less unendurable' by referring to Gloucester's guilt in begetting Edmund,[2] he could justify the scene. But his criticism is significant. In his view tragic terror is something totally different from pure horror.

Because he finds that Shakespeare keeps a moral balance in his plays, and does not run counter to moral values, Coleridge writes that one of Shakespeare's virtues as a dramatist is that he keeps *'at all times the high road of life'*. And, as we have seen, in his view this constitutes one of the greatest virtues of a dramatist. It is this, and not prudery, which he has in mind when on several occasions, he goes out of this way to defend the morality of Shakespeare.[3] In fact, to make his meaning clear Coleridge draws a distinction between what he calls 'manners' or 'decency' and 'morals'. By manners he understands 'what is dependent on the particular customs and fashions of the age'.[4] But morality is something permanent; it belongs to the concept of man, so to speak: 'Even in a state of comparative barbarism as to manners, there may be, and there is, morality.' An offence against decency or manners is grossness, not immorality. Of grossness the examples are rife in Shakespeare's plays, as well as in the works of his contemporaries, even though there are less of them in his work than in theirs;[5] but of immorality there are none. 'Shakespeare may sometimes be gross', but he is always moral. Yet his grossness is the 'mere sport of fancy, dissipating low feelings by exciting the intellect'. Unlike what we find in the works of Beaumont and Fletcher it is 'all head-work, and fancy-drolleries, no sensation supposed in the speaker, no itchy

---

[1] *Ibid.* p. 372.
[2] *SC*, I, 57: He confessed 'that he was at the time a married man and already blest with a lawful heir of his fortunes'.
[3] *SC*, II, 266, 268. See Lucas, *Decline and Fall of the Romantic Ideal*, pp. 191ff.
[4] *SC*, II, 125–6.   [5] *MC*, p. 48.

wriggling'. It is committed 'for the sake of merriment' and not 'for the sake of offending'.[1] But while offending our decencies (for manners have changed) Shakespeare never runs counter to our moral sense. He is the opposite of the contemporary writer who 'tampers with the morals without offending the decencies'. In spite of his impersonal art, he 'always makes vice odious and virtue admirable'.[2] His plays are based upon a scheme of moral values which is not repugnant to moral sensibility. It is still basically our own scheme, and has relevance to 'frail and fallible Human Nature'. That is why one rises from their attentive perusal 'a sadder and a wiser man'.[3]

Importance of morality

Such is the importance which Coleridge attaches to morality that even in his discussion of dramatic illusion, where he believes that the power of judgement is suspended, he still asserts that we can never 'suspend the moral sense'. And in the fragment of an essay on beauty, he maintains that whereas in music and painting it may be possible occasionally to do without moral feeling, in poetry this is impossible.[4] In his criticism of Shakespeare's plays he is always looking upon the characters as the incarnations of moral values: 'Shakespeare's sublime morality . . . pervades all his great characters.' In a character like Richard III or Iago we are meant to see a dramatic representation of 'the dreadful consequences of placing the moral in subordination to the intellectual'. Cressida represents the turbulence of passion arising from 'warmth of temperament', while in Troilus we have the moral profundity of love. Hamlet stands for the excessive deliberation which paralyses action, and Macbeth for the diseased will which ends in self-deception. This preoccupation with moral issues leads him to find a moral significance even in a minor character in a play which is not a tragedy. Caliban, we are told, is 'all earth, all condensed and gross in feelings and images'; he is the representation of 'the dawnings of understanding without reason or the moral sense'. In him 'as in some brute animals, this advance to the intellectual faculties, without the moral sense, is marked by the appearance of vice'. His poetry does not redeem

[1] *SC*, I, 135; II, 126–7; *MC*, p. 83. [2] *Omniana*, II, 24; *SC*, II, 34.
[3] *Method*, p. 33. [4] *BL*, II, 197, 252.

him morally but only endows him with a certain degree of nobility which raises him 'above contempt'.[1]

Limitations of Coleridge's moral approach

This moral earnestness in Coleridge, however, causes him sometimes to be too solemn in his approach to some of Shakespeare's characters. He would find a particular moral meaning in a character, which can never be justified by the total impression. Thus he says that in both Falstaff and Richard III we have 'the subordination of the moral to the intellectual being'.[2] Apart from the debilitating lack of humour which it reveals, there is something seriously wrong in an interpretation that finds *essentially* the same values in Falstaff's character as in that of Richard III. But it is not because Coleridge's conception of humour is erroneous that he fails to see it in the character of Falstaff. The analysis which he has left us of humour is not devoid either of merit or of perceptiveness, despite the fact that he draws heavily on Jean-Paul Richter.[3] But these are the shortcomings of an excessively serious moral approach, for it is the moralist in Coleridge who

---

[1] *SC*, I, 232, 109, 134; II, 178.   [2] *Ibid.* I, 234; cf. *ibid.* II, 209, and *BL*, II, 189.

[3] When Coleridge writes that in humour 'the little is made great, and the great little, in order to destroy both, because all is equal in contrast with the infinite', he is simply reproducing Richter in English (*MC*, p. 119; cf. Jean-Paul Richter, *Vorschule der Aesthetik* (1804), section 32). But on the whole he follows Richter wisely and even adds to his master's analysis. The result is that his analysis of some of the qualities of Sterne's humour, for instance, illuminates not only the humour of Sterne, but humour in general. Coleridge distinguishes between wit and humour, showing that the former is purely a product of an 'intellectual operation' and that its field is thoughts, words and images (*MC*, pp. 440–1). Humour, on the other hand, is related to pathos, and it is the expression of an attitude of the whole man to life. Its domain is therefore human life, not so much as a set of social assumptions, rules and habits, but primarily as human. Humour is free from all notions of utility. The soul of a humorist is given to some pursuit or other totally abstracted from any interest or utility (although he himself may think otherwise), which is given by him 'some disproportionate *generality* and universality'. Hence the dependence of humour upon the particular temperament. Whereas wit is 'impersonal' humour 'always more or less partakes of the character of the speaker' (*ibid.* pp. 111–13). 'No combination of thoughts, words, or images will of itself constitute humour, unless some peculiarity of individual temperament and character be indicated thereby, as the cause of the same', and there must be 'a growth from within' (*ibid.* p. 443). Coleridge proceeds further in his analysis, showing how humour is free even from moral *effect* (*ibid.* p. 118). In humour, he says, we get 'a sort of dallying with the devil', and an 'inward sympathy with the enemy', 'a craving to dispute and yet agree' (*ibid.* p. 121). In a humorous character we witness a mode of living which makes

blinds him to the humour in the character. Similarly his moral zeal, coupled with his idolatry, drive him to make the preposterous statement that 'Shakespeare became all beings but the vicious'. 'The great prerogative of genius,' he writes, again in a bardolatrous mood, '(and Shakespeare felt and availed himself of it) is now to swell itself to the dignity of a god, and now to subdue and keep dormant some part of that lofty nature, and to descend even to the lowest character – to become everything, in fact, but the vicious.'[1] It is difficult to see what Coleridge means by such statements. If by a 'vicious' character he understands a 'pure monster', then it is possible to agree with him, for as he himself says, 'in every one of his (Shakespeare's) characters we still feel ourselves communing with the same human nature'.[2] But then this will be a strange and rather misleading use of the word 'vicious'.

Yet, despite the limitations of his moral approach, it cannot be said that Coleridge often applies moral criteria in his criticism of Shakespeare's characters as crudely as the eighteenth-century critics did. Of course, several cases of crude moral judgement unassisted by artistic sensibility can be pointed out in his criticism. The obvious case is that of Angelo in *Measure for Measure*, already referred to.[3] Likewise his moral sensibility is wounded by Isabella's behaviour in the same play,[4] and by Lady Anne's

civilized life a topsy-turvy universe in which all the social and moral values are turned upside down, and in which 'the hollowness and farce of the world' is made apparent (*ibid.* p. 119). That Coleridge could see all this, at least partly in germ, in what constitutes humour and yet refrain from calling Falstaff a humorous character is very strange indeed. The reason he adduces for his opinion that Falstaff is not a humorous character is significantly the very reason from which such a judgement should follow. Unfortunately it does not fit the facts of the case: 'The character of Falstaff, as drawn by Shakespeare, may be described as one of wit, rather than of humour. The speeches of Falstaff and Prince Henry would, for the most part be equally proper in the mouth of either, and might indeed, with undiminished effect, proceed from any person. This is owing to their being composed almost wholly of wit, which is impersonal, and not of humour, which always more or less partakes of the character of the speaker' (*ibid.* p. 111). Because he could see in Falstaff only the 'subordination of the moral to the intellectual being', and because wit is purely the product of an 'intellectual operation', Coleridge wrote that 'this character [i.e. Falstaff] so often extolled as the masterpiece of humor, contains, and was not meant to contain, any humor at all' (*ibid.* p. 50).

[1] *SC*, ii, 204, 133; cf. ii, 217.   [2] *Method*, p. 27.   [3] *SC*, i, 113ff.; ii, 352.
[4] *MC*, p. 49.

in *Richard III*. He even dismisses the scene in which she 'yielded to the usurper's solicitations' as non-Shakespearean,[1] although he has the honesty to admit that *Measure for Measure*, painful as he finds it, is 'Shakespeare's throughout'.[2] But these are exceptional cases, and as a rule Coleridge's application of moral criteria in his judgement of characters is not so crude. This is largely due to his peculiar conception of the creative imagination, which, although it is based upon a serious view of art, does not confuse art with life.

[1] *SC*, ii, 209.　　[2] *Ibid*. i, 113.

6

Shakespeare's poetry

Language an integral part of the plays

Coleridge's theory of the imagination led him to the belief that a truly imaginative work is a complete organic whole in which the constituent parts mutually explain and support each other. His criterion of artistic excellence, is the complete interdependence of these parts. A mature Shakespearean play, in his view, is always marked by its totality of interest; in it the main theme pervades all its constituent elements. In his search for its 'meaning' therefore Coleridge does not abstract elements like character or plot or language from the whole context, and discuss them *in vacuo*, so to speak. Indeed, in this study, for the sake of convenience only, we have attempted a distinction (but not a 'division' as Coleridge would say) between these constituent elements, in order to understand fully Coleridge's conception of the nature of Shakespearean drama. We have considered his treatment of plot or structure and of character, and must now proceed to discuss his views on the language of Shakespeare's plays, bearing in mind all the time that these constituent elements are in reality inseparable. We have noticed how in his discussion of the form of Shakespeare's plays Coleridge is led to the question of their meaning and that in turn brings him to considerations of character. Similarly his treatment of character leads him at certain points to considerations of the language of the plays. This is clearly a symptom of his organic approach.

As with plot or character, so it is with language. The relation between the dramatic vision which the plays embody and the language in which this vision is expressed is an intimate one. Dramatic poetry, Coleridge says, 'must be poetry *hid* in thought and passion, not thought or passion disguised in the dress of poetry'.[1] Coleridge's view of Shakespeare's language is there-

---

[1] *MC*, p. 343.

fore essentially dramatic. Because the poetry is not an external addition, but is born in the same act as the dramatic vision, it is an integral part of the drama. On this aspect of Shakespeare's language Coleridge's contribution to Shakespearean criticism is incalculable.

To say that Coleridge was one of the first critics who fully understood the dramatic nature of Shakespeare's language is no exaggeration. Ever since Dryden, English critics entertained a tight conception of the language of poetry which valued polish and correctness above any other quality, and which was not easy to reconcile with the greatest English dramatic poetry exemplified by Shakespeare. In order to make room for Shakespeare, however, eighteenth-century critics were eventually to develop another antithetical standard, which by its very nature was intractable to the dominant critical rules, namely the standard of the sublime. For our present purpose we may sum up the eighteenth-century view of poetry saying that it was a view which on the whole favoured the poetry of statement.[1] Although it must be raised above the level of prose by certain stylistic devices, poetry must possess primarily all the clarity and unambiguity of prose statement.

But the dramatic poetry of Shakespeare, which aims above all at immediacy and urgency, and which works simultaneously on a variety of levels, cannot, except to the loss of its complexity, afford to be as clear as prose statements. It cannot be as 'correct' as the champions of correctness would have liked it to be. That is why Shakespeare was often blamed by eighteenth-century critics, and his sublimity and his bathos were considered inseparable. Even Dr Johnson complained in the *Preface* that 'the stile of Shakespeare was in itself ungrammatical, perplexed and obscure'.[2] If the eighteenth-century critics generally took exception to the lack of perfection in Shakespeare's style, to his ambiguity and grammatical incorrectness, it was largely because they misunderstood the nature of his poetry. Even when his poetry was praised the fact that it is essentially *dramatic* poetry was universally overlooked. Not even Daniel Webb, probably the most sympathetic critic of Shakespeare's poetry in the eighteenth century, showed much awareness of it in his book, *Remarks on the*

[1] F. R. Leavis, *The Common Pursuit* (1952), p. 110. [2] *Raleigh*, p. 42.

157

Beauties of Poetry (1762). Webb refused to be 'brought to consider the beauties of a poet in the same light that' one does 'the colours of a tulip', and did most to elevate Shakespeare the poet to the rank of 'conscious artist'. He compared Shakespeare's versification with that of Pope to the latter's disadvantage. In what he called 'sentimental harmony', which is the coordination of rhythm and sense, he found Shakespeare to be 'equal, if not superior to any other English poet'. The variety in his versification, commonly thought a sign of weakness and inequality, he regarded as a conscious means to achieve the desired effect. But Webb told us virtually nothing about the *dramatic* function of the poetry, about the relationship between rhythm and imagery to character and to the whole. There is one solitary example in the book, however, in which he tried to relate an image to the character and situation, namely his comment on the line from the Queen's speech to Hamlet:

> Good Hamlet, cast thy *nighted* colour off:

'This metaphor,' he wrote, 'seems, at first, to reach no farther than the gloominess of Hamlet's dress; but if our ideas go along with the poet's, we shall extend it to the melancholy of his mind.' Unfortunately this is the only exception to Webb's usual approach.[1]

Coleridge, on the other hand, fully realized that Shakespeare was writing not just poetry, but *dramatic* poetry, and he clearly understood that dramatic poetry has its own exigencies. The editors, he once said:

> are all of them ready enough to cry out against Shakespeare's laxities and licences of style, forgetting that he is not merely a poet but a *dramatic* poet – that when the head and heart are swelling with fullness, a man does not ask himself whether he has grammatically *arranged*, but only whether (the context taken in) he has *conveyed*, his meaning.[2]

And he took to task those critics who would explain 'by ellipses and *subauditurs* in a Greek or Latin classic' what they would 'triumph over as ignorance' in a modern writer such as Shakespeare. Whatever is 'in the genius of vehement conversation', he explained, should not be forced to conform to the cold

---

[1] Webb, *Remarks on the Beauties of Poetry*, pp. 36, 32, 48–50, 79.   [2] *SC*, I, 84–5.

language of statement. Dramatic poetry obeys a logic of its own, other than the logic of formal grammar, and in it grammar itself is often subservient to expressiveness. Because Shakespeare wrote a kind of verse which was meant to be 'recited dramatically' he sometimes 'broke off from the grammar' in order to 'give the meaning more passionately'.[1] That is why any comparison between the poetry of Shakespeare and that of any other non-dramatic poet as Milton or Spenser is considered by Coleridge to be 'heterogeneous'. Even at its most lyrical the poetry in Shakespeare's plays is still dramatic: *A Midsummer Night's Dream* is not pure lyrical verse; it is 'one continued specimen of the lyrical dramatized'. And we have seen how Coleridge considers even the songs part and parcel of the plays in which they are introduced.[2]

There are, of course, reasons why Coleridge was generally more sensitive than his predecessors to the virtues of Shakespeare's style. Coleridge was an enthusiastic admirer of Shakespeare's language. He was constantly conscious of the fact that Shakespeare was a poet and that his plays are poetic drama. Unlike his predecessors he was deeply interested in Shakespeare's non-dramatic poetry, and although he left us little or no criticism on the sonnets a glance at his *Notebooks* (see *Notebooks*, II, Notes, 2428) will show that he knew and admired them greatly. More importantly his view of the language of poetry is free from the prejudices and limitations which attend the ideal of clarity. Apart from its failure to accommodate Shakespeare's dramatic poetry, the ideal of clarity and 'prose statement' involves certain basic misconceptions regarding the nature of the language of poetry. Clarity and distinction are the virtues ultimately advocated by the rational spirit and the Royal Society; they are in their proper place in the language of science. But in poetry language fulfils a different function from what it does in a scientific exposition. By setting a great value on clarity and distinction, not only in prose but in poetry as well, eighteenth-century critics consciously or unconsciously relegated poetry to the position of handmaid to rational thinking. Side by side with the pleasure theory

---

[1] *Ibid.* I, 159. Coleridge is using the word 'grammar' here in the sense of a 'formal' science. For his own dynamic and functional view of grammar see *Ph L*, p. 50.   [2] *SC*, I, 226–7.

we find in this complex century the view that the object of poetry is to give instruction. The case is really more complicated than the Horatian *utile et dulce*. Poetry should propagate what is true, not indeed what is poetically true, but what has been proved to be true either by science or by commonsense. Poetry therefore becomes a means of propaganda, only an excellent means, since it sets forth truth in a pleasant garb. Stylistically the eighteenth-century view is a dualistic view which sharply separates form from content. The content is a hard core of clear thought, what oft was thought; and the form is the beautiful and decorous verbiage in which this thought is expressed, an outer clothing and a mere trapping. But this sharp separation of form and content is ultimately the mark of scientific and not poetic language. If the language of eighteenth-century poetry has generally struck critics from Arnold to Leavis as a language of 'prose statement', it is really because in it the referential element is used at its highest potency. Basically the referential element in language is all that matters in science and even in everyday life. Of this difference between the poetic and other uses of language Coleridge is aware.

Words and meaning in poetry

Coleridge draws a distinction between two kinds, or uses, of language. There is what he calls 'the language of man', which is in fact the language of everyday life and of science. In it 'the sound, *sun* [e.g.], or the figures, *S,U,N*, are pure arbitrary modes of recalling the object, and for visual mere objects not only sufficient, but have infinite advantages from their v[ery no]thingness *per se*'. At the other extreme from this language is the world of living objects as they exist in all their reality and concreteness, what Coleridge metaphorically calls 'the language of nature'. The language of poetry, at its best as in Shakespeare, is 'a something intermediate' between the cold referential use and the concrete living objects, 'or rather it is the former blended with the latter, the arbitrary not merely recalling the cold notion of the thing, but expressing the reality of it'. Again in *Biographia Literaria* Coleridge points out the difference between the two kinds of language: 'the difference is great and evident,' he writes,

160

between words used as the *arbitrary marks* of thought, our smooth market-coin of intercourse, with the image and superscription worn out by currency; and those which convey pictures either borrowed from *one* outward object to enliven and particularize some *other*; or used allegorically to body forth the inward state of the person speaking; or such as are at least the exponents of his peculiar turn and unusual extent of faculty.[1]

The distinction is between the language of pure reference and the language of poetry. The former is bare, and because of its bareness it is best fitted for purposes of mere reference, whereas the latter is soaked in experience; its function is not just to refer but to put the mind in possession of reality in all its concreteness. That is why at its best every element in it is functional 'In my opinion,' Coleridge writes in one of his letters, 'every phrase, every metaphor, every personification should have its justifying clause in some *passion*, either of the poet's mind or of the characters described by the poet.'[2]

At one point Coleridge defines poetry as 'the *best* words in the best order'.[3] This is not a mere rhetorical assertion as it is sometimes taken to be. It has a serious meaning, and for that we go to Coleridge himself. 'Whatever lines,' he writes, 'can be translated into other words of the same language, without diminution of their significance either in sense, or association, or in any worthy feeling, are so far vicious in their diction.' Again he says that the excellence of verse is that 'it is untranslatable into any other words without a detriment to the beauty of a passage'. He is reported by H. N. Coleridge to have said that 'the removal of a word out of the finished passages in Shakespeare or Milton will alter the thought, or the feeling, or at least the tone'.[4] Because thought and expression are in this way inseparable it will not do to have as a substitute for 'poetic thoughts', 'thoughts translated into the language of poetry'. We have travelled a long way indeed from the position of Dryden and his tradition, with its sharp separation between thought and expression. Coleridge has already laid the basis of

[1] *Ibid.* i, 209; *BL*, ii, 98.   [2] Letter to W. Sotheby (13 July 1802), *CL*, ii, 812.
[3] *MC*, p. 403; F. L. Lucas, *Decline and Fall of the Romantic Ideal*, pp. 189–90.
[4] *BL*, i, 14; *SC*, ii, 179; *MC*, p. 439; J. R. de J. Jackson (ed.), *Coleridge the Critical Heritage* (1970), p. 626.

the theory of the indissoluble union of form and content, which is to be developed and explained later by De Quincey:

if language were merely a dress (for thought), then you could separate the two; you could lay the thoughts on the left hand, the language on the right. But, generally speaking, you can no more deal thus with poetic thoughts than you can with soul and body. The union is too subtle, the intermixture too ineffable, – each is existing not merely *with* the other, but each *in* and *through* the other.[1]

In insisting, as he often does, that great poetry such as Shakespeare's cannot be translated into other words 'without injury to the meaning', Coleridge does not mean by 'meaning' merely the bare 'sense', using the technical term of I. A. Richards in his *Practical Criticism*. By meaning Coleridge, in fact, understands practically all of the latter's four kinds of meaning:

I include in the *meaning* of a word not only its correspondent object, but likewise all the associations which it recalls. For language is framed to convey not the object alone, but likewise the character, mood and intentions of the person who is representing it.[2]

Not only the character, mood and intentions of the speaker, but the situation as well has to be taken into account, for the whole passage or context is also a part of the meaning. And we find him writing of 'the elements of meaning – their double, triple and quadruple combinations'. In poetry these combinations are tighter and more closely woven. The main purport of Coleridge's controversy with Wordsworth over poetic diction is that poetry differs from prose in that in it language has a different function to fulfil: 'the architecture of the words is *essentially* different from that of prose'.[3] By 'architecture' Coleridge has in mind not only metre, but the kind of order and interrelation between the different elements of meaning which he points out in his own famous analysis of Shakespeare's lines from *Venus and Adonis*, and which he puts forward as an example of the effect of the secondary imagination. The function of poetic imagination is precisely to fuse these different elements together, making of them one unified whole.

[1] H. Darbishire (ed.), *De Quincey's Literary Criticism* (1909), p. 187.
[2] *BL*, ii, 115–16; cf. *BL*, i, 5; *MC*, p. 221, 439; *SC*, ii, 179; *TT*, 3 July 1933.
[3] *AP*, p. 204; *BL*, ii, 48.

After this brief account of Coleridge's conception of meaning and the role of language in poetry several features of his criticism of Shakespeare's language become explicable. In his defence of imagery and metaphor we do not find the underlying primitivist assumption, common enough in the late eighteenth century, that figures of speech whatever they may be, are a mark of original genius. In fact there is nothing primitivist about Coleridge's attitude to poetry, as can easily be seen from his discussion in *Biographia Literaria* (ch. 22) of the reasons Wordsworth gives for his choice of simple and rustic characters in the preface to the *Lyrical Ballads*. Coleridge defends imagery and metaphor only when after a thorough critical examination he finds them to be strictly functional. 'Formal similes', he believes, are only '*sermoni propriora*'; they may be a product of 'pleasing moods of the mind', but not of the 'highest and most appropriate' poetic moods.[1] If imagery does not extend the meaning, then it is a mere trapping, and as such it ought to be condemned by the critic and eschewed by the poet. In order to see whether or not a figure extends the meaning it is not enough to examine the expression in itself, so to speak. A critic must likewise consider the expression in relation to the speaker and to the whole situation, since these also form part of the meaning. It is therefore easy to see how Coleridge's view of poetic meaning makes him a far better qualified critic than his predecessors of the *dramatic* poetry of Shakespeare.

Imagery and metaphor

Similarly in Coleridge's criticism we cease to hear about Shakespeare's lack of decorum in his use of the English language. Because of the eighteenth-century rule that in the high 'kinds' of poetry no familiar or mean word or image should be introduced, Johnson, we remember, condemned Lady Macbeth's soliloquy, 'Come, thick night...' because Shakespeare used words like 'dun' ('an epithet now seldom heard but in the stable') and 'knife' ('an instrument used by butchers and cooks in the meanest employments'), and Goldsmith (or whoever wrote the essay 'On Metaphors') found the words 'Ay, there's the rub' in the soliloquy 'To be or not to be' 'a vulgarism beneath the

[1] Letter to W. Sotheby (10 September 1802), *CL*, II, 864.

dignity of Hamlet's character'.[1] But this rule is really based upon an inadequate and highly artificial view of poetic language: if the thought is separable from expression, then it can be expressed adequately in more than one way, and it is the poet's business to choose the most 'sublime' way. Thanks to Coleridge, we have now come to regard it as a critical commonplace that thought and expression form an indivisible unity, and that great poetry is untranslatable into other words of the same language. Images are not important in themselves, they become important only when they mean something to the poet. A familiar image acquires significance when it is transformed by the poet's emotional apprehension: 'The most familiar images' are given novelty 'by a new state of feelings'.[2] In fact, 'one of the purposes and tests of true poetry', Coleridge maintains, is 'the employment of common objects in uncommon ways – the felicitous and novel use of images of daily occurrence', and of such 'familiar images and illustrations' Shakespeare is 'full'.[3] Here is implied a criticism of the eighteenth-century view of sublime poetry, which considered the sublime to exist in certain objects and which advised a poet to introduce in his poetry images of certain objects and avoid others in order to merit the epithet 'sublime'. Again this is a criticism directed by the dynamic or organic view against the mechanical. In the former no image is mean or grand *per se*, and consequently unless every image is melted down and fused by the poet's emotional experience in the heat of the creative process no amount of adding one so-called grand image to another can be sufficient to produce a sublime effect. Thus an image acquires significance only in its context.

Because his view of metaphor is radically different from that of eighteenth-century critics, Coleridge managed to put an end at long last to the universal attacks on Shakespeare's metaphorical style, which were repeated *ad nauseam* from the time of Dryden to that of Whately. For the sake of his general thesis in *Modern Poetry and the Tradition*, Cleanth Brooks claims that Coleridge's conception of metaphor is substantially the same as that of the eighteenth-century critics. But nothing could be

[1] *The Rambler*, No. 168; Oliver Goldsmith, *Complete Works* (1867), p. 227.
[2] *SC*, i, 75.   [3] *Ibid*. ii, 43; cf. ii, 203.

further from the truth.[1] The eighteenth-century ideal of clarity led to a conception of metaphor which narrowly limited its possibilities and levelled out its complexity. The aim of metaphor in Dr Johnson's definition is to illustrate or aggrandize (according to Goldsmith, or to be exact, the author of the essay 'On Metaphors', 'to illustrate and beautify'). But if metaphors are regarded simply as ornaments of diction then they are deemed out of place in tragedy. 'To the sublime of sentiment', which it is the business of tragedy to provide, 'images are superfluous', says one critic. Another writes that 'in expressing any severe passion that totally occupies the mind metaphor is unnatural', and he therefore condemns Macbeth's speech on sleep after the murder of Duncan.[2] The attack on the images in Hamlet's soliloquy 'To be or not to be', in the essay 'On Metaphors' attributed by some to Goldsmith is, or ought to be, well-known. But nothing could be easier than to multiply examples of this condemnation of imagery in the eighteenth century.

Coleridge is aware of the complexity of the function of Shakespeare's imagery. Unlike the eighteenth-century critics, he does not relegate the function of metaphor to illustration and embellishment. In *Biographia Literaria* he tells us that figures and metaphors must have their 'justifying reasons', and should not be 'mere artifices of connection or ornament', they should not 'degenerate into mere creatures of an arbitrary purpose, cold, technical artifices or ornament or connection'.[3] The relation which imagery bears to its context should be primarily organic. For the organic quality, which in Coleridge's view characterizes Shakespeare's plays, is also manifest very clearly in his style. The style of the plays, Coleridge writes, is 'so peculiarly vital and organic'. 'In Shakespeare one sentence begets the next naturally; the meaning is all inwoven'; he 'goes on creating and evolving B out of A, and C out of B, and so on, just as a serpent moves, which makes a fulcrum of its own body, and seems for ever twisting and untwisting its own strength'. But because style is not the mere outward dress of thought, this feature is

[1] Cleanth Brooks, *Modern Poetry and the Tradition* (1948), pp. 18, 26.
[2] W. Hodson, *Observations on Tragedy* (1780), pp. 98–100; Kames, *Elements of Criticism*, I, 497.   [3] *BL*, II, 28, 64.

not really purely stylistic; it is the feature of the whole artistic creation: 'The construction of Shakespeare's sentences, whether in verse or prose, is the necessary and homogeneous vehicle of his peculiar manner of thinking.'[1] The result of this peculiar quality of style, or perhaps the cause of it, is the organic nature of Shakespeare's metaphors. Metaphors in Shakespeare seem to be closely tied together by the most subtle bonds. He generates one metaphor 'by unmarked influences of association from some preceding metaphor'. Shakespeare's conceits, he says, 'not only arise out of some *word* in the lines before, but they *lead* to the thought in the lines following'. To illustrate his meaning Coleridge quotes the lines from *As You Like It*, which describe the wounded stag (II. i. 38–40):

> The big round tears
> Cours'd one another down his innocent nose
> In piteous chase:

where the image in 'cours'd' comes 'naturally from the position of the head, and most beautifully, from the association of the preceding image of the chase, in which "the poor sequester'd stag from the hunter's aim had ta'en hurt"'.[2]

Before Coleridge the associationist Walter Whiter had noted the unconscious association in Shakespeare's imagery as well as the image-clusters which E. A. Armstrong has made better known and collected more systematically in his book *Shakespeare's Imagination* (1946). But Whiter was so intent on showing the unconscious working of Shakespeare's mind that he failed to see how Shakespeare's mode of associating one image with another makes his style a complex organic texture, and he actually denied Shakespeare deliberate intention in some of his most obvious puns. In his preoccupation with 'the most indubitable principle in the doctrine of metaphysics' (i.e. the principle of the association of ideas) he lost sight of Shakespeare's poetic skill and artistry, his 'esemplastic' power and fusing imagination. And how could he avoid that if his view of poetic imagination was that of eighteenth-century passive associationism? One

---

[1] *SC*, 112; *TT*, 7 April 1833; 5 March 1834; 15 March 1834.
[2] *SC*, I, 112, 17; *BL*, II, 198n. It may be pointed out here that Walter Whiter also quotes these lines to show the working of unconscious association in Shakespeare's mind (Whiter, *Specimen of a Commentary*, p. 97).

should not therefore exaggerate the modernity of Whiter's approach as some scholars have done in the past few years.[1] Coleridge, on the other hand, by maintaining that great poetry is the product of a nice balance between the conscious and unconscious, restored the dignity of conscious artistry to Shakespeare's works, and was able to ask intelligent questions about the significance and effect of a particular mode of associating or introducing imagery. It is customary nowadays to think that Walter Whiter was the first critic to point out the importance of Shakespeare's imagery. But it is important to realize the limitations of Whiter's interest and treatment. Whiter was interested in the images as such, their tendency to cluster and their revelation of Shakespeare's mind as well as of the background of his times. His interest was therefore psychological, sociological and textual; but it was never really artistic. The question whether imagery is an integral part of the structure of a play, whether it spontaneously arises from, and in turn reacts immediately or obliquely upon a particular situation or character, and is ultimately fused into the organic structure of the whole play as a poetic and dramatic vision – that question does not arise anywhere in his book. For the realization of the complex nature of Shakespeare's imagery we had to wait until Coleridge's time. Coleridge was the first English critic to see the dramatic value of Shakespeare's imagery. As for the German enthusiasts, despite their belief in the principle of organic unity they said nothing on the imagery. 'In the great admirers of Shakespeare among the German poets, like A. W. Schlegel or Ludwig Tieck,' says Wolfgang Clemen, 'we seek in vain for a single remark on Shakespeare's imagery.'[2] One finds, for instance, that, with the exception of puns, Schlegel's lack of interest in the minutiae of Shakespeare's style, such as imagery, is striking.

[1] See S. K. Sen, 'A Neglected Critic of Shakespeare. Walter Whiter', *Shakespeare Quarterly*, XIII, no. 2 (Spring 1962); A. M. Eastman and G. B. Harrison (eds.), *Shakespeare's Critics from Jonson to Auden* (1964), p. xiii; Mary Bell, 'Walter Whiter's Notes on Shakespeare', *Shakespeare Survey*, no. 20 (1967), and Whiter, *Specimen of a Commentary*. Being the text of the first (1794) edition revised by the author and never previously published, edited by Alan Over, completed by Mary Bell (1967). Surely Barbara Hardy is nearer the mark when she states that Whiter 'had no concept of a creative imagination'. See her article 'Walter Whiter and Shakespeare', *Notes and Queries*, 198 (1953), pp. 50–4.
[2] Wolfgang Clemen, *The Development of Shakespeare's Imagery* (1951), p. 14.

Even in Shakespeare's earliest non-dramatic writings Coleridge pointed to the artistic significance of the imagery. In *Venus and Adonis* and *Lucrece* the 'series and never broken chain of imagery, always vivid and, because unbroken, often minute' serve to add an extra dimension to the narrative. They 'provide a substitute for that visual language, that constant intervention and running comment by tone, look and gesture, which in his dramatic works he was entitled to expect from the players'. It is through the imagery in these poems that Coleridge could see 'the great instinct, which impelled the poet to the drama', and because of the imagery Venus and Adonis 'seem at once the characters themselves, and the whole representation of those characters by the most consummate actors'.[1] When imagination is working at its highest, even in those early works of Shakespeare, the imagery bears a closer and more organic relation to its context. The image in the lines from *Venus and Adonis*, made famous by Coleridge's quotation and analysis, is really the epitome of the whole situation. All the elements of the situation are fused and unified by the image itself:

> Look! how a bright star shooteth from the sky,
> So glides he in the night from Venus' eye (II. 815–16)

'How many images and feelings,' says Coleridge, 'are here brought together without effort and without discord – the beauty of Adonis – the rapidity of his flight – the yearning yet hopelessness of the enamoured gazer – and a shadowy ideal character thrown over the whole.'[2]

This latter type of imagery is what characterizes the plays of Shakespeare, at least in the period of his maturity. There the imagery 'moulds and colors itself to the circumstances, passion, or character, present and foremost in the mind'. And for 'unrivalled instances of this excellence' Coleridge refers the reader not only to *Lear* and *Othello*, but to practically all the 'dramatic works' of Shakespeare.[3] Shakespeare's imagery is part and parcel of the plays; it is rooted in its dramatic context. Amongst other reasons, it is because the serious eighteenth-century critics regarded Shakespeare as a poet, and not as a dramatic poet, that they condemned his imagery. Instead of placing a metaphorical

---

[1] *BL*, II, 15; cf. *SC*, II, 92–3. [2] *SC*, I, 213. [3] *BL*, II, 18.

expression in its dramatic context and asking themselves whether or not it then becomes functional, they often wrenched the expression from the dramatic situation and examined it by itself, as if it occurred in a poem written purely in the first person. Thus Pope and Arbuthnot, Coleridge reminds us, chose Prospero's lines to Miranda when he directs her attention to Ferdinand:

> The fringed curtains of thine eye advance
> And say what thou seest yond. (I. ii. 408–9)

as an illustration of the 'Art of Sinking in Poetry'. But remembering his golden rule of the untranslatability of good poetry Coleridge writes, 'Taking these words as a periphrase of "Look what is coming yonder" it certainly may to some appear to border on the ridiculous.' And this is precisely how the tradition that considers the object of metaphor to be either illustration or embellishment can take the lines. But by examining the dramatic context in which the lines occur, Coleridge tries to show how the metaphor is neither strained nor bombastic, but is in fact born of the tone and nature of the particular character uttering it.[1]

In Coleridge's treatment we notice that the function of imagery is not limited to the negative role of according with the situation and the character. Imagery can play a more positive part. By being the most concentrated form of expression it is especially suited to dramatic poetry. A single image can create a vivid picture of a situation in the mind of the reader. Coleridge quotes Prospero's words to Miranda:

> One midnight,
> Fated to the purpose, did Antonio open
> The gates of Milan; and i' the dead of darkness,
> The ministers for the purpose hurried thence
> Me, and thy crying self. (I. ii. 128–31)

to show how 'by introducing a single happy epithet, "crying", in the last line, a complete picture is presented to the mind'. And besides being an echo to the characters, imagery sometimes enforces and clinches the impression of a whole character. Thus

[1] *SC*, II, 178–80.

169

Caliban who is 'a sort of creature of the earth' 'gives us images from the earth' while Ariel himself 'a sort of creature of the air' – 'in air he lives, from air he derives his being, in air he acts; and all his colours and properties seem to have been obtained from the rainbow and the skies' – 'gives us images from the air'.[1]

Imagery can also have a revelatory function: Coleridge shows how it becomes itself a means of characterization. The imagery in the speeches of Lady Macbeth illuminates to us certain aspects of her character of which she herself is not conscious. In spite of her endeavours to rise above the moral law 'by inflated and soaring fancies, and appeals to spiritual agency', the imagery in which she expresses herself reveals sufficiently that she is no 'moral monster'.

So far is the woman from being dead within her, that her sex occasionally betrays itself in the very moment of dark and bloody imagination. A passage where she alludes to 'plucking her nipple from the boneless gums of her infant', though usually thought to prove a merciless and unwomanly nature, proves the direct opposite . . . She brings it . . . as the most horrible act which it was possible for imagination to conceive, as that which was most revolting to her own feelings . . . Had she regarded this with savage indifference, there would have been no force in the appeal . . . Another exquisite trait was the faltering of her resolution, while standing over Duncan in his slumbers: '*Had he not resembled My father as he slept*, I had done't.'[2]

Moreover, in a single image we may find the crystallization of a whole inner conflict in a character. The example Coleridge points out is the image in Othello's final speech, in which he takes stock of the whole of his tragic situation, describing himself as:

> one whose hand,
> Like the base Indian, threw a pearl away
> Richer than all his tribe. (v. ii. 346–8)

Not only Theobald, Warburton, Steevens and Farmer, but

---

[1] *SC*, ii, 174–8. Schlegel remarks that Caliban signifies the heavy element of earth while Ariel's name 'bears an allusion to air' (Schlegel, *Dramatic Art and Literature*, p. 395). But of course he mentions nothing about the imagery. Joseph Warton, however, it may be pointed out, wrote in *The Adventurer* (no. 93), that 'Ariel . . . has a set of ideas and images peculiar to his station and office, a beauty of the same kind with that which is justly admired in the Adam of Milton, whose manners and sentiments are all paradisaical.'

[2] *MC*, p. 449; *SC*, ii, 271.

strangely enough, some modern scholars prefer to follow the Quarto and read 'Judean' for 'Indian'. Theobald's reason for adopting 'Judean' is that 'no Indian was so ignorant as not to know the value of pearls', and that Shakespeare would have called an Indian 'rude' and not 'base'. Against this 'rational' explanation one has only to set Coleridge's reasons for defending the Folio version 'Indian', to see the essential difference in the attitude of the two critics to imagery. In the first place Coleridge is against the purely illustrative function of the image, and he therefore rejects the reference to the story of Herod, saying contemptuously: 'To make Othello say that he, who had killed his wife, was like Herod, who had killed his!' Secondly, his defence of 'base' shows an understanding of the complex nature of Shakespeare's imagery, which arises from an insight into the working of the mind, not only of Othello, but also of Shakespere. 'Othello,' he says, 'wishes to excuse himself on the score of ignorance, and yet not to excuse himself – to excuse himself by accusing.' This struggle of feeling in Othello, Coleridge thinks, is finely conveyed by the word 'base'. The word 'base', he goes on, 'is applied to the *rude* Indian, not in his own character, but as the momentary representative of Othello', taking 'Indian' to mean '*savage in genere*'.[1] In this way the image reveals the contradictory feelings of the character; it is born naturally out of the dramatic situation, which in its turn it illuminates.

Puns

Like his imagery Shakespeare's puns bear an organic relation to his dramatic poetry. Because the eighteenth-century conception of the poetic language of Shakespeare was not particularly dramatic, the nature and function of puns were not understood, and they were accordingly denounced by Shakespearean critics of the period. Those who defended Shakespeare on this score merely exonerated him from responsibility for such degradation of his sublime style. They declared that Shakespeare's faults were only the faults of his times, and that his misfortune was that he prostituted his genius in this respect. They were only too anxious to defend the man, and in doing so they forgot that the charge against the plays as works of art still held.

[1] *SC*, I, 54.

Of course, there were one or two attempts to defend Shakespeare's puns, based not on the familiar general reference to the bad custom of the times, but on a close treatment of the text. Both Morgann and Whiter attempted an analysis of the Shakespearean pun. Of the two Morgann, as is to be expected, is more to the point. Like Morgann's, Whiter's treatment of puns is incidental, but, unlike Morgann's, his defence consists in vaporizing most of the puns he encounters in Shakespeare's poetry. As his object is to point out the unconscious working of Shakespeare's mind by reference to the principle of the association of ideas, Whiter attributes most of his puns to the working of this principle, thus denying Shakespeare's conscious intention behind them. He undertakes 'to defend our Poet in a variety of instances against the charge of an intended quibble, which the Commentators have often unjustly imputed to him'.[1] He therefore denies the presence of an intended quibble, for instance, in the lines from *As You Like It*, on the words 'suit' and 'coat':

JACQUES   I am ambitious for a motley coat.
DUKE S.   Thou shalt have one.
JACQUES   It is my only suit;
              Provided that you weed your better judgments
              Of all opinion that grows rank in them
              That I am wise.   (II. vii. 43–7)

By exculpating Shakespeare from the charge of conscious punning Whiter makes him more palatable to the eighteenth-century taste in poetry, but he does not realize that by doing so he also thins out the rich texture of Shakespeare's verse. Whiter's own attitude to 'puns' as such is no less censorious than that of his age, as his recent enthusiastic editor admits.[2]

Less purely psychological and more literary and artistic is Morgann's criticism of the Shakespearean pun. Like the rest of the eighteenth-century critics, he believes that puns *qua* puns are 'base things'. But because he is one of the very few critics of the

---

[1] Whiter, *Specimen of a Commentary* (1794) pp. 83–4.,
[2] In the introduction to her edition Mary Bell describes Whiter's attempt to defend the Shakespearean pun as 'half-hearted' (p. lvi), but in her article 'Walter Whiter's Notes on Shakespeare', *Shakespeare Survey*, no. 20, p. 86 she is more explicit: 'In his attitude to the pun, too, Whiter is closer to the age of Johnson than to the age of Coleridge.'

century – if not the only one – who seems to believe consistently in the conscious artistry of Shakespeare, he admits that Shakespeare converts these base things into excellence. He maintains that some of the puns are not his, but those of them which are undoubtedly his can, with very few exceptions, be justified. The sole example he offers:

> For if the Jew doth cut but deep enough
> I'll pay the forfeiture *with all my heart*[1]

he defends on the grounds that it is natural for one 'who affects gaiety under the pressure of severe misfortunes' to play on words, and that the pun itself, because it is an unsuccessful effort of fortitude, 'serves the more plainly to disclose the gloom and darkness of the mind'. This is an excellent defence of this particular pun, to be sure. Unfortunately Morgann's criticism of Shakespeare's puns is very brief and relegated to a footnote: he offers only one example for analysis and illustration, and points only to one of the many functions of puns.

It is not until we come to Coleridge that we get any detailed and clear understanding of the role of puns in Shakespeare's verse, and of their immediate dramatic relevance. As in the case of imagery there seems to be no question of any foreign influence here. Indeed Schlegel, whose influence upon Coleridge is considerable and explicit at times, defended and justified Shakespeare's puns at the same time as Coleridge. But in their treatment the two critics pursued entirely different methods, and one can say that Coleridge's is the more valuable and suggestive for purposes of literary criticism. Schlegel's defence of puns is based on an onomatopoeic theory of the origin of language. There is a desire in the human mind when deeply excited to go back to a primitive stage, when language exhibits 'the object which it denotes, sensibly, by its very sound'. In the more developed stages of language, this desire finds its gratification when the excited imagination seizes 'any congruity in sound which may accidentally offer itself', thus restoring 'for the nonce the lost

---

[1] *The Merchant of Venice*, IV. i. 280–1. The actual lines are:

> For if the Jew do cut but deep enough,
> I'll pay it presently with all my heart.

Morgann, *Falstaff*, p. 106n.

resemblance between the word and the thing '.[1] This is the main argument of Schlegel in justification of puns. There is of course his other argument, which consists merely in an appeal to the classic authors: 'Whoever, in *Richard II*, is disgusted with the affecting play of words of the dying John of Gaunt on his own name, should remember that the same thing occurs in the *Ajax* of Sophocles.' But this argument does not really deserve serious examination. Schlegel's main argument, however, rests on a doubtful theoretical basis. We do not know what part onomatopoea plays in the genesis of a language. But even if the theory was true, it would only give us an anthropological or psychological explanation for the general phenomenon of punning. Schlegel does not provide any useful analysis why certain puns are more valuable than others in certain poetic contexts, or what role they play, or why Shakespeare's puns are relevant to his poetic drama.

These questions Coleridge attempted to answer. He himself was keenly interested in puns; in fact, one of his innumerable unrealized projects was a whole essay in defence of punning.[2] In his discussion of Shakespeare's puns he remains within the bounds of literary criticism, introducing general psychology only as far as is necessary for the clarification of our responses to the plays. Wellek is therefore wrong when he says that Coleridge's theory of punning 'seems irrelevant to the uses of punning in poetry'. Puns, Coleridge explains, are first of all the expression of exuberance of mind. An age in which punning is the fashion must be marked by 'vigour of intellect'. Coleridge was surely correct about the intellectual quality of Shakespeare's age. But to be of artistic value, a pun has to observe certain laws, otherwise it becomes the blemish, the mark of pedantry and affectation which the eighteenth-century critics took all puns to be. Shakespeare himself, Coleridge notes, satirizes the habit in *Love's Labour's Lost* as well as in Osric in *Hamlet*. In a serious play a pun has to become an integral part of the whole; it has to illuminate or intensify character and situation. When Coleridge fails to see the relation between a pun and its context, he condemns it, as we find in the Porter's scene in *Macbeth*. Here it is important to realize that he does not dismiss the puns (and the

---

[1] Schlegel, *Dramatic Art and Literature*, pp. 366–7.   [2] *AP*, p. 225.

best part of the speech in which the puns occur) because they are puns. That would be exceedingly improbable, considering his constant defence of puns. He dismisses them because he fails to see the relation between them and the whole situation. 'Resort to this grace,' i.e. pun, he says, 'may, in some cases, deserve censure, not because it is a play upon words, but because it is a play upon words in a wrong place and at a wrong time.' Coleridge's fault here is in perception and not in principles or attitude of mind, as it is commonly understood. Had anyone pointed out to him the ironic relation the whole speech bears to the situation, he would have been first to acclaim the artistry and design of the poet. Of course, Coleridge does not pretend that every individual pun in Shakespeare is justifiable on artistic grounds. He admits that 'even in those which bear the strongest characteristics of his mind, there are some conceits not strictly to be vindicated', that 'they detract sometimes from his universality as to time, person and situation'. But what he is constantly combating is the notion that 'whenever a conceit is met with it is unnatural'.[1]

When they are functional, puns in Shakespeare's plays serve various purposes. In the comedies, when his aim is other than the explicit satire on affectation and fashion, puns are a means of characterization, and express 'exuberant activity of mind' in the character given to them. In the serious plays, apart from indicating the mental vigour of the speaker, puns become a manifestation of excess of passion. A pun may be a mark of contemptuous and evil nature, which seizes the occasion to mock and sneer at what is good, as in the scornful expressions which Antonio and Sebastian direct at the good Gonzalo in *The Tempest*. With them punning is 'a mode of getting rid of their own uneasy feelings'. Or it may be 'the language of suppressed passion' as in the case of John of Gaunt's celebrated quibble on his own name. Or again it may be 'the language of resentment in order to express contempt', which, together with 'suppressed passion, especially hardly smothered dislike' is to be found in Hamlet's quibble, when he says to the king that he is 'too much in the *sun*'.[2]

---

[1] Wellek, *History of Modern Criticism*, ii, 176; *SC*, ii, 140, 186, 121.
[2] *SC*, i, 22–3, 135. See a MS note on pp. 103–5 of vol. ii of Coleridge's own copy of *Omniana* in the British Museum, in which he writes that 'vindictive anger striving to ease itself by contempt' is 'the most frequent origin of Puns'.

In all these examples the mind of the character is wrought to a high pitch of passion, and:

He that knows the state of the human mind in deep passion must know, that it approaches to that condition of madness, which is not absolute frenzy or delirium, but which models all things to one reigning idea; still it strays from the main subject of complaint, and still it returns to it, by a sort of irresistible impulse.[1]

The phraseology of the passage and the contrast between madness and delirium are strongly reminiscent of Coleridge's distinction between imagination and fancy. The stress, as always with Coleridge, is on the organic aspect of expression and experience. In the successful examples of puns in serious drama the play on words is organically related to the feeling which dominates the situation. Both Hamlet and John of Gaunt pun successfully because both are shown in an impassioned state of mind, and there is a 'natural tendency' in 'the mind immersed in one strong feeling to connect that feeling with every sight and object around it, especially when [it is] opposed and the word addressed to it [is in] any way repugnant to the feeling'. Coleridge seems to have been aware (indeed he does not state it in this connection, but it is apparent from his favourite principle of the reconciliation of opposites) that the tension which arises from the attempt to relate the feeling to whatever is 'repugnant' to it is peculiarly dramatic. But apart from that, he realizes that the play on words which is the manifestation of excess of passion, fulfils a function similar to that of 'gesticulations, looks or tones'. Not only is it, when it is 'congruous with the feeling of the scene', appropriate to drama, and 'allowable in the dramatic dialogue', but it is 'oftentimes one of the most effectual intensives of passion'.[2] Like gesticulations, looks or tones, puns intensify and illuminate the passions, and because they are such concentrated forms of intensification, they are an important and integral part of Shakespeare's dramatic poetry. It is therefore wrong to regard them as the unhappy and distracting results of complying with the vulgar taste of the frequenters of 'paltry taverns'.

Of course, we who have lived in an age interested in poetic

---

[1] *SC*, ii, 185.   [2] *Ibid.* i, 153, 150.

176

wit and verbal athleticism, have been taught that there are other uses of pun as well as deeper motives. But it is fair to remember that we have travelled a long way from Coleridge, although along the Coleridgean line; he is, after all, the initiator of critical interest in the complexity of poetic meaning. He is familiar with the multiple levels of meaning, of the Empsonian ambiguities in Shakespeare's poetry. 'The meaning one sense chiefly,' he says, 'and yet keeping both senses in view, is perfectly Shakespearean.'[1] For instance, in Bolingbroke's address to the Lords in *Richard II*:

> Go to the rude ribs of that ancient castle;
> Through brazen trumpet send the breath of parle
> Into his ruin'd ears, and thus deliver . . . (iii. iii. 32–4)

Coleridge feels that 'ruin'd ears' apply both to the castle and to the fallen king: 'Although Bolingbroke was only speaking of the castle, his thoughts dwelt on the king.'[2]

In his treatment of puns Coleridge seems to distinguish between two kinds: what we may call here organic and inorganic puns. They can both be functional. But the organic has a more complex function to fulfil. The inorganic is largely verbal: it consists in 'connecting disparate thoughts purely by means of resemblances in the words expressing them'. Its function is to 'display wit' in the speaker. It is then only a means of characterization, but has no necessary relation to the whole situation. Consequently, although it is 'in character in lighter comedy' it would disfigure the 'graver scenes', as it 'sometimes' does in

[1] *Ibid.* i, 105.
[2] *Ibid.* ii, 190. Coleridge actually maintained that Shakespeare purposely used the personal pronoun 'his' to convey this effect. This, of course, is an error caused by Coleridge's unscholarly training, and it was quite rightly pointed out by F. L. Lucas (*Decline and Fall of the Romantic Ideal*, p. 196): '"His" is not necessarily a personal pronoun at all, being the regular possessive also of the *impersonal* "it".' But to charge Coleridge with 'false subtlety' in this account is unfair. We all know that we do not go to Coleridge for scholarly information: in this he is most unreliable. Nevertheless the subtlety and pertinence of the remark remain unimpaired, whether or not the pronoun 'his' has a personal reference, and Shakespeare may well have meant both Richard and the castle by the epithet. Even Lucas himself could not deny that. Shakespeare in fact is full of this type of ambiguity: the classic example, if example be needed, is in Macbeth's speech to the Doctor (v. iii. 39–45) in which he is thinking as much of his own 'diseased' mind and 'stuffed bosom' as of Lady Macbeth's.

Shakespeare – since the latter are normally far more organically conceived.[1]

The organic pun which Shakespeare uses 'more often', unlike the inorganic, loses a great portion of its force and meaning if it is detached from its dramatic context. It is not purely verbal, but it 'doubles the natural connection or order of logical con-sequence in the thoughts'. It is not just 'witty', though it fulfils its function by 'the introduction of an artificial and sought for resemblance in the words'. It is a forceful and proper means of intensifying the emotional impact of a situation, and is justified by 'the law of passion which, inducing in the mind an unusual activity, seeks for means to waste its superfluity'. Under an emotional stress the words themselves become, as it were, living things, 'the subjects and materials for that surplus action, and for the same cause that agitates our limbs'.[1] Coleridge finds ex-amples of organic pun even in an early work of Shakespeare, which is also a comedy. In the King's opening speech in *Love's Labour's Lost*, which is significantly a solemn one, Coleridge finds in the line

And then grace us in the disgrace of death (i. i. 3)

an organic pun. The relation between 'grace' and 'disgrace' is not purely verbal. Although the expression arouses a sufficient degree of surprise, the dramatic context and the intention of the speaker taken into consideration, 'disgrace' seems to be the only apt word to describe the peculiar effect death is going to produce. The pun here 'doubles the natural connection or order of logical consequence in the thoughts' of the speaker, and by so doing gives it greater emphasis. Shunning the life of action, the King of Navarre decides to set up his court as an 'academe' for learning and contemplative life, thereby hoping to win the im-mortal glory which knowledge brings to its bearer after death. He is thus giving up the transitory and temporal glory of a life of action for the greater glory after death which is the fruit of knowledge and the contemplative life. To him therefore death would be a grace, whereas to those who lead an active life it would mean disgrace, i.e. the loss of worldly goods, glory etc. Or 'grace' may be taken in the religious sense, and in this case

[1] *SC*, i, 95–6.

it can be obtained more by a life of study and contemplation than by an active life. The pun here is organic in the sense that it derives its meaning from, and in turn lends significance to, the context of the situation.

Like his organic puns Shakespeare's wit is often 'blended with the other qualities of his works, and is, by its nature, capable of being so blended'. It is often not purely verbal, but 'most exquisite humour, heightened by a figure, and attributed to a particular character'. It works on the level of imagery: without ceasing to produce the degree of surprise we obtain from 'an unexpected turn of expression', the general effect it has is not simply that of surprise, but is often accompanied with a gratification arising from the juxtaposition of imagery. The example Coleridge offers is the comparison Falstaff draws between the flea on Bardolph's nose and a soul suffering in purgatory (*Henry V*, ii. iii. 42–4).[1]

Coleridge's examination of the minutiae of Shakespeare's style

It is clear that Coleridge does not regard Shakespeare as a primitive dramatist, who complied with the popular and vulgar taste of the times. On the contrary, he believes he is the supreme dramatic poet in English. Of course, Coleridge does not pretend that Shakespeare's whole dramatic output is of equal excellence, nor is he blind to the development and improvement in Shakespeare's handling of dramatic poetry. Indeed, he does not trace the growth in his mastery in every individual play. But he points to the occurrence of such marked development. For instance, in a play like *Romeo and Juliet*, he says, 'the poet is not entirely blended with the dramatist, – at least not in the degree to be afterwards noticed in *Lear*, *Hamlet*, *Othello* or *Macbeth*'. Capulet and Montague 'not infrequently talk a language only belonging to the poet, and not so characteristic of, and peculiar to, the passions of persons in the situations in which they are placed'. In such passages Shakespeare 'for a moment forgetting the character, utters his own words in his own person'.[2] But in the more mature works Shakespeare is no 'ventriloquist', and his poetry becomes truly dramatic. He varies his style according to the nature of the character and the dramatic situation.

[1] *Ibid.* ii, 123–4; cf. *MC*, p. 42.   [2] *SC*, ii, 136–7.

In such works, therefore, Coleridge reads Shakespeare's minutiae of style with the greatest care and attention. He praises 'Shakespeare's *instinctive* propriety in the choice of words'.[1] For instance, he finds that the repetition of a word may be meant by the poet to carry an important weight, and to point to the meaning of a whole play, as in the case of the epithet 'honest' in *Othello*. A stylistic detail may be intended to illuminate a certain aspect of a character. For example, in the words of Macbeth to Angus and Ross, who have just brought him the news of the honours Duncan has bestowed upon him:

> Kind gentlemen, your pains
> Are registered where every day I turn
> The leaf to read them. (*Macbeth*, I. iii. 150–3)

he finds 'the *promising courtesies* of a usurper in intention'. And in his replies to Duncan's joyful welcome to him on his arrival from the victorious battle against Cawdor, Macbeth, we are shown, has 'nothing but the commonplaces of loyalty, in which he hides himself in the "air"; and in the...language of effort'. Macbeth expresses '*reasoning*, instead of joy, stammering repetition of "duties"', using 'a hollow hyperbole'.[2] This type of criticism, which reads the text with the utmost sensitivity and intelligence, is rare in the eighteenth century. Indeed Dr Johnson himself provides one of the few examples. Of Macbeth's hypocritical exclamations, when he tries to explain why he killed the king's chamberlains:

> Here lay Duncan
> His silver skin laced with his golden blood, etc. . . .
> (*Macbeth*, II. iii. 117–24)

Dr Johnson writes:

It is not improbable, that Shakespeare put these forced and unnatural metaphors into the mouth of Macbeth as a mark of artifice and dissimulation, to show the difference between the studied language of hypocrisy, and the natural outcries of sudden passion.[3]

But Dr Johnson's hesitation in making the suggestion is fairly obvious: we remember his severe condemnation of the whole passage. Coleridge's remarks, on the other hand, often reveal

---

[1] *SC*, I, 148. [2] *Ibid.* I, 70–3. [3] *Raleigh*, p. 172.

this sensitive textual criticism in a highly developed form. Coleridge would even find the very rhythm of a speech expressive of some fine shade of feeling or other. He sees in Lady Macbeth's welcome to Duncan in her castle 'a laboured rhythm and hypocritical overmuch in which you cannot detect a ray of personal feeling'. Or he would contrast the 'forced flurry of talkativeness' of Macbeth, when he attempts to explain the reasons that led him to the murder of the grooms, with the terse remarks of Macduff.[1]

Moreover, Shakespeare varies his style and diction to suit the dramatic situation. The players' speeches in *Hamlet*, Coleridge points out, differ materially in style and diction from the speeches of the chief characters. Here the difference in style is conditioned by the difference in planes of reality. Of the preliminary speech of the actor he writes:

This admirable substitution of the epic for the dramatic, giving such a *reality* to the impassioned dramatic diction of Shakespeare's own dialogue, and authorized too by the actual style of the tragedies before Shakespeare (*Porrex and Ferrex, Titus Andronicus*, etc.) is worthy of notice.[2]

Similarly in the *Mousetrap* itself rhymed verse is used instead of blank verse with the same effect. Style is also varied in accordance with the degree of dignity and solemnity of what is spoken. *The Winter's Tale* opens with the two lords of Sicilia and Bohemia, Camillo and Archidamus, engaged in pleasant polite conversation, but in the scene immediately following we have the two kings and the queen with their royal courtesies, which will soon develop with grave consequences. The royal conversation is therefore marked by a 'rise of diction' so that it may be

---

[1] *MC*, p. 449.
[2] *SC*, I, 27, 31. Coleridge may indeed have taken the hint from Schlegel: see Schlegel, *Dramatic Art and Literature*, pp. 406–7. But it may be pointed out that before Coleridge Lord John Chedworth (*Notes Upon Some of the Obscure Passages in Shakespeare's Plays* (1805), p. 351), though not quite confidently, had also remarked on the effect of this distinction: 'I have sometimes fancied that Shakespeare has made these lines elaborately tumid for the purpose of marking a distinction between the diction of this supposed tragedy, and that of the personages of the drama, whose language he would have taken to be that of real life, and by this artifice, to give the greater appearance of reality to his play.' The critic's hesitation about the conscious artistry of the poet is, nevertheless, significant.

distinguished from the 'chit-chat' of the lords.[1] But the rise in diction can serve other and deeper purposes in Shakespearean drama. In moments of extreme stress, Coleridge notes, rhetoric may be resorted to by a character as a means of mastering his or her emotions. The effort of Marcellus 'to master his own imaginative terrors', when he tells Horatio the story of the Ghost's appearance, is revealed in the marked 'elevation of the style'. Likewise, rhetoric and inflated language may betray an attempt on the part of the speaker to escape from an unpleasant reality. This sort of self-deception can be seen in the 'affected bravado' of Lady Macbeth.[2]

Versification

The same organic approach which considers language in relation to character and dramatic situation can be seen in Coleridge's treatment of Shakespeare's versification. Once more, Coleridge's view of metre is essentially dramatic, and once more that is what distinguishes it from the eighteenth-century conception. Because their view of metre was largely formal and undramatic, eighteenth-century critics found a great deal of irregularity in Shakespeare's verse, and editors and adaptors endeavoured to smooth some of the lines which their ears felt to be excessively harsh. Indeed in some of the passages corrected the attempts amounted to a complete recasting. This charge of irregularity was levelled not against Shakespeare solely, but against Elizabethan dramatic verse in general, and also, naturally, verse like Donne's, which was written in a dramatic vein. And the critics who complained of the irregularity and uncouthness of Shakespeare's versification were not only those haunted by a demon of correctness, like Hurdis[3] and Seymour;[4] they included sympathetic critics as well. William Dodd, the author of *The Beauties of Shakespeare*, remarked that Shakespeare 'did not study versification' as much

[1] *SC*, I, 122.   [2] *Ibid*. I, 20–1, 80.

[3] James Hurdis, *Cursory Remarks upon the Arrangement of the Plays of Shakespeare* (1792), e.g. pp. 18, 38.

[4] E. H. Seymour, *Remarks Critical, Conjectural and Explanatory upon the Plays of Shakespeare* (1805), I, 5–6. Seymour in fact believes that Shakespeare is 'an exemplar of metrical harmony'; but his text is corrupted (*ibid*. I, 11). However, his conception of metrical harmony is such that the number of passages in the canon which he attempts to regularize is colossal. See, e.g. vol. I, pp. 16, 36; vol. II, pp. 79, 97, 150, etc.

as, for instance, Milton, and that he did not 'remember in him any striking instance of this species of beauty'. Even Malone and Francis Douce complained of the irregularity of Shakespeare's metre.[1]

This eighteenth-century conception of metre formed part and parcel of its general conception of poetry. Because critics then held a dualistic view of poetry which separated form from content, metre, together with expression, was thought of largely as something of an external mould, which a line should be made to fit.[2] A line in which syllabic perfection does not obtain (and Shakespeare's works abound with such lines) was therefore considered faulty. On the other hand, because of his particular view of form Coleridge's approach to metre is primarily organic and dynamic. In English verse, he writes: 'we have first, accent; secondly, emphasis; and lastly, retardation and acceleration of the times of syllables according to the meaning of the words, the passion that accompanies them, and even the character of the person that uses them'.[3] In his treatment metre becomes part of the meaning of dramatic poetry. He shows how in the poetry of Shakespeare, and of the best Elizabethans, metre is a rich tool with immense and varied potentialities, which the poet manipulates dynamically, in order to render a precise expression to his experience:

Since Dryden, the metre of our poets leads to the sense: in our elder and more genuine poets, the sense, including the passion, leads to the metre. Read even Donne's satires as he meant them to be read and as the sense and passion demand, and you will find in the lines a manly harmony.

In this connection Coleridge's theory of the origin and function of metre is significant. If metre is to hold passion in check,[4] then

---

[1] William Dodd, *The Beauties of Shakespeare* (1752), vol. II, p. 202 n.; Edmond Malone, *A Letter to the Rev. Richard Farmer* (1792), p. 35; Francis Douce, *Illustrations of Shakespeare and Ancient Manners* (1807), I, 373.

[2] In spite of its syllabic correctness it cannot be said, of course, that in the hands of a great eighteenth-century poet metre was an external rigid mould into which the substance of content had to be poured. Any analysis of the best of Pope's poetry will show how absurd such a notion is. But the case of critics and minor poets is different and throughout the century the irregularity of Shakespeare's verse was a commonplace of criticism.

[3] *MC*, p. 67; cf. pp. 94, 133ff.   [4] *BL*, II, 49–50.

the greater and more intense the passion the less regular metre becomes. At the opposite end of metre is pure unbridled passion, which cannot be checked: an emotional chaos, as in the case of the ravings of the mad Lear which Shakespeare did not attempt to formalize in metre. We also remember Coleridge's own experiment in versification in *Christabel*, which is based upon a truly organic conception of metre. In his preface to the poem he writes that its metre is 'properly speaking irregular', for it depends not on the number of syllables, but of accents in each line. 'Nevertheless,' he continues, 'this occasional variation in number of syllables is not introduced wantonly, or for the mere ends of convenience, but in correspondence with some transition in the nature of the imagery or passion.'

The intimate relation between metre and the other constituent elements of the plays is always emphasized whenever Coleridge comes to discuss Shakespeare's versification. 'We must observe,' he writes, Shakespeare's 'varied images symbolical of moral truth, thrusting by and seeming to trip up each other, from an impetuosity of thought, producing a metre which is always flowing from one verse into the other, and seldom closing with the tenth syllable of the line.' And again, he says that 'such fullness of thought . . . gives an involution of metre so natural to the expression of passion'. In one of his lectures, we are told by a reporter, he demonstrates 'with truth and beauty' 'the connection between the character of the versification and of the language, and between the metre and the sense, one elucidating and assisting the other'.[1] The body of the lecture is missing, and it would seem that a great deal of his practical criticism on this point, as on others, is lost. But such was Coleridge's belief in the organic nature of Shakespeare's versification that he regarded his blank verse 'as criteria of his plays'. One of Shakespeare's characteristics, he again said, is 'impetuosity of thought – so strongly influencing his metre, and furnishing a criterion of what is and is not Shakespeare's'.[2] It is because Coleridge looked upon metre as an organic part of the meaning and the whole that he could say that 'the sense of musical delight, with the power of producing it, is a gift of imagination'.[3] For it is only the imagination that can produce a really organic whole.

[1] *SC*, ii, 267–8, 314, 323.   [2] *Ibid.* i, 93, 232.   [3] *BL*, ii, 14.

In Shakespeare's plays verse is a strictly functional element. For instance, it can be used as a means of characterization. At its lowest level, it indicates the rank of the speaker. Characters of a higher social status use verse, while others use prose, as can be seen in the different conversations of the lords and the kings in *The Winter's Tale*, already alluded to. For the same reason Coleridge tries to cast Marullus's words in *Julius Caesar* (I. i. 20) into blank verse, so that the tribune may be distinguished from the rabble. But in this Coleridge is no believer in eighteenth-century 'decorum'; he is by no means oblivious of the subtleties of Shakespeare's prose. Shakespeare, Coleridge is well aware, preserves the same social distinction between any two characters even when they both speak their minds in the same medium. There is a great difference between Hamlet's prose passages and the grave-digger's or the cobbler's in *Julius Caesar*: in this case the difference lies, among other things, in the rhythm of the prose they use.[1]

But metre does more than simply imitate the 'personal rank' of a character. It may suggest the temper and quality of the speaker. The peculiar measure of the song of the Fairy in *Midsummer Night's Dream* (II. i. 2ff.), Collier reports, is appropriate 'to the rapid and airy motion of the Fairy by whom the passage is delivered'. A line of irregular length may have artistic justification. In *Richard II* (III. iii. 35), Bolingbroke in a speech to be delivered to the King, makes his name 'Henry Bolingbroke' occupy a whole line. By that, Coleridge comments, Shakespeare meant to 'convey Bolingbroke's opinion of his own importance'. A syllable may be meant to be dwelt on in reciting, so as to be equivalent to a dissyllable to characterize a certain quality in a character. A defective line may detach and draw attention to a certain speech, 'giving it the individuality and entireness of a little poem'. In the rhythm of a line by Brutus he detects 'that sort of mild philosophic contempt characterizing Brutus'.[2] In Lady Macbeth's speech of welcome to Duncan, we have seen, he notes 'a laboured rhythm' revealing insincerity and affectation.

This is how Coleridge treats Shakespeare's versification. He may be oversubtle in some of his remarks, but he certainly does

[1] *SC*, I, 13. [2] *Ibid.* II, 190; I, 157, 14.

not regard the metre as an element super-added. Underlying his criticism is the assumption that Shakespeare 'never avails himself of the supposed license of transposition merely for the metre'.[1] This may be an exaggeration if Coleridge really means it to apply to whatever Shakespeare wrote. But it is an exaggeration of an important truth, and Coleridge is right when he contrasts Shakespeare's use of the spoken rhythm with the artificial and forced expressions which he thinks a modern tragic poet resorts to in order to suit the metre. And at least it has made him attentive not only to the significance of the position of every word in the line, but also to the significance of every stress. He decides whether the position of a stress in a line is right or wrong from its appropriateness to the character and the dramatic situation. In Marullus's retort to the cobbler's playful suggestion that he should mend him (*Julius Caesar*, I. i. 20–1) – a line which for psychological reasons Coleridge assigns quite rightly to Marullus, as the First Folio shows, and not to Flavius as Theobald does – he suggests that the stress should fall on the word 'mend' and not on 'me' since the dramatic situation implies that Marullus in a mixture of *surprise* and anger is echoing the cobbler's words.[2] This, it may be remarked, is a criticism of minutiae. But such criticism, based on a thorough and detailed knowledge of the text, is responsible for his often masterly analysis of Shakespeare's poetry. We still remember the '*credibilizing* effect' he finds in the word 'again' in Horatio's question regarding the Ghost:

What, has this thing appeared again tonight?[3]

Rhyme

Coleridge stops to ask himself about the dramatic function and meaning of the smallest features of Shakespearean drama. He enquires into the purpose of 'the occasional interspersion of rhymes, and the more frequent winding up of a speech therewith'. It is not that he believes in a dramatic purpose where there is none, for he knows that the frequency of rhyme in the early works of the dramatist is not so much a deliberate device as a sign of immaturity. But the question concerns the more

[1] *Ibid.* I, 16. [2] *Ibid.* I, 14. [3] *Ibid.* I, 20.

mature works, in which there is reason to believe in the conscious artistry and intention of the poet. He notes that rhymes are sometimes used to mark the patterned sententious speeches, and in such cases 'the rhyme answers the purposes of the Greek chorus, and distinguishes the *general* truths from the passions of the dialogue'.[1] But rhymes may have a deeper significance. In a serious play a speech that is formalized by rhymes may express 'deliberateness' in the speaker. On such artistic grounds Coleridge tries to solve the mystery of Hamlet's harsh treatment of Ophelia in the nunnery scene, which Dover Wilson attempts to explain away by supplying what he thinks to be a missing stage direction. The manner and form of Ophelia's speech to Hamlet on returning to him his love tokens (iii.i. 97ff.), the 'penetrating' Hamlet perceives to be 'forced', and he therefore realizes that she is not 'acting a part of her own', that 'he is watched and Ophelia a decoy'.[2] Accordingly he assumes his madness. Rhyme also has another purpose. Like rhetoric and 'elevation of style', it expresses the effort of the speaker to master his emotions. The winding up of a speech with a rhyme indicates in the character 'an attempt . . . to collect himself, and *be cool* at the close'.[3] Of course, in some cases, there may be purely stage reasons for the rhyme coming at the end of a speech : a rhyme, we know, may serve simply as a reminder to the other actor that his part is due to begin. But it is significant that Coleridge concentrates on purely artistic considerations.

Poetry is not the mere outpouring of passion, but even in its minutest detail, it has a logic of its own, as severe as that of science. This logic is what Coleridge describes as 'aesthetic logic'. On the grounds of aesthetic logic he would judge an expression incorrect or a line faulty. And by virtue of this logic a work of art becomes an absolutely self-consistent entity, a complete organism. Such is the mature Shakespearean play. Its complete meaning is to be looked for not in the characters or in the plot alone, but in every minute detail, from rhythm and versification to the single word and image. For all these elements are complementary, and have their particular function. Such an

1 *Ibid.* i, 146, 92.
2 *Hamlet*, ed. J. Dover Wilson (1948), p. lvi; *SC*, i, 30; ii, 195.
3 *SC*, i, 146.

organic work, however, can only be the product of the imaginative power of a genius, for only a genius can produce a work that is 'effected by a single energy, modified *ab intra* in each component part'.[1]

[1] *SC*, I, 5.

Conclusion

What, exactly, is Coleridge's contribution to English Shakespearean criticism? I think this study has made it clear that it is impossible to accept Dr Babcock's conclusions on the subject. The thesis of Dr Babcock's book on the Shakespearean critics of the last quarter of the eighteenth century is that:

Point for point, from all the different angles, the early nineteenth century merely echoed the late eighteenth. In short, if the question were raised as to whether the nineteenth century produced any *new* criticism of Shakespeare, the answer would have to be – no.

The 'only possible new point' which he concedes to the nineteenth-century critics, and which, he corrects himself, 'is not strictly new', is 'Coleridge's emphasis on first scenes' – as if Coleridge's criticism of first scenes could be isolated from his general critical position. He even goes so far as to deny that Coleridge said 'some glorious things' on Shakespeare.[1] I suppose if one applied Dr Babcock's method, breaking any apparently new system crudely into small pieces, one would soon reach the conclusion that there is nothing new under the sun. This is perhaps the unintended effect of the analytic chemistry method advocated by Professor Lovejoy on literary studies.

Criticism, like any other rational pursuit, becomes valuable, not when it brings something out of nothing, but when it introduces a new approach. The problems of criticism have, in a sense, been fundamentally the same from times immemorial – those of dramatic poetry are mostly there in the *Poetics*. But who can deny that we have travelled a long way from Aristotle? That the unit ideas: form, plot, character, imagery etc. meant different things in different ages? With every new approach, the basic facts, which remain more or less the same, assume a new significance; they acquire a different meaning in every new system. To

[1] Babcock, *Genesis of Idolatry*, pp. 226–7.

189

say therefore, as Dr Babcock does,[1] that Coleridge meant the same thing as the eighteenth-century critics when he called Shakespeare an original genius, is obviously a misrepresentation of facts – since the conception of original genius is ultimately bound up with that of the creative imagination. To deny the difference between Coleridge's conception of imagination and that of the eighteenth century is to deny, among other things, all the difference that there is between a mechanical and a dynamic philosophy. But that is clearly untenable.

Coleridge's contribution to English Shakespearean criticism is precisely the introduction of a new approach. There is much of eighteenth-century opinion in his principles and practice, but, as this study shows, there is in him a dichotomy between what belongs to the eighteenth century, and what is essentially his own. Besides, Coleridge sometimes betrays a critical irresponsibility of the gravest order. Indeed his shortcomings and limitations should not be mitigated or glossed over, although we should try to understand them if our appraisal of his criticism is to be just. And although well known, they deserve to be mentioned in this summing up of his contribution.

Perhaps the most disconcerting feature of his criticism today is his occasional idolatry, and the tendency to consider Shakespeare entirely by himself without any relation to his time and place. We must remember, however, that it was understandable that Coleridge should react against the misguided and uncritical enthusiasm which scholars and editors of Shakespeare's contemporaries felt for the subject of their studies in his day. Coleridge had to go to extremes in order to stress Shakespeare's superiority when contemporary scholars lavished praise indiscriminately on Beaumont and Fletcher, or Ford and Massinger at the expense of Shakespeare. For instance, Gifford, a serious and influential scholar, wrote in the introduction to his edition of Massinger's works (1805) that Shakespeare's superiority to his contemporaries 'rests on his superior wit alone', but 'in all the other, and as I should deem, higher excellencies of the drama, character, pathos, depth of thought, etc., he is equalled by Beaumont and Fletcher, Ben Jonson, and Massinger'.[2] Before Gifford, J. Monck Mason had maintained in his volume of com-

[1] Babcock, *Genesis of Idolatry*, p. 218. [2] *MC*, p. 41.

190

mentary on the plays of Beaumont and Fletcher (1797) that 'if we descend to a comparison of particular plays, many of theirs will be found superior to many of his' [i.e. Shakespeare's].[1] That is at least one reason why Coleridge spared no occasion to explode the preposterously inflated opinion of Beaumont and Fletcher's works, and to point out to his age their true worth. Without underrating the importance of Shakespeare's contemporaries Coleridge emphasized all the time his overwhelming superiority to them. 'Shakespeare's eminence,' he said, 'is his own and [not] his age's – as the pine-apple, the melon, and the gourd may grow in the same bed; nay, the same circumstances of warmth and soil may be necessary to their full development, but do not account for the golden hue, the ambrosial flavour, the perfect shape of the pine-apple, or the tufted crown of its head,' and 'the more we reflect and examine, examine and reflect, the more astonished we are at the immense superiority of Shakespeare over his contemporaries – and yet what contemporaries!'[2]

Similarly Coleridge's idolatry, which is sometimes couched in rapturous terms unbearable to the modern ear, is not a compound of primitivist enthusiasm and uncritical emotionalist appreciation; but it is essentially the result of a critical approach that had confirmed for him the greatness of Shakespeare and based it on secure grounds. When Coleridge maintained that 'the task [of Shakespearean criticism] will be genial in proportion as the criticism is reverential',[3] we must remember that he wrote after the repeated experience of finding aesthetic reasons for and merits in parts of Shakespeare's works with which he had previously found fault. It must be difficult for a critic to curb his enthusiasm, when after an analysis of the plays, he is led to the conclusion that 'in all points from the most important to the most minute, the judgement of Shakespeare is commensurate with his genius'. Besides, Coleridge believed the first duty of a critic to lie in the analysis and explanation of the beauty of a work, and not in the drawing up of a balance sheet of beauties and faults, weighing the ones against the others. 'He who tells me,' he said, 'that there are *defects* in a new work, tells me nothing which I should not have taken for granted without his information. But

---

[1] J. Monck Mason, *Comments on the Plays of Beaumont and Fletcher* (1797), p. v.
[2] *MC*, pp. 42, 53–4. [3] *SC*, I, 126.

he, who points out and elucidates the *beauties* of an original work, does indeed give me interesting information, such as experience would not have authorized me in anticipating.[1] The attitude is essentially Longinian. As a reader his *'golden rule'* was *'until you understand a writer's ignorance, presume yourself ignorant of his understanding'*.[2]

Coleridge's idolatry, however, does not always reveal itself in harmless and meaningless statements. It can lead him to frankly false criticism, and here is the danger. His occasional tendency to disengage Shakespeare from his historical context and see him as a being wholly above his times sometimes ends in distortion and misrepresentation. It is not that Coleridge is unaware of the importance of the historical method. In 1807 he writes to Humphry Davy about his first course of lectures, telling him that his intention is to discourse 'on the genius and writings of Shakespeare relatively to his Predecessors and Contemporaries'.[3] But it cannot be said that in his criticism of Shakespeare he often resorts to the historical method. On the contrary, we find him asserting at some point that Shakespeare is 'least of all poets colored in any particulars by the spirit or customs of his age'. This is true, if Coleridge means that the values of Shakespeare's work transcend his time and place. Again, when he points out that there is in him 'who lived in an age of religious and political heat' 'nothing sectarian in religion or politics', we agree with him, because he has shown us the essentially impersonal nature of Shakespeare's art. But Coleridge goes further; he asserts that 'there is nothing common to Shakespeare and to other writers of his day – not even the language they employed',[4] thus unwittingly making Shakespeare the almost superhuman phenomenon he very sensibly attacks and explodes in other places. Not even the recent attempt made by one of his idolators to relate it to his philosophy or theology can justify the language Coleridge uses when he describes Shakespeare as 'self-sustained, deriving his genius immediately from heaven, independent of all earthly or national influence' or turn it into literary criticism in any meaningful sense of the term.[5] And when

[1] *BL*, I, 44.   [2] *BL*, I, 160.   [3] *CL*, III, 29.   [4] *SC*, II, 125.
[5] J. R. de J. Jackson, *Method and Imagination in Coleridge's Criticism* (1969), p. 129.

Coleridge maintains that although he lived in an age of misers, witchcraft and astrology Shakespeare presented to us neither misers, nor witches, we realize how far his critical irresponsibility can go.[1]

Such statements are the product partly of his bardolatry, partly of his occasional tendency to make facile and ill-grounded generalizations. He would say, for instance, that 'there is no character in Shakespeare in which envy is portrayed, with one solitary exception – Cassius in *Julius Caesar*'.[2] But, we may ask, what about Iago, Edmund or the numberless characters in the history plays? Or, driven by his idealization of womanhood, he would declare that in Shakespeare 'all the elements of womanhood are holy', having forgotten Goneril and Regan or Lady Macbeth, about whom he elsewhere made many penetrating observations. His dictum that Shakespeare's female characters are characterless is proverbial, and was swallowed hook, line and sinker by Hazlitt.[3] But what of Beatrice, Portia or Cleopatra? Although he realized the functional nature of double-epithets and compounds, when they are not reduced to the status of 'mere printer's devils' tricks', he would dismiss them on the ground that English is 'in its very genius unfitted for compounds', and would claim that their number grows remarkably smaller in Shakespeare's mature plays like *Lear*, *Macbeth*, *Othello*, and *Hamlet*, in comparison with early works like *Love's Labour's Lost*, *Romeo and Juliet*, and *Venus and Adonis*,[4] which is clearly not true. This tendency to make easy generalization explains why the man who realized as early as 1796 that we should not 'pass an act of *Uniformity* against Poets',[5] adopted not only Schlegel's distinction between classic and romantic, but his sweeping condescension to what is Greek – although to be fair to Coleridge we must point out that later on, in his conversation with Henry Crabb Robinson, he 'accused Schlegel of *Einseitigkeit* in his exclusive admiration of Shakespeare'. 'Sublimity is Hebrew by birth', he declared as a general statement; but not long afterwards we find him talking of 'the sublime simplicity of Aeschylus'.[6] Similarly, Coleridge's antipathy to what is French may

[1] *SC* I, 245; cf. II, 145–6.   [2] *Ibid.* II, 146.   [3] *Ibid.* I, 133; *Hazlitt*, xx, 83.
[4] *MC*, p. 307; *BL*, I, 2n.   [5] *CL*, I, 215, 279.
[6] *SC*, II, 160ff.; *MC*, p. 395; *TT*, 25 July 1832; 1 July 1833.

have a political basis, but it would not have been possible to make the sweeping statements about French literature and drama, which he often made, had it not been for his almost constitutional tendency to say such things. Coupled with that tendency there is his digressive habit. Shakespeare's treatment of love in *Romeo and Juliet* serves as an occasion to deliver a long sermon about his own view of love. Instead of applying his keen powers to an analysis of Shakespeare's play he *will* provide us with material which may be interesting in itself, but which has no relevance to Shakespeare's dramatic poetry. One can also add Coleridge's annoying habit of repeating himself, his tendency to confine his detailed remarks to a relatively small number of Shakespeare's plays, his predominantly solemn approach which must have been responsible for the little criticism he left us on the comedies, and for his inability to feel the humour of Falstaff. One could go on.

However, it is neither fair nor instructive to judge Coleridge's criticism solely by his failings. For that matter what critic is wholly reliable at all times? With all his faults Coleridge brought a new approach to Shakespearean drama, an approach which has become part and parcel of most of the subsequent criticism of Shakespeare. I do not think that Eliot was exaggerating when he wrote that 'it is impossible to understand Shakespeare criticism to this day, without a familiar acquaintance with Coleridge's lectures and notes'.[1] The value of Coleridge as a Shakespearean critic lies in the introduction of a new and serious understanding of creative imagination, resulting in a new attitude to Shakespearean drama. This new attitude regarded each play as the poet's dramatic vision of human existence – a vision which forms an essentially organic whole. The dramatic interest and meaning of the mature Shakespearean play, Coleridge has taught us, is only to be arrived at through a careful consideration of every word, scene and act. For the vision penetrates its whole fabric, and finds expression in plot, character and poetry alike. A consideration of any one of these constituent elements, by itself and dissociated from the others, would seriously distort the dramatic vision. It is therefore dangerous to concentrate on the so-called

[1] *A Companion to Shakespeare Studies*, ed. Granville-Barker and G. B. Harrison, p. 298.

beauties of Shakespeare. Coleridge considered the beauties of any sort 'objectionable works – injurious to the original Author, as disorganizing his productions – pulling to pieces the well-wrought *Crown* of his glory to pick out the shining stones, and injurious to the Reader, by indulging the taste for unconnected, and for that reason unretained single Thoughts'.[1] This is what Coleridge taught us, as well as his contemporaries. Without him, one ventures to say, the course of English Shakespearean criticism would have been different. It is difficult to imagine that without his influence Lamb would have been able to say in the preface to his *Specimens of English Dramatic Poets* (1808): 'I have chosen wherever I could to give entire scenes, and in some instances successive scenes, rather than to string together single passages and detached beauties.' For we have seen what the 'Beauties of Shakespeare' meant until Coleridge's time.

That this is an advance in the history of Shakespearean criticism none but the prejudiced can really deny. Mr Isaacs' valuable essay on Coleridge's critical terminology has shown us the host of new critical terms which Coleridge introduced in the body of his criticism, and most of which have taken root in the English language, becoming an indispensable part of the vocabulary of any critic.[2] I suppose one does not need to explain what the introduction of a new critical term means, but Coleridge himself once said, quite rightly, that 'every additament of perception requires a new word'.[3] It is difficult for us now to realize the extent of Coleridge's contribution, because it has been incorporated into Shakespearean criticism. Most of his remarks, like his terminology, have been taken into the main body of critical opinion both in the nineteenth and the twentieth centuries, to such an extent that they often form tacit assumptions in our minds. But it is fair, if we want to give Coleridge his due, to point out that modern critics owe him more than they generally realize or care to admit. Who, for instance, would have thought that he was the first critic to perceive the role of tragic irony in Shakespearean drama? Perhaps we ought to feel grateful even for some of his excesses. To take one example, it was obviously

[1] *CL*, v, 200.
[2] J. Isaacs, 'Coleridge's Critical Terminology', *Essays and Studies*, xxi (1936).
[3] *AP*, p. 267.

necessary to concentrate on showing the greatness of the tragedies, if only in order to counteract the effect of the eighteenth-century critical tradition, with its distinct preference for Shakespeare's comedies. After Coleridge no one could seriously say again that Shakespeare's tragedy 'seems to be skill, his comedy to be instinct'.

We have seen, in the opening chapter, how eighteenth-century criticism resulted eventually in the breaking up of the organic unity of Shakespearean drama. Coleridge's supreme service lies in the new attitude which he adopted both in theory and in practice to Shakespeare, and which treated the works with more critical respect. The restoration of the organic unity of the plays is a significant event in the history of Shakespearean criticism. By introducing a new conception of form, Coleridge was able both to write, and to point the way to formal criticism in the best sense, and to provide a more satisfactory view of poetic drama in general. And one result of this view, and not the only result, is the reinstatement of poetry – not in the sense of shining passages which have a value in themselves other than their dramatic value – but as an indivisible part of drama. In his sensitive and subtle analysis of this poetry Coleridge tried to show the dramatic function and meaning of the minutest features of Shakespeare's style. More particularly because of his new, dynamic and complex conception of metaphor and imagery Coleridge was able to put an end at long last to the attacks on Shakespeare's metaphorical style which had been a common feature of *all* serious Shakespearean criticism since Dryden's time. Likewise, by his insistence that in imaginative activity a nice balance is kept between the conscious and the unconscious, that Shakespeare's works reveal superb judgement and conscious artistry, he managed to explode the popular notion that Shakespeare was an inspired but wild genius, and to encourage the serious reader to ask intelligent questions about the meaning of Shakespeare's plays.

Besides, in his criticism of Shakespeare Coleridge raises fundamental questions – a thing which makes reading it invigorating and inspiring. Coleridge does not dissociate his experience of Shakespeare from the serious business of life. He discusses the problem of science and poetry, the problem of poetic belief, the

196

nature and function of poetic imagination. His new approach to Shakespeare is one aspect of his approach to the problems of the spirit. If his conception of form is organic, it is because his philosophy is a dynamic philosophy. Very often his Shakespearean criticism is more than a literary interpretation of the plays. While still regarding them as works of art, it attempts to relate them to the whole world of the spirit. But, to remain within the bounds of literary criticism proper, Coleridge once explained to a correspondent that one of the objects of his lectures on literature was to 'leave a *sting* behind, i.e., a disposition to study the subject anew, under the light of a new principle'.[1] One can safely say that his lectures, notes, and marginalia on Shakespeare's works have left that sting.

[1] Letter to J. Britten, *SC*, ɪɪ, 325.

APPENDIX A

Coleridge and acting

It is generally assumed, too easily, I think, that Coleridge was hostile to the idea of performing Shakespearean drama on the stage, and to acting in general. Of course, there is some justification for this general opinion in Coleridge's own writings. In *Omniana* we read an account of a visit he made to the theatre to see *The Beggar's Opera*, in which we are told of the 'horror and disgust' aroused in him by the performance of a work that had always 'delighted' him with 'its poignant wit and original satire'. The 'immorality' of the work which had not given him 'any offence' in reading became palpable in the stage representation, and it is then, he wrote, that he 'learnt the immense difference between reading and seeing a play'. A play acted seems to be more real than a play read *silently*. 'Even the sound of one's own or another's voice takes them [the thoughts of which a play consists] out of that lifeless, twilight realm of idea, which is the confine, the *intermundium*, as it were, of existence and non-existence. Merely that the thoughts have become audible, by blending with them a sense of *outness* gives them a sort of reality' (*Omniana*, I, 20–2). Here, it is true, Coleridge deprecates the representation of what is immoral and in no way refers to Shakespeare. But the distinction between the world of the stage and the mental world is significant, and in this fragment of Coleridge's we notice the highest point of awareness of, and withdrawal from, the world of the senses. But is this the whole story?

In his writings on Shakespeare Coleridge does not reveal any deep interest in the theatrical production of his plays. In this respect he differs from either Lamb or Hazlitt. Of course, he cannot be charged with initiating the attitude that made of Shakespeare's works the object of the study alone, for the attitude existed long before his time and we know of Dr Johnson's hatred

198

for the stage: 'A play read affects the mind like a play acted', Dr Johnson writes in the *Preface* (*Raleigh*, p. 28), and Boswell reports him as saying that 'many of Shakespeare's plays are the worse for being acted' (*Boswell's Life of Dr Johnson*, ed. G. Birkbeck Hill, revised by L. F. Powell (Oxford, 1934), II, 92). Yet complete denunciation of the stage representation of Shakespeare at any time came, not from Coleridge, but from Lamb and Hazlitt. In spite of his enthusiasm for the stage, in his essay 'On the Tragedies of Shakespeare considered with Reference to their Fitness for Stage Representation' Lamb declared that 'the plays of Shakespeare are less calculated for performance on the stage than those of almost any other dramatist whatever' (*The Works of Charles Lamb*, ed. William Macdonald, 1903, III, 20). Again he said that 'Lear is essentially impossible to represent on the stage. But how many dramatic personages are there in Shakespeare which though more actable and feasible (if I may so speak) than Lear, yet from some circumstance, some adjunct to their character, are improper to be shown to our bodily eye' for 'what we are conscious of in reading is almost exclusively the mind, and its movement' (*ibid.* III, 33, 34). Clearly the critic shrinks from the world of the senses, from seeing 'an old man tottering about the stage with a walking stick etc.' pass for Shakespeare's Lear, from having a 'fine vision' materialized and brought down 'to the standard of flesh and blood' (*ibid.* III, 19). Similarly Hazlitt states categorically that 'Poetry and the stage do not agree together. The attempt to reconcile them fails not only of effect, but of decorum. The *ideal* has no place upon the stage, the imagination cannot sufficiently qualify the impressions of the senses' (William Hazlitt, *The Complete Works*, ed. P. P. Howe, V, 234). For this distrust of the senses, Coleridge who attacked materialism in all its aspects and scoffed at the 'despotism of the eye' in Hartley's psychology (*BL*, I, 74), seems to me to be chiefly responsible. He himself said that 'so little are images capable of satisfying the obscure feelings connected with words' (*BL*, II, 142). Yet there are several points which need clarification in Coleridge's attitude to the stage representation of Shakespeare's plays, and it does seem to me unfair to declare summarily and without any qualification, as Miss Bradbrook does, that 'Coleridge, Hazlitt and Lamb all three rejected the stage' (M. C. Bradbrook, *Elizabethan Stage Conditions*, p. 12).

Coleridge does not reject the idea of representing Shakespeare on the stage as such, but a *particular mode* of performing the plays. In his view, dramatic poetry is not essentially incompatible with stage representation. In fact we know that he actually contemplated writing a long essay on 'Dramatic Poetry exclusively in its relation to Theatrical Representation' (Letter to John Murray, 8 May 1816, *CL*, IV, 637). What Coleridge objects to is the *naturalistic* style of performing Shakespeare, which treated his poetic drama as if it were the same kind of thing as the contemporary realistic drama. Indeed, in his preoccupation with the lasting element in Shakespeare's works, Coleridge sometimes goes so far as to say that the stage Shakespeare wrote for is really 'that of the universal mind' (*SC*, I, 4). But such a statement, in spite of the weight it carries, should not be taken to mean that Coleridge did not recognize that Shakespeare wrote for a 'particular stage'. Coleridge undoubtedly benefited from the facts recently unearthed by the late eighteenth-century scholars about Elizabethan stage conditions. Capell and Malone had already pointed to the bareness of Shakespeare's stage, and its freedom from the modern sophisticated paraphernalia of scenery and decor, as well as to the fact that the appeal of the plays was made to the ear and the imagination. Coleridge therefore felt justified in believing that the plays were acted originally as dramatic poetry. He realized the essential difference between the stage, and consequently the manner of acting, in Shakespeare's times and his own. 'The circumstances of acting,' he said, 'were altogether different from ours; it was much more of recitation, or rather a medium between recitation and what we now call recitation. The idea of the poet was always present, not of the actors, not of the thing to be represented. It was at that time more a delight and employment for the intellect, than [an] amusement for the senses.' But this was possible when 'the theatre . . . had no artificial, extraneous inducements – few scenes, little music . . . Shakespeare himself said: "We appeal to your imagination"' (*SC*, II, 85). Again he said, 'how different from modern plays, where the glare of the scenes with every wished-for object industriously realized, the mind becomes bewildered in surrounding attractions; whereas Shakespeare, in place of ranting, music, and outward action, addresses us in words that enchain the mind, and carry on the attention from scene to scene' (*SC*, ii, 279–80).

Coleridge may have tended to minimize the importance of the visual appeal of Elizabethan stage performances, but there is no doubt that he believed that the peculiar structure of the Elizabethan stage and the manner of Elizabethan acting emphasized the poetic nature of drama. It is not true, therefore, to say, as Miss Bradbrook does, that he 'condemned Shakespeare's age and stage by implication' (*Elizabethan Stage Conditions*, p. 14). On the contrary, he explicitly said that if Shakespeare 'had lived in the present day and had seen one of his plays represented, he would the first moment have felt the shifting of the scenes' and 'he would have constructed [his plays] on a different model'. But Coleridge was grateful that Shakespeare lived at a time when theatrical conditions were more favourable to poetic drama, for he would much rather have poetic drama than mere stage plays in the modern naturalistic style (*SC*, ii, 85, 97, 278). Through the lips of a satirical portrait of a defendant of the contemporary practices of the stage he said, in the second of his 'Satyrane Letters': 'And what is *done* on the stage is more striking than what is acted. I once remember such a deafening explosion, that I could not hear a word of the play for half an act after it; and a little real gunpowder being set fire to at the same time, and smelt by all the spectators, the naturalness of the scene was quite astonishing' (*BL*, ii, 163).

The naturalistic performance of Shakespeare's plays, which relied more upon scenery and colours than upon poetry was therefore one reason why Coleridge was averse to the contemporary stage representation of them. But there were other reasons as well. Coleridge objected to the star performances of Shakespeare, which seemed to have been common in his days. He deplored the custom of giving the important roles to celebrated and gifted actors and actresses like Kemble and Mrs Siddons, while allotting the minor parts to completely incompetent persons, who were singularly incapable of reciting poetry, and 'who owed their very elevation to dexterity in snuffing candles' (*SC*, ii, 97). The result of the custom was a serious distortion of the

201

pattern of the plays, since Shakespeare 'shone no less conspicuously and brightly' in the minor characters. Indeed it would seem that the public in its turn came to expect this type of performance, as contemporary criticism shows. Even intelligent theatre critics like Lamb and Hazlitt wrote their essays, not on the production of a certain play, but on this or that eminent actor in this or that important role. But, according to Coleridge, this was evidently the wrong approach to the plays. He lamented the fact that few people went to the theatre 'to see a *play*, but to see Master Betty or Mr Kean, or some one individual in some *one* part' (*MC*, p. 339). Again he complained that 'those who went to theatre in our own day, when any of our poet's works were represented, went to see Mr Kemble in *Macbeth*, or Mrs Siddons' Isabel' (*SC*, II, 97). What Coleridge obviously wanted was an integrated and unified performance, a thing which the theatres of his time did not provide. And when we recall the mangled version in which the plays were acted, we cannot wonder that they should be condemned by a critic who valued above anything else the organic unity of a work. For one who strongly believed that 'the fairest part of the most beautiful body will appear deformed and monstrous, if dissevered from its place in the organic whole' (*BL*, I, 162), it was quite natural to write: 'To the disgrace of the English stage, such attempts have indeed been made on almost all the dramas of Shakespeare. Scarcely a season passes which does not produce some ὕϲερον πρότερον of this kind in which the mangled limbs of our great poet are thrown together in most admired disorder' (*SC*, II, 350). We must remember that it was not until 1838 (i.e. after Coleridge's death) that Macready restored, for example, Shakespeare's *Lear* and the *Tempest*, or rather produced them with a minimal number of alterations (see *Shakespeare Adaptation*, with introduction and notes by Montague Summers, 1922, pp. vii, cv).

Coleridge's view of Shakespearean acting forms an inseparable part of his general Shakespearean criticism. What he wanted in the first place was Shakespeare's own works, and these interpreted by a group of uniformly competent actors in such a way that the pattern of the play should not be distorted. The plays should be represented primarily as poetic drama without any of the pernicious and prosaic effect of naturalism. 'A great actor, comic or tragic,' he wrote, 'is not to be a mere *copy*, a *fac simile*, but an *imitation* of Nature . . . A good actor is Pygmalion's Statue, a work of exquisite *art*, *animated* and gifted with *motion*; but still *art*, still a species of Poetry' (*CL*, III, 501). But in order to ensure the intimate and appropriate atmosphere for the exercise of the imaginative power in an audience it is best that the performance should take place in a fairly small theatre (*SC*, II, 278).

On his return from Germany Coleridge was full of enthusiasm for Lessing's critical powers. Not only did he for long contemplate the writing of his biography but he also intended to follow his example in England. In January 1800 he wrote to Thomas Wedgwood from London, telling him that he was spending his evenings in the theatres because he was about 'to conduct a sort of Dramaturgy, a series of essays on the Drama both its general principles, and likewise in reference to the present state of the English Theatres' to be published in the *Morning Post* (*CL*, I, 559). We do not know if he actually wrote any, but if he did, then the loss is great, judging by the excellent sample of his contemporary dramatic criticism, which he published on Maturin's play, *Bertram*. (See E. K. Chambers, *Samuel Taylor Coleridge*, 1938, p. 122: 'If he wrote any, they have not been identified.') This, to say nothing of his own attempts at writing plays, may be sufficient to refute any notion that Coleridge was not interested in the theatre as such or that he had a strong aversion to the stage. And in the body of his criticism there are to be found here and there indications (they may be of little importance in themselves, still they are there) that he did go to see Shakespeare on the stage, as well as suggestions as to how parts should be acted, or lines should be delivered (see, e.g. *SC*, I, 31, 83, 87, 107, 122).

APPENDIX B

Coleridge's projected edition of Shakespeare

(A note on Coleridge's scholarship)

At one time in his life Coleridge contemplated working on an edition of Shakespeare. On 7 September 1825 he wrote to the Rev. Edward Coleridge, 'Montague has undertaken to arrange engagement with his publisher for an edition of Shakespeare by me' (*CL*, v, 493). This prospective edition was to contain 'properly critical notes, prefaces, and analyses, comprizing the results of five and twenty years' study' (*CL*, vi, 695). As is to be expected, this project, like the many other projects his mind was only too fertile in producing, never materialized. However, from the marginal notes scribbled on the pages of the Stockdale and Theobald editions which he used, we know enough about his editorial method to guess what that edition would have been like.

The textual problems Coleridge tackles are mainly problems of prosody and problems of interpretation and emendation of obscure or incomprehensible words. Coleridge's criticism of Shakespeare's versification reveals certain assumptions about his art, which have already been discussed in the last chapter of this book. A word on his textual criticism will not be amiss here, particularly as Coleridge's reputation has suffered probably more on account of this part, than of the rest, of his work on Shakespeare (see, for instance, F. L. Lucas, *The Decline and Fall of the Romantic Ideal*, p. 191, n.1). It is undeniable that, because of his lack of scholarship, Coleridge's weakness shows itself most clearly in his handling of the question of emendation and textual interpretation; but his lack of scholarship has been rather exaggerated. I am not trying to make out a case for Coleridge's abilities as a scholar; my aim is only to remind the reader that his editorial blunders are not as many as they are made out to be, and that for every blunder in his textual interpretation there are several sound points which deserve to be mentioned.

While Coleridge's knowledge of Elizabethan literature was not like that of Thomas Warton, the historian of English poetry, it yet was not the very superficial acquaintance Swinburne, for instance, assumed (see A. C. Swinburne, *Three Plays of Shakespeare*, 1919, p. 64: 'Coleridge, whose ignorance of Shakespeare's predecessors was apparently as absolute as it is assuredly astonishing in the friend of Lamb . . .'). Moreover, it was a living knowledge. The late eighteenth-century commentators on Shakespeare, it is true, knew immeasurably more than he did; but theirs was often an accumulated mass of information, an unwieldy heap of names and dates without shape or system, which smacked of an antiquarian interest, and was very often closely allied to it. How many of these commentators were members of the Society of Antiquaries? With Coleridge, on the other hand, whatever he knew was vital to him, and was soon reduced to order and system in his own mind. In this sense, it can be said that what he knew of Elizabethan and Jacobean literature developed his sensibility.

And it was not so very little after all. In his recorded criticism Coleridge refers to *Gorboduc*, to the work of Kyd (he is aware of some similarity between *The Spanish Tragedy* and some parts of Shakespeare's work), Marlowe, Chapman, Raleigh, Harington (the translator of Ariosto), Sidney, Spenser, Davies, Daniel, Drayton, Ben Jonson, Beaumont and Fletcher, Ford and Massinger, Donne and the metaphysical poets (who, apart from Dr Johnson, whose verdict was so often echoed, knew the last in the eighteenth century?). Besides, he is acquainted with the work of some of the eighteenth-century scholars. He knows Johnson, Farmer, Tyrwhitt, Whalley, Ayscough, Steevens and Malone, not to mention early editors like Pope, Theobald and Warburton. From these as well as from his close friend Lamb he must have had at least a second-hand knowledge of the background of Shakespeare. And who can honestly say for certain that such an omnivorous reader as Coleridge did not know this book or that?

Perhaps we may start with those questions of emendation and elucidation of text which require scholarship, and in which Coleridge appears to go wide of the mark. Let us take, for instance, the 'fishmonger' of *Hamlet* (ii, ii. 172). Coleridge's interpretation of the passage is: Hamlet insinuates that Polonius is sent to fish out the secret from him (*SC*, I, 26). Coleridge perhaps never read such books as Barnaby Rich's *Irish Hubbub* to discover with Malone what the true meaning of the word is. But we may do well to remind ourselves that until Malone's edition none of the previous editors questioned the meaning of the expression. And both Whiter and Gifford resorted to conjecture. The explanation of the now much publicized Whiter is:

Probably it was supposed that the daughters of these tradesmen, who dealt in so nourishing a species of food, were blessed with extraordinary powers of conception (Whiter, *Specimen of a Commentary*, p. 152).

At least Coleridge's interpretation, given no other clue, is the only reasonable sense the passage can yield; far from being a pure conjecture, it is intimately related to the context of the dramatic situation. And in spite of the fact that we know now from the multiplicity of evidence that the word means 'a seller of woman's chastity', I am not sure whether to an Elizabethan ear, trained in subtleties, puns and ambiguities, some implication of fishing out secrets, arising from the situation itself, does not remain in the word.

There are other examples in which Coleridge relies on intuitive rather than historical or scholarly grounds. In *King John* (III. ii. 1–2) he defends the word 'ayery', which he prefers to Warburton's suggested 'fiery', accepted by Theobald:

> This day grows wondrous hot
> Some ayery devil hovers in the sky.

Coleridge's reason for rejecting 'fiery' is that it is implied in the word 'devil' if 'a full and strong emphasis' is laid on it in reading, and the alteration is therefore 'useless and tasteless' (*SC*, I, 142). Bishop Percy, being a scholar, had pointed out the possibility of Shakespeare's alluding to the 'distinctions and divisions of some of the demonologists, so much regarded in his time' and quoted in support of his suggestion Burton's *Anatomy of Melancholy*. Yet modern scholars are almost agreed on the authenticity of 'ayery' which Coleridge defends for non-scholarly reasons.

The typical Coleridgean non-scholarly approach in textual criticism is perhaps best seen in his defence of the word 'fool' in *The Winter's Tale* (III, ii. 186–8). Paulina addresses Leontes:

> That thou betrayd'st Polixenes, 'twas nothing;
> That did but show thee, of a *fool*, inconstant
> And damnable ingrateful.

Theobald finds it 'too gross and blunt' in Paulina to call the king a fool and he accordingly suggests reading instead 'of a soul' since 'it is more pardonable in her to arraign his morals, and the qualities of his mind, than rudely to call him *ideot* to his face'. Coleridge, on the other hand, like Johnson, rejects this emendation; but the reasons he adduces are so characteristic of one part of his textual criticism that they deserve to be quoted at length:

I think the original [he says] to be Shakespeare's. 1 – My ear feels it Shakespearian; 2 – the involved grammar is Shakespearian – i.e., 'show thee, being a fool naturally, to have improved your folly by inconstancy,' etc. 3 – the alteration is most flat and un-*Shakespearian*. As to grossness, [she calls him] 'gross and foolish' below (*SC*, I, 120).

In this example 'fool' happens to be the right word, and it has been accepted by editors since. But the method which relies exclusively or even largely on 'my ear' is, we immediately perceive, an extremely precarious method. It is this which makes Coleridge fall into error. The 'my ear' approach is indispensable to a good critic; but to overemphasize it, one hardly needs to say, is soliciting trouble, even for a critic, and of course most of all for an editor, since no individual ear is an infallible judge in matters of poetry.

When Coleridge's ear errs, it then errs egregiously. The porter soliloquy in *Macbeth* is a notorious example. The eighteenth-century critics had condemned the porter scene altogether, because it offended their idea of decorum. Bad as it was found to be, its authenticity was not disputed. Coleridge, on the other hand, finds the greater part of the soliloquy 'low' and declares his belief that it was 'written for the mob by some other hand' (*SC*, I, 75). His reason for considering it 'an interpolation of the actors' is none other than the personal impression that 'not one syllable has the ever present being of Shakespeare'. Similarly in *Antony and Cleopatra*, Coleridge suggests an absurd emendation in the passage in which Enobarbus describes Cleopatra's barge:

> Her gentlewomen, like the Nereides,
> So *many mermaids*, tended her i' the eyes,
> And made their bends adornings: at the helm
> A seeming mermaid steers: (ii. ii. 211–14).

In order that the epithet 'seeming' may not become as he finds it 'so extremely improper' and that 'the fine image' of the seeming mermaid at the helm may not be 'weakened by so useless an anticipation', he strongly suspects that Shakespeare wrote either 'sea-queens' or 'sea-bridges' instead of 'mermaids' or still worse 'submarine graces' in place of 'so many mermaids' (*SC*, i, 88). Not even the likelihood that Coleridge obtained the word 'graces' directly from North's *Plutarch* could redeem the proposed emendation. The other notorious emendation of Coleridge is in *Henry IV*, Part II, ii. ii. 182:

> This Doll Tear-sheet should be some Rode.

where he proposes to read 'Tear Street' for 'Tear-sheet' (*SC*, i, 158). Taking 'Rode' to mean just a 'road', he asks whether Shakespeare did not 'name this street-walker Doll Tear-street – *terere stratam* (*viam*)'. This is largely, but not wholly, a fault of scholarship – although some excuse may be made on behalf of Coleridge in that the word 'road', which, as Coleridge rightly finds it, is problematic without an explanatory note, did not trouble the previous editors, and that the figurative meaning pertinent to this text was not discovered until late in the nineteenth century by Skeat.

These, together with his equally absurd suggestion of 'blank height of the dark' for 'blanket of the dark' (*SC*, i, 73) in Lady Macbeth's soliloquy (*Macbeth*, i, v. 54) are the only major examples of unscholarly work that strike one in the body of his textual criticism. There are minor instances, of course. In Hamlet's words to Laertes over Ophelia's grave:

> Woo't drink *up* eisel? (*Hamlet*, v. i. 299)

208

Coleridge, like Steevens, understands 'drink up' to mean necessarily 'totally to exhaust', oblivious, as Malone was not, of Sonnet 114, where, the latter points out, 'drink up' means simply 'drink' (*SC*, I, 36). Against these, however, we ought to set Coleridge's contribution. It is a small contribution indeed, but then Coleridge never actually worked on his intended edition. His approach, when not purely intuitive, is a tentative one in which he does not hesitate to make use of the modicum of scholarship at his command. Even in the 'drink up eisel' question – although he could not reconcile himself to the use of the particle 'up' – his contribution to the understanding of the passage cannot be overlooked without loss. His suspicion that Hamlet is alluding to 'the cup of anguish at the Cross' will appear to us all the more strongly grounded when we know that Skelton says of Jesus:

He drank eisel and gall.

(see *The Sonnets of William Shakespeare*, ed. Edward Dowden, 1883, p. 222). Undoubtedly this allusion will enhance the significance and solemnity of the various ways of showing grief Hamlet enumerates, and the sarcastic crescendo will appear the more powerful by the contrast between the sincere manifestation of grief, so deepened by the sacred association, and the eating of crocodile to induce hypocritical tears.

In *King John* (I. i. 231) where the bastard Philip resents being called Philip by Gurney, Coleridge's reading causes him to rail against Warburton's emendation, accepted by Theobald, of 'sparrow' into 'Spare me':

Philip! sparrow: James.

'Had Warburton read old Skelton's *Philip Sparrow*,' he says 'an exquisite and original poem, and no doubt popular in Shakespeare's time, even Warburton would scarcely have made so deep a plunge into the bathetic as to have deathified "sparrow" into "spare me"' (*SC*, I, 141). There may be an allusion to Skelton's poem here, or Philip may be just a common onomatopoeic appelation of a sparrow at the time. What is important, however, is that Coleridge is using his learning to justify his point. And when he finds that his learning does not help, he often suggests a reasonable emendation, as in the line in *Julius Caesar* (II. i. 83):

> For if thou path thy native semblance on,

where he proposes to read 'put' instead of 'path', since he fails to find a text where Shakespeare or any other writer of his age 'uses "path" as a verb for "walk"' (*SC*, I, 16). Even Steevens' discovery of a similar, though not altogether identical use of 'path' in Drayton, does not make Coleridge's 'put' (which to my mind is more satisfactory than 'hadst' suggested by some scholars) less acceptable. But if he can find for an obscure word in one play a parallel in another play of Shakespeare, he often resorts to it to elucidate the text. The common sense of his comparative approach is clear in his interpretation of the word 'unbonneted' in Othello's words to Iago (*Othello*, I. ii. 22–4):

> my demerits
> May speak unbonneted to as proud a fortune
> As this that I have reach'd

by reference to a similar one in *Coriolanus* (II. ii. 30), while at the same time being aware of the danger of 'the assumption that Shakespeare could not use the same word differently in different places' (*SC*, I, 48). His rejection of Theobald's interpretation, which is based on an analogy from *King Lear*, shows how mature his employment of this comparative method is: he maintains the need for an editor to distinguish between a 'direct' use of a word in one context, and a 'metaphorical' use of it in another. On the other hand, when the text does not yield him any sense, he not infrequently admits his inability to understand it (see, e.g. *SC*, I, 90).

When, however, the question is to be decided not so much by scholarship as by critical insight, Coleridge is most reliable. The best example of this is his defence of the word 'Indian' in Othello's final speech (*Othello*, v. ii. 347), discussed earlier (see above, pp. 170f.). This is Coleridge at his best. But he can be blinded by a prudish sense of morality: he sees a 'very indelicate anticipation' put in the mouth of Rosalind when she speaks of 'my child's father' (*As You Like It*, I. iii. 10–12), a thing which makes him find the phrase 'strange' (*SC*, I, 105).

Similarly his view of the characters can prejudice his interpretation of the text. Although he realizes that Hamlet's words to Polonius (*Hamlet*, II. ii. 181–2):

For if the sun breed maggots in a dead dog, being a god-kissing carrion – Have you a daughter?

are purposely obscure, yet his interpretation of the words, which are admittedly difficult, does suffer from the idealization of Shakespeare's female characters. The lines, he writes:

refer to some thought in Hamlet's mind contrasting the lovely daughter with such a tedious old fool, her father, as *he* represents Polonius to himself. 'Why, fool as he is, he is some degrees in rank above a dead dog's carcase; and if the sun, being a god that kisses carrion, can raise life out of a dead dog, why may [not] good fortune that favours fools, have raised a lovely girl out of this dead-alive old fool.' (*SC*, I, 26–7)

Coleridge accepts Warburton's 'noble emendation', as Dr Johnson calls it, but he attacks his interpretation for his 'attention to general positions without the due Shakespearean reference to what is probably passing in the mind of his speaker, characteristic and expository of his particular character and present mood'. Yet he himself, in his attention to his view of the character of Ophelia and what Hamlet, as he conceives him, should think of her, misses Hamlet's cynical mood. And just as Warburton's error consists in relating the passage to what precedes it alone, Coleridge's lies in linking it only with what follows – Warburton prejudiced by his moral bias, Coleridge by his idealistic view of Ophelia and Hamlet.

After this sketchy view of the characteristics of Coleridge's editorial method, we may conclude that the value of his intended edition of Shakespeare would have been critical rather than scholarly. Although Coleridge, as has been shown here, does not infrequently apply some sort of scholarship, we have seen how much his method is fraught with dangers, and how much it is unscholarly in the modern, or even in the eighteenth-century, sense of the term (we have no evidence that he once consulted any early folio or quarto). This appears most clearly in his attempts to establish a chronological order of Shakespeare's plays.

Coleridge fully realizes the importance of the chronological order for the understanding of a poet's whole output: 'After all you can say, I still think the chronological order the best for arranging a poet's works. All your divisions are in particular instances inadequate, and they destroy the interest which arises from watching the progress, maturity, and even the decay of genius' (*TT* 1 January, 1834). But he starts by flouting the authority of the scientific, historical or factual method. 'Various attempts', he says:

have been made to arrange the plays of Shakespeare, each according to its priority in time, by proofs derived from external documents. How unsuccessful these attempts have been might easily be shown, not only from the widely different results arrived at by men, all deeply versed in the black-letter books, old plays, pamphlets, manuscript records and catalogues of that age, but also from the fallacious and unsatisfactory nature of the facts and assumptions on which the evidence rests (*SC*, I, 235).

If Coleridge rejects the historical method for its failure to give us absolute certainty as to the order of Shakespeare's plays one may sympathize with him. Yet what can be more certain in such matters than the date of the publication of a play or its entry in the Stationers Register – if only we get to know it? It is symptomatic of the subjective nature of the 'internal evidence' method that if one relies solely upon it, one is likely to conceive a different order for the plays every time one develops, changes, or sees the plays in a new light. Coleridge himself has not left us only one scheme of arrangement. Of course, Coleridge is right when he points out that the question of deciding the actual date of every play is not an easy one, that the plays of Shakespeare 'both during and after his life were the property of the stage, and published by the players, doubtless according to their notions of acceptability with the visitants of the theatre' (*SC*, I, 236; cf. II, 87ff.). We admit with him that in such an age 'an allusion or reference to any drama or poem in the publication of a contemporary cannot be received as conclusive evidence'; but all we can conclude from this is that we should be extremely wary in applying the historical method, and not, as Coleridge believes, that the method itself is useless and ought to be discarded in favour of the internal evidence approach of his.

Having tried to excuse himself for not meddling in 'black-letter' scholarship, Coleridge proceeds to construct an order for Shakespeare's plays, 'turning his researches towards the internal evidence furnished by the writings themselves', though not completely rejecting the fruit of historical research, since he accepts Malone's dating of the commencement of Shakespeare's dramatic career. From internal evidence he gathers that *Venus and Adonis* was the first heir of his invention. After that Coleridge divides up Shakespeare's plays into different periods, or rather epochs or aeras, as he prefers to style them. These periods differ from one time to another. Coleridge has left us three main and other subsidiary attempts: the first is undated; but the other two were made in 1810 and 1819 respectively. And the weakness of his method manifests itself in the fact that he could never make up his mind definitely about the placing of some plays in the perspective of the whole output. For instance, in the first attempt, apart from placing three spurious plays in the first period, i.e. *The London Prodigal, Cromwell* and *Edward III* (which he drops in the two other main attempts), he assigns, quite rightly, *The Tempest, Winter's Tale* and *Cymbeline* to the last period (*SC*, I, 237–8); yet in the classification attempted in 1810 he relegates *The Tempest* to the second class, together with *A Midsummer Night Dream, As You Like It* and *Twelfth Night*, immediately after his earliest period which includes *Love's Labour's Lost, All's Well, Comedy of Errors* and *Romeo and Juliet*; and *Cymbeline* is promoted to the third class together with *Troilus and Cressida* (*SC*, I, 239). In the fragment designed for his lecture at the Crown and Anchor in 1819 he again changes his mind and includes *Troilus and Cressida* and *Measure for Measure* in the last period of Shakespeare's creative activity (*SC*, I, 241).

If we compare these attempts of Coleridge with any of the schemes drawn up by the late eighteenth-century scholars, the difference of method at once becomes salient. It is true that the scholars themselves differed from one another in their proposed arrangements. Compare, for example, the schemes of Capell and Malone. Edward Capell (*Notes and Various Readings to Shakespeare*, 1783, vol. II, part IV) dates *The Winter's Tale* 1613, whereas Edmond Malone (*The Plays and Poems of William Shakespeare*, ed. Edmond Malone, 1790, vol. I, part I, pp. 266ff.)

fixes it at 1604; the former assigns to *Hamlet* the probable date
of 1605 while the latter suggests 1596, and so on. Yet each has
an argument, which is often based on some fact or other. In their
method there is room for argument: you are at liberty to accept
or reject the fact, to be convinced by, or refute the argument.
Coleridge's method is not like that. Of course occasionally, and
only occasionally, he gives what is near to a scholarly argument
for placing a play in a particular period. Consider for example his
reasons for deciding that *Love's Labour's Lost* is an early play,
'the earliest of Shakespeare's dramas' (*SC*, I, 92; cf. II, 106–7).
Coleridge here puts forward as an argument the number of the
rhymes with which the play abounds – just as Malone does (*op.
cit.* vol. I, part I, p. 294). But Coleridge moves further and takes
into account, not strictly scholarly, but directly aesthetic, considerations. 'The characters', we are told, 'are either imperson-
ated out of his own multiformity, by imaginative self-position,
or of such as a country boy and a schoolboy's observation might
supply – the curate, school-master...' We are asked to notice
the satire on 'follies of words', the abundance of 'acute and
fancifully illustrated aphorisms', the 'sweet' and 'smooth'
metre; we are shown that the characters of Biron and Rosaline
are 'evidently the pre-existent state of his Beatrice and Benedict'.
All these belong to the strict category of aesthetics. They become dangerous in pure scholarship; and, after all, attempting a
chronological order of Shakespeare's plays is a matter which a
disciplined scholar is the only fit person to undertake. In Coleridge's hands the aesthetic method does not go far wrong very
often, but that is because he is a critic of the first order. In its
general features Coleridge's scheme does not strike us as completely unfamiliar or totally unperceptive. For instance, we tend
to agree with him when he links together the four great
tragedies, *Hamlet*, *Othello*, *Macbeth* and *Lear* and places them at
the summit of Shakespeare's fourth period, the period which
'gives all the graces and faculties of a genius in full possession
and habit of power', and when he assigns to *Antony and Cleopatra*
an even later date. This is nearer to us than Malone's fixing the
date of *Hamlet* in 1596, immediately after *Romeo and Juliet* and
in the same year as *King John* (*op. cit.* vol. I, part I, p. 266). And
when he groups together *The Tempest*, *Winter's Tale* and

Cymbeline, we know that he is justified, that these plays have common aesthetic elements. The value of Coleridge's arrangement lies not in presenting an accurate time scheme for the plays, but in suggesting certain landmarks in the development of Shakespeare's dramatic power. The periods or epochs into which Coleridge divides Shakespeare's work are not divisions in time; in proposing them Coleridge is motivated by aesthetic rather than temporal considerations, and that is why they vary from one time in Coleridge's life to another. His scheme is therefore the parent of such schemes as Dowden's later on in the century. When we find that Dowden places *Troilus and Cressida* and *Measure for Measure* in the 'serious, dark, ironical' period, (Edward Dowden, *Shakespeare, His Mind and Art*, 1889, p.x.), we should not forget that Coleridge in the first scheme classifies *Troilus and Cressida* under the phrase '*Ubergang in die Ironie*', and he later links it with *Measure for Measure* (*SC*, I, 238).

But in the hands of an incompetent critic this aesthetic method can be disastrous. The example of James Hurdis, who was appointed Professor of Poetry at Oxford in 1793, immediately suggests itself. Hurdis was not satisfied with Malone's proposed order, and accordingly he published a slim volume in which he offered a 'new disposition of the plays' (James Hurdis, *Cursory Remarks upon the Arrangement of Shakespeare's Plays*, 1792, pp. 45–6). But what he suggested was almost completely the reverse of the present accepted order. He believed that Shakespeare had begun his dramatic career by writing *Antony and Cleopatra*, *The Winter's Tale*, *Cymbeline*, *Coriolanus* and *The Tempest*. Of *Antony and Cleopatra*, a play which Coleridge describes as 'one of the most gorgeous and sustained of all Shakespeare's dramas' (Thomas Allsop, *Letters, Conversations and Recollections of S. T. Coleridge*, 1836, II, 138), and in which he finds 'a formidable rival of the *Macbeth*, *Lear*, *Othello* and *Hamlet*' (*SC*, I, 86) Hurdis wrote:

Of all Shakespeare's plays, that which most abounds with faulty lines, is *Antony & Cleopatra* . . . Add to this that *Antony & Cleopatra* is, in almost every scene, dull and tedious. There is action enough, but it is not made interesting by any nice discrimination or elevation of character, nor by artful display of nature. The dialogue is always flat and often foolish, abounding with passages which provoke a smile by their absurdity, when the action is solemn and important (Hurdis, *op. cit.* p. 40).

Since of Shakespeare's works there is none written 'with less spirit and less knowledge of his art', Hurdis concludes that it is the earliest of Shakespeare's plays (*ibid.* p. 41). Likewise, he has no doubts that the *Two Gentlemen of Verona* was 'certainly written after *The Winter's Tale, Cymbeline, Antony & Cleopatra, Timon, Coriolanus* and *The Tempest*', because he finds that all these plays 'abound in defects of stile and rhythm', whereas the *Two Gentlemen* is 'so generally good in both' (*ibid.* p. 9). But such are the vagaries of the aesthetic method, when it encroaches on scholarship and is used by someone not competent enough to pass just judgements.

Coleridge did not entertain much respect for scholarship. This was his weakness, although he prided himself on not being one of the Malones. In various parts of his work he directs bitter invective against the Shakespearean scholars, editors and commentators, ranging from Theobald and Warburton down to Malone (see, e.g., *SC*, II, 165ff.). His notes on the plays abound in such attacks delivered sometimes in the harshest language. Of Warburton and Theobald he says in contempt and indignation, 'Thus it is for no poets to comment on the greatest of poets' (*SC*, I, 54).

The disregard for scholarship, however, was growing rapidly universal by Coleridge's time. The general reader was getting tired of the endless volumes of notes and commentaries, and sometimes long-winded discussions of minute textual points that hardly deserve such a ponderous treatment. Even the scholars themselves were becoming conscious of this growing impatience of the public. Francis Douce, in his valuable book written to illustrate Shakespeare, had to defend himself against the abuse levelled at learning in the periodicals of the time (*Illustrations of Shakespeare,* 1808, II, xi). Another scholar, John Croft, prefaced his very slim book of notes with an apology for the number of notes that had already appeared on Shakespeare. 'The press,' he wrote, 'has groaned and not stood still for near half a century past under the pressure, though clogged with the weight of such an enormous multifarious mass of notes' (*Annotations on the*

Plays of Shakespeare, York, 1810, p. iii). The author admitted he was aware 'that Shakespeare was so bewildered with Notes, and the Text so stormed that it appears contrived for a Peg for the Notes to hang upon, that there is not any elbow room left to add to the already amplified list or *levee en masse* of commentators' (*ibid,* p. iv). Even Malone complained that the 'idle notion' that Shakespeare has been buried under his commentators was being propagated by the 'tasteless and the dull' (*The Plays and Poems of William Shakespeare,* ed. Edmond Malone, 1790, vol. I, part I, p. lv).

From the closing years of the eighteenth century onwards there poured a flood of satires, skits, parodies and burlesques on the commentators of Shakespeare. A few examples will suffice to show this trend of opinion at the time. In 1794 S. T. Mathias published a satirical poem called *The Pursuits of Literature,* in which he likens Shakespeare being torn to pieces ruthlessly by his commentators to Actaeon in the Greek legend devoured by his own hounds. The popularity of these verses may be measured by the fact that they were known even to a German critic. In 1799 a parody appeared under the title of *Capell's Ghost* (published in *The School for Satire,* 1802), in which we read:

> On a sudden strangely sounding,
> Dubious *notes* and yells were heard,
> Grammar, sense and points confounding
> A sad troop of *Clerks* appeared.

In 1800 and 1801 the two skits of G. Hardinge were published, called respectively *The Essence of Malone* and *Another Essence of Malone,* or *The Beauties of Shakespeare's Editor.* Lastly, a certain author writing under the pen name of Martinus Scriblerus produced an even more ferocious and ironical attack on the commentators in 1814, called *Explanations and Emendations of Some Passages in the Text of Shakespeare and of Beaumont and Fletcher.*

Of course, Coleridge should have known better; but against such a background his disrespect for the scholars ought, in all fairness, to be set.

Index